HOWARD I. SHAPIRO, M.D., is a practicing gynecologist and serves as a medical advisor to the National Organization for Women and the Committee of Planned Parenthood of Southern Fairfield County, Connecticut. A Fellow of the American College of Obstetricians and Gynecologists, Dr. Shapiro is Director of the Colposcopy Clinic and Associate Attending Physician at Norwalk Hospital, Connecticut; Attending Physician of the Outpatient Department at Yale New Haven Hospital; and author of several works on obstetrics and gynecology. Dr. Shapiro has also received an Ettinger Fellowship for Cancer Research from the Cancer Society.

THE BIRTH CONTROL BOOK

Howard I. Shapiro, M.D.

A DISCUS BOOK/PUBLISHED BY AVON BOOKS

AVON BOOKS
A division of
The Hearst Corporation
959 Eighth Avenue
New York, New York 10019

First Avon Trade Printing, September, 1978
First Discus Printing, February, 1982

DISCUS TRADEMARK REG. U. S. PAT. OFF. AND IN
OTHER COUNTRIES, MARCA REGISTRADA, HECHO EN
U. S. A.

Printed in the U. S. A.

OP   10   9   8   7   6   5   4   3   2   1

To Betsy, My Love and Inspiration

ACKNOWLEDGMENTS

The author is indebted to Joan Sjostrom and Jean Botts, librarians at Norwalk Hospital, for helping me locate the innumerable references which were vital to the completion of this book. Special thanks are extended to Mary Dattalo for the hundreds of hours she devoted to the flawless typing and preparation of the manuscript. The late Barbara Maclean also helped to prepare the manuscript in addition to working as my invaluable secretary and receptionist. Most importantly, she was a dear friend.

The members of the editorial staff of St. Martin's Press are to be congratulated for instantly recognizing the value and potential of my work. Marcia Markland's enthusiasm and guidance has been responsible for bringing this effort to its successful conclusion.

I am extremely grateful to Dr. S. Bruce Schearer for his careful review of the manuscript and his valuable suggestions. Dr. Schearer is Assistant Director, Biomedical Division, The Population Council, and serves as Secretary to the International Committee for Contraception Research.

Finally, to my wife, Betsy, and daughters Suzanne and Marjorie, I offer my thanks for the love, patience, and encouragement I received during the preparation of the manuscript.

CONTENTS

CONTENTS

PREFACE

This book represents one gynecologist's response to the Women's Health Movement in America. The growing rift between women and their doctors, and the resentment women feel toward the medical establishment—gynecology in particular—is not surprising. For too many years, male gynecologists have been making vital decisions for women based on little more than their personal preferences and prejudices. Until recently, few women had the temerity to question that "Father knows best" attitude, and if they did, it was often interpreted as an affront to the physician's authority.

Times have changed. Today's woman is demanding complete control over her body, because those who were entrusted with this responsibility have failed her miserably. Who is responsible? Physicians naturally place the blame on the manufacturers of those ingenious products devised to be swallowed, inserted, and injected without proper or honest research evaluation beforehand. Why should women maintain confidence after they learn about another new complication of birth control pills while reading the morning paper? How could the initial supplies of Cu-7 IUDs have been packaged incorrectly so that they were all contaminated? How did the Dalkon Shield receive such glowing reports by the manufacturer, yet do so poorly when used by women who suffered the consequences? The list is endless, but these examples should suffice to help us understand the reasons for a woman's skepticism and anger.

Physicians are as responsible as the manufacturers. We are only too willing to accept a new product introduced in a memorized speech by a drug salesman who possesses absolutely no knowledge of medicine. Millions of dollars are spent by manufacturers in marketing products with catchy names and attractive colors as a means of attracting both doctor and patient.

The Food and Drug Administration, or FDA, must also share the blame. Their premature announcements of drug approval in one bulletin, followed by embarrassing retractions in the next bulletin, would make anyone skeptical of their efficiency. The attempt of the FDA to allow redistribution of the Dalkon Shield despite objections from their own medical advisors makes one wonder if their sentiments are with big business or with the health of women.

It becomes obvious that women will be better able to control their own destinies if accurate medical information is made available to them. Many of the health care needs of women involve not disease or illness, but education, consisting of support and counsel about the anatomy and physiology of reproduction, methods of contraception, and abortion. Gynecologists must undertake to raise the level of patients' understanding of those and other subjects.

The purpose of this book is to share my knowledge of the vital subjects of contraception, sterilization, and abortion with the reader. I hope this text will help to demystify, elucidate, and educate until that time when the perfect contraceptive is developed.

The information in each chapter is presented in a question-and-answer form. The vast majority of these questions are those of the many women I have had the privilege of treating during the past seven years. This project, therefore, belongs to them as well as to me. My greatest personal pleasure will be in knowing it has found a place as a much-needed reference source for all women.

1
THE
REPRODUCTIVE
SYSTEM

Before you can understand contraceptive methods and gynecological surgery, some knowledge of the basic anatomy and physiology of reproduction is essential. In teaching my patients about their normal external or outer genital anatomy, I use a magnifying mirror while I point out the various parts. Follow the diagrams in the text and compare this with your own normal anatomy (Figure 1–1).

When you view the external genitals, you can readily identify the *mons pubis* as that triangular area covered with hair. By pressing down on the lower part of the mons on a line directly in the middle of the abdomen, you can touch the pubic symphysis bone.

What are the labia?

The labia are paired folds of skin on either side of the vaginal opening. There are two types: the outer, larger labia, called the labia majora; and the inner, more delicate labia minora. The former are covered with hair and contain sweat glands and *sebaceous*, or oil, glands. In women who have never had children, the labia majora often meet in the middle, but following childbirth they may remain farther apart. They protect and cushion the more fragile structures of the vulva within them against injury. The enlarged healthy size of these labia is dependent upon hormonal factors, and women in the menopausal years who lack estrogen

1

often note a flattening and even a disappearance of these structures.

The labia minora are hairless, more delicate folds lying inside the labia majora. They are supplied with oil glands, numerous blood vessels, and erectile tissue, which is tissue that becomes swollen during sexual arousal. There are many nerve endings in the labia minora, making it very sensitive to sexual stimulation. The foreskin or hood of the clitoris is formed by the joining of the two labia minora.

How large is the normal clitoris?

The clitoris is a small organ of erectile tissue lying under the hood formed by the labia minora. The length of the clitoris varies from less than one quarter of an inch to as much as one inch during sexual excitation. This sensitive structure plays a most important role in female orgasm.

Why can't I find my urethra?

The urethra, or urinary opening, always appears easy to locate in textbooks, but it is difficult to find on people. Honest doctors and nurses will readily admit that they occasionally

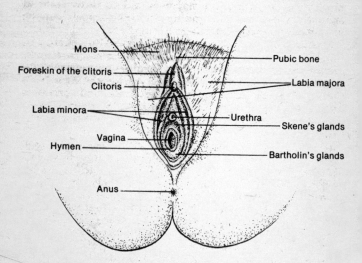

Figure 1-1.   The External Genitals (Vulva)

have trouble finding the urethra of a patient when inserting a catheter or urinary tube. To find your urethra, separate as well as lift the labia minora with the index and middle finger of one hand while focusing the mirror with the opposite hand. Then you can find it between the vagina and clitoris, but closer to the vagina. If that doesn't work, passing urine while viewing with the mirror always proves successful.

Are there any other openings into the vaginal opening?
On each side of the urethra are two tiny openings leading from two mucus-secreting glands named *Skene's*. Two other openings at the lower part of the vagina on each side enter into glands named *Bartholin's*. It is often difficult, if not impossible, to see these with the mirror. These glands have little, if any, function. However, inflammation may block their openings, causing a large, painful swelling in the areas involved.

What is the shape of the normal hymen?
The hymen is a thin membrane lying across the opening to the vagina, and any one of many different shapes may be considered normal (Figure 1–2).

It should be noted that an easily stretched hymen may be intact or unbroken in a sexually active woman, or may be almost totally absent in a virgin. Usually, however, initial intercourse will produce tearing of the hymen. This heals quickly, leaving little tags of tissue. Childbirth produces further tearing of these tags, and following delivery they may become fewer in number and flatter in appearance.

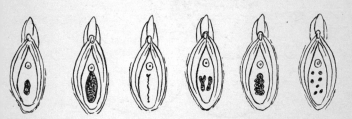

Figure 1-2. Variations of the Normal Hymen

Carunculae myrtiformes is the name given to the appearance of the hymenal remnants following childbirth (Figure 1–3).

An *imperforate* hymen is one that has no opening in it, with the consequence that menstrual blood can't pass out of the vagina, so it may accumulate in both the vagina and the cavity of the uterus. When a young woman of menstruating age complains of monthly cramping but no bleeding, this condition should be immediately suspected. Treatment consists of opening the hymen with a small incision, under anesthesia.

How can I examine my inner vagina and cervix?
You can accomplish this easily by using a viewing instrument called a *speculum*. If you can't get a speculum from a doctor or a clinic, you can buy a plastic or metal one from most surgical supply stores. The speculum may be used over and over again by the same individual, but must be rinsed with warm water after each use. When using a speculum, you must place a light and a mirror near the vulva in order to see the inner vagina and cervix.

A more elaborate speculum with its own detachable light

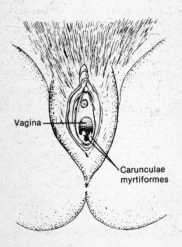

Figure 1-3.   Carunculae Myrtiformes

source is also available. This speculum has the advantage of being prelubricated and is available in both regular and small sizes. (Figure 1–4).

Can venereal diseases be transmitted by a speculum?
Contrary to popular belief, it is almost impossible to contract venereal disease by inserting a vaginal speculum that was used several hours before by an infected individual. The organisms that cause gonorrhea and syphilis are very delicate and are unable to survive for more than a few minutes outside the body. Other bacteria, viruses, and protozoa capable of causing other types of VD are slightly more hardy than those causing gonorrhea and syphilis; however, most bacteriologists would agree that it would be most unusual for these organisms to survive for several hours on a speculum, especially a dry one.

This does not mean that one should abandon sensible precautions when using a speculum. If a plastic speculum is believed to have been in contact with a person with VD, it should be scrubbed with an antiseptic solution (Betadine, Phisohex) and left to dry. Metal speculums may be sterilized

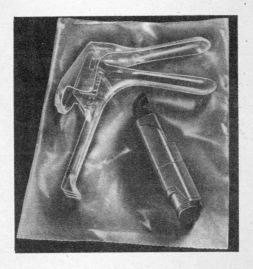

Figure 1-4. Speculum with Light Source

by placing them in boiling water for five minutes. Since VD may be present in a totally asymptotic individual, a speculum should never be passed from woman to woman.

How do I use a speculum?

Lying on your back with knees bent, and thighs as far apart as possible, insert the index finger of your left hand (if you're right-handed) into the vagina, exerting firm downward pressure in the direction of the rectum. Insert the closed speculum (Figure 1–4), held in the right hand, over this finger into the vagina. Turn the handle of the speculum in the direction of your right side while it is being inserted. For the woman who is not using a prelubricated speculum, insertion will be easier if K-Y Lubricating Jelly, purchased at any pharmacy without prescription, is liberally applied to the speculum and inner labia before insertion. Gently advance the speculum as far as it can comfortably go. Usually that is its full length of four inches. Then rotate it so that the handle faces the floor. Open the speculum by pressing the lever with the thumb (Figure 1–4).

What do I see when using a speculum?

The slightly reddened side walls of the vagina are easily seen, and by gently rotating the speculum back to its insertion position while it remains open in the vagina, the upper and lower vaginal walls may also be visualized. If you experience pressure on the urinary bladder or rectum during these maneuvers, it is only natural, since the vagina is in such close proximity to these structures, as you can see from a side view of a woman's pelvis (Figure 1–5).

At the end of the vagina is the lower part of the uterus, called the *cervix*, and its opening, the *cervical os*, which leads into the cavity of the uterus (Figure 1–6).

It is through the os that sperm pass on their journey toward fertilizing the egg in the upper, outer part of the Fallopian tube. The glands within the cervix discharge mucus into the os throughout the month. The amount of mucus and its consistency is dependent upon the female hormones *estrogen* and *progesterone*. Estrogen causes an abundance of thin, watery, and stretchable mucus very receptive to sperm as they pass through the cervix at the time of ovulation. Progesterone, on the other hand, produces a thick, nonstretchable mucus that prevents sperm from entering the os.

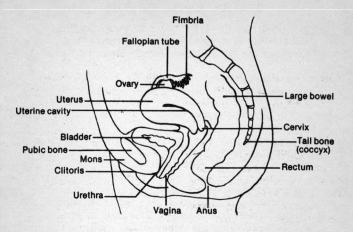

Figure 1-5. Side View of the Pelvis

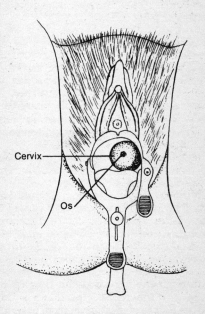

Figure 1-6. Cervix and Os As Seen Through the Speculum

When you touch the cervix, notice that it has the consistency of the cartilage at the tip of the nose. If you want to do this, first remove the speculum and then insert the index finger as far as possible into the vagina. During pregnancy, the cervix softens considerably, becomes swollen, and takes on a bluish color due to an increase in its blood supply. In labor, it has a tremendous capacity to dilate, or open, in order to accommodate the baby's head. After childbirth, the appearance of the cervix is changed, since the small, pinpoint opening has been stretched (Figure 1–7).

For many women the appearance of the cervix is not perfectly smooth. On the contrary, the reddened, mucus-secreting glandular tissue of the inner cervix may actually turn outward, or *evert*. Eversion is a perfectly normal and harmless situation in which the only symptom produced is increase in mucus secretion, especially at the time of ovulation.

What is the upper part of the uterus called?

The upper part of the uterus is called *corpus*, or "body". In the adult woman this structure is smaller than her fist and weighs approximately two ounces. By the end of pregnancy it may weigh two and one-quarter pounds, and its muscle layer, or *myometrium*, has stretched to a point at which it can hold a huge infant or two, amniotic fluid, and a placenta. Figure 1–8 demonstrates a nonpregnant uterus as

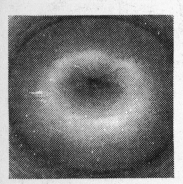
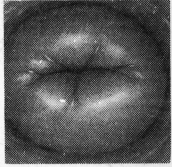

Figure 1-7.   Cervix Before and After Childbirth

it appears from the inside, showing the myometrium and the very important endometrium.

Why is the endometrium so important?
The glands in the endometrium, as in the cervix, undergo changes in response to estrogen and progesterone, which circulate in a woman's body. Though not seen by the naked eye, those changes are clearly visible under the microscope. It is the endometrium, under the influence of progesterone, which accepts and nourishes the fertilized egg at the onset of pregnancy. When the egg is not fertilized, the upper layer of the endometrium detaches from its blood supply, and bleeding, or *menstruation*, begins.

What is the function of the Fallopian tubes in the process of conception?
The two oviducts, or *Fallopian tubes,* are of vital importance in grasping the egg with their finger-like projections, called *fimbria* (Figure 1–8), as it is released from the ovary. Fertilization, or the uniting of the egg and the sperm, takes place shortly after the egg enters the Fallopian tube. The muscles of the tube then transport the egg in the direction of the endometrium. The journey takes approximately forty-eight hours. Proof of the fimbria's efficiency is demonstrated by

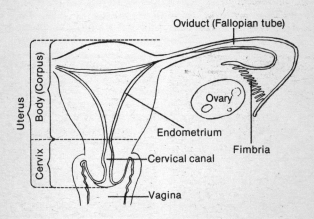

Figure 1-8.   Uterus

several reports of successful pregnancy following surgical removal of the ovary on one side of the body and the tube on the opposite side.

What are the ovaries like?

The two ovaries are white and oval-shaped. In the adult woman they measure about one and one-half inches in length and three-quarters of an inch in breadth. They are attached to the uterus by the *ovarian ligament*. Though each ovary may contain as many as 400,000 egg cells only one of these eggs, which is surrounded by fluid and called a *follicle*, develops to maturity each month. The follicle pushes through the surface of the ovary at the time of ovulation. Occasionally two different eggs will do this at the same time, and if both are fertilized the result is fraternal twins. The newer fertility drugs responsible for multiple births cause several eggs to pop at once, so that all the offspring are fraternal. Identical twins are conceived when a single fertilized egg divides and separates into two equal parts.

It is strictly a matter of chance as to which egg of the several thousand will next become a mature follicle. Contrary to popular belief, the ovaries do not alternate ovulations each menstrual cycle. It is more like a random flip of a coin, and one ovary may get the assignment several times in a row. Furthermore, surgical removal of one ovary should not present a problem, since the one remaining has more than enough eggs to last for a lifetime. Under such circumstances the one ovary works at full capacity in producing an ovulation every month. Most scientists believe that the egg cannot live beyond 24 hours, and its ability to be fertilized is probably no more than 15–18 hours. Healthy sperm may be capable of movement for twenty-four to forty-eight hours (and on rare occasions even longer), though their ability to fertilize is believed to last considerably less time.

The ovary makes estrogen and progesterone, the two female hormones. Estrogen, which is produced in the cells of the developing follicle, is responsible for breast development, thinning of the cervical mucus, and microscopic growth of the endometrium prior to ovulation. This growth begins after menstruation and is referred to as the *proliferative* phase of the menstrual cycle (Figure 1–9).

Following ovulation, the now-empty follicle in the ovary becomes a yellow structure called the *corpus luteum* (Figure

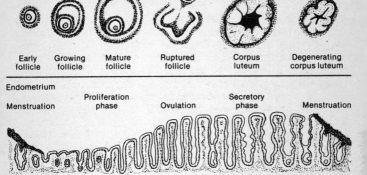

Figure 1-9. The Follicle and Endometrium During the Menstrual Cycle

1–9). Progesterone is produced by the corpus luteum and is responsible for turning the endometrium into a lush receptor and supporter of the fertilized egg. That is termed the *secretory* phase of the menstrual cycle (Figure 1–9). If the egg is fertilized, the corpus luteum continues to produce progesterone in support of the pregnancy. In the absence of pregnancy, the corpus luteum dies and no more progesterone is produced.

As I've said, when the support of the endometrium collapses, menstruation ensues.

How is the cycle regulated? What makes all this happen?

It all begins in a small but vital area of the brain called the *hypothalamus*. The hypothalamus contains substances called *releasing factors*, which travel via small veins to the pituitary gland. The releasing factor believed to be most responsible for ovulation is named *luteinizing hormone-releasing factor* or LRF. The function of LRF is to stimulate the pituitary gland to release two of its hormones named *luteinizing hormone* (LH) and *follicle stimulating hormone* (FSH). While LRF has been isolated and identified in the laboratory by scientists, the existence of follicle stimulating hormone-releasing factor or FRF is theorized by some and denied by others. If FRF does exist, it is believed to function along with LRF in stimulating the pituitary gland to release its FSH. Scientists have also synthesized another factor which they have named *gonadotropin releasing factor* (GnRF). This substance also has the capacity to elicit pituitary release of FSH and LH.

During the typical menstrual cycle, FSH acts by traveling through the blood stream to the ovary, where it stimulates the follicle to grow and produce estrogen (Figure 1-10).

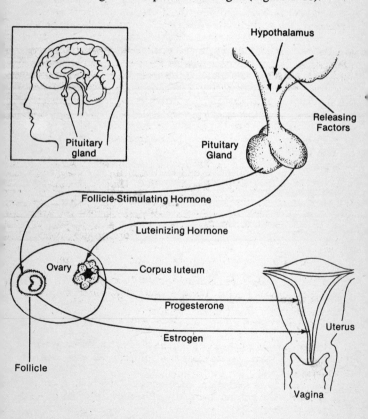

Figure 1-10.   The Control of Ovulation and Menstruation

Immediately before ovulation a large amount of estrogen, combined with LRF, is responsible for a sudden increase of LH. It is this surge of LH which ejects the egg from the ovary.

Since I have an unlimited number of eggs, why will I stop ovulating at menopause?

It is not known why the ovary suddenly ages and is no longer able to produce mature follicles from the thousands of surplus eggs. It is also a mystery why some women menstruate as late as their late-fifties while other women experience premature menopause before the age of forty. Menopause, by definition, is the end of menstruation, but many women are actually unable to conceive long before that. It is only natural that women over fifty who are menstruating are deeply concerned that they will conceive. However, pregnancy in this age group is rare, because most menses are preceded by inadequate follicle growth without actual ovulation. When ovulation does take place in a woman over fifty, the corpus luteum appears to be unable to sustain a pregnancy.

Practically speaking, a woman need not use contraceptives after the age of fifty, or when she has had no period for one year and is over forty-five years of age. It should be mentioned that neither birth control pills nor any other hormones are able to either accelerate or postpone the onset of menopause. The new ovulation-stimulating drugs, when given to a woman past menopause, are also unable to stimulate ovulation.

How does the male reproductive system function?

The external genitals of the male consist of the *penis* and the *scrotum*, which is the skin covering the two testes. The penis is composed of two parts: the *glans* and the *body* (Figure 1–11).

If you follow the corona of the glans to its undersurface in a circumcised male, you'll see a fold of skin called the *frenulum* (Figure 1–12).

In an uncircumcised man, the *prepuce*, or foreskin, completely covers the corona, frenulum, and most—if not all—of the glans (Figure 1–13).

Sperm cells, or *spermatozoa*, are produced by the two testes from adolescence until old age. The sperm are passed

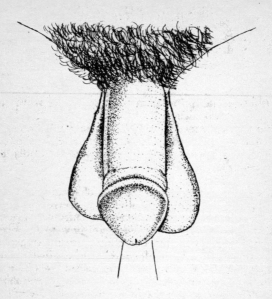

Figure 1-11.   External Male Genitals

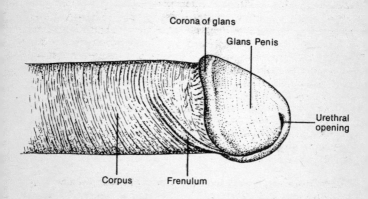

Corona of glans

Glans Penis

Urethral opening

Corpus

Frenulum

Figure 1-12.   Penis of Circumcised Male

14

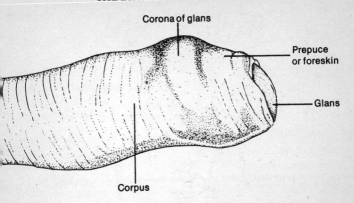

Figure 1-13.   *Penis of Uncircumcised Male*

up from each testicle to a lower tube, called the *epididymis*. From there, they pass through a second tube, called the *vas deferens*. The spermatozoa are then temporarily stored in the upper part of the vas deferens, or in a small sac called the *seminal vesicle*. When a man reaches orgasm, the sperm and other secretions are pushed out from these two locations, and into the urethra (Figure 1–14). From there, they are ejaculated from the end of the erect penis.

The fluid ejaculate is called *semen* and usually equals about a tablespoon in volume. Though a normal ejaculate contains between 40 million and four hundred million sperm, this amount is not excessive, since many are lost on their long journey, and only a few survivors reach the outer part of the Fallopian tube. Of these, only one sperm fertilizes the egg, by breaking through its protective coating.

Testosterone is the hormone produced by the testes that is responsible for masculine characteristics, libido, and sexual potency. The production of testosterone and spermatozoa are both under the control of the same pituitary gland hormones—FSH and LH—found in women.

What do normal sperm look like under the microscope?
Spermatozoa look like small, worm-like creatures. The head is oval and contains the chromosomes which determine one half of the traits of the potential child. The tail is vital for

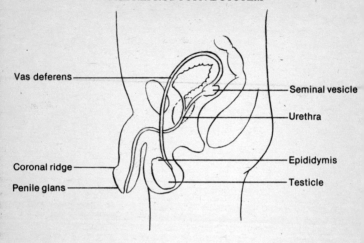

Vas deferens

Seminal vesicle

Urethra

Epididymis

Testicle

Coronal ridge

Penile glans

Figure 1-14.   Internal Male Anatomy

forward movement of the sperm. Even the slightest changes in the shape or movement of the sperm adversely affect a man's fertility (Figure 1–15).

What determines the sex of a fetus?
The sex of the fertilized egg is determined by the type of sex chromosome present in the head of the sperm. The adult

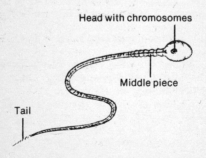

Head with chromosomes

Middle piece

Tail

Figure 1-15.   Appearance of Sperm under the Microscope (Enlarged)

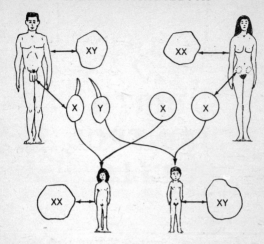

Figure 1-16. Sex Chromosomes of Sperm and Egg

male has two sex chromosomes in his body cells; they are called X and Y (Figure 1-16). Each sperm can carry only an X or a Y. The adult woman contains two X sex chromosomes in each of her body cells, but no Ys. Therefore, her egg always contributes an X to the future offspring (Figure 1-16). If a sperm cell carrying a Y chromosome fertilizes the X egg, the result is an XY male. However, if a sperm cell carrying an X gets there first, the result is an XX female (Figure 1-16).

What does all this basic anatomy have to do with contraception?

Throughout this book I will refer to this chapter when describing how the various contraception, sterilization, and abortion techniques work.

2

BIRTH CONTROL PILLS

Since the FDA approved their use in 1960, birth control pills have become the most common form of contraception used in the United States. In 1974 it was estimated that ten million American women—or 30 percent of all American women between the ages of eighteen and forty-four—were "on the Pill." More recent estimates are that there are eight million oral contraceptive users in this country. Despite these statistics, many women know little about the medications in the various pills, or the complications and side effects that these hormones may produce.

Which birth control pill is best?
Unfortunately, no one birth control pill is suitable for all women. A physician familiar with the ingredients of each of the many products on the market must prescribe individually for each patient. For some reason women who do request a specific pill usually ask for Ovral. If I ask them why, they say that a friend, or another doctor, said it had the "lowest dose" of hormones. Ovral certainly is an effective contraceptive pill and is ideal for many patients. However, contrary to popular belief, it does not have the "lowest dose" of hormones, and may be less than ideal for many women.

   Table 2–1 lists all the birth control pills currently available in the United States, as well as the amount of estrogen and progestogen in each pill. All products, with the exception of the minipills, contain estrogen, and this estrogen is either mestranol or ethinyl estradiol. The progestogen is either norethynodrel, norethindrone, norethindrone acetate, ethynodiol diacetate, or norgestrel. A description of each pill, along with a breakdown of its ingredients, is given in Table 2–1.

How do birth control pills prevent pregnancy?

Birth control pills that combine estrogen and progestogen are thought to prevent conception by inhibiting the release of LRF from the hypothalamus. That in turn stops FSH from stimulating an ovarian follicle to grow, and stops LH from triggering ovulation. In addition, both components of combination pills change the endometrium in such a manner that even if ovulation did take place, implantation of the fertilized egg would be unsuccessful. Furthermore, the progestogen in each of those pills produces a cervical mucus that is thick and hostile to sperm trying to penetrate and migrate through the cervical os. Minipills, which contain only progestogen, do not always prevent ovulation, but they exert the dual action of thickening the cervical mucus and making the endometrium unreceptive.

Is one of the two types of estrogen in the Pill stronger than the other?

Recently published studies conducted with the .05 milligram dose suggest that both estrogens are equally potent. However, earlier studies indicated that ethinyl estradiol was 1.7 to 2 times as potent as mestranol in its effect on the endometrium. Since breakthrough bleeding (bleeding which occurs on days that the pill is being taken rather than at the normal time during the days that the pill is stopped) is more common as the dose of estrogen is decreased, manufacturers of the newer low dose birth control pills that contain less than .05 milligrams of estrogen prefer ethinyl estradiol rather than mestranol.

Whether ethinyl estradiol is more potent than mestranol in areas of the body other than the endometrium remains an unanswered question. Several authorities believe that .05 milligrams of ethinyl estradiol is actually equal to .08 milligrams of mestranol, and that women using an oral contraceptive containing .03 milligrams of ethinyl estradiol are

TABLE 2-1 — THE PILLS: WHAT'S IN THEM

BRAND NAME	NUMBER OF TABLETS	DESCRIPTION	ESTROGENS (MILLIGRAMS)*		PROGESTOGENS (MILLIGRAMS)*				
			MESTRANOL	ETHINYL ESTRADIOL	NORGESTREL	NORETHINDRONE	NORETHINDRONE ACETATE	ETHYNODIOL DIACETATE	NORETHYNODREL
		COMBINATIONS							
Brevicon (Syntex)	21	In blue compact; blue tablets		0.035		0.5			
Brevicon (Syntex)	28	In blue compact; 21 blue tablets with "2110" on one side, 7 beige placebos		0.035		0.5			
Demulen (Searle)	21	In yellow compact; white tablets with "71" on one side		0.05				1.0	
Demulen-28 (Searle)	28	In yellow compact; 21 white tablets with "71" on one side, plus 7 pink placebos		0.05				1.0	
Enovid 5 (Searle)	20	In white calendar packet; pink tablets with "51" on one side	0.075						5.0
Enovid-E (Searle)	20	In white compact; pink tablets with "131" on one side	0.1						2.5
Loestrin 1/20 (Parke, Davis)	21	In yellow compact; 21 white tablets with "915" on one side		0.02			1.0		
Loestrin 1.5/30	21	In white compact; 21 green tablets with "916" on one side		0.03			1.5		
Loestrin 1/20 (Parke, Davis)	28	In yellow compact; 21 white tablets with "915" on one side, 7 brown 75-milligram ferrous fumarate (iron) tablets		0.02			1.0		

*.05 milligrams = 50 micrograms

TABLE 2-1 — THE PILLS: WHAT'S IN THEM (CONTINUED)

| BRAND NAME | NUMBER OF TABLETS | DESCRIPTION | ESTROGENS (MILLIGRAMS) | | | PROGESTOGENS (MILLIGRAMS) | | | |
			MESTRANOL	ETHINYL ESTRADIOL	NORGESTREL	NORETHINDRONE	NORETHINDRONE ACETATE	ETHYNODIOL DIACETATE	NORETHYNODREL
		COMBINATIONS							
Loestrin 1.5/30 (Parke, Davis)	28	In white compact; 21 green tablets with "916" on one side, 7 brown 75-milligram ferrous fumarate tablets		0.03			1.5		
Lo/Ovral (Wyeth)	21	In comb case; white tablets		0.03	0.3				
Norinyl 1 + 50 (Syntex)	21	In blue compact; white tablets	0.05			1.0			
Norinyl 1 + 50 (Syntex)	28	In yellow compact; 21 white tablets, 7 orange placebos	0.05			1.0			
Norinyl 1 + 80 (Syntex)	21	In beige compact; yellow tablets	0.08			1.0			
Norinyl 1 + 80 (Syntex)	28	In green compact; 21 yellow tablets, 7 orange placebos	0.08			1.0			
Norinyl 2 (Syntex)	20	In white compact; white tablets with "2" on one side	0.1			2.0			
Norlestrin 21/1 (Parke, Davis)	21	In green compact; yellow tablets with "904" on one side		0.05			1.0		
Norlestrin 28/1 (Parke, Davis)	28	In green compact; 21 yellow tablets with "904" on one side, 7 white placebos		0.05			1.0		

21

TABLE 2-1 — THE PILLS: WHAT'S IN THEM (CONTINUED)

BRAND NAME	NUMBER OF TABLETS	DESCRIPTION	ESTROGENS (MILLIGRAMS)		PROGESTOGENS (MILLIGRAMS)				
			MESTRANOL	ETHINYL ESTRADIOL	NORGESTREL	NORETHINDRONE	NORETHINDRONE ACETATE	ETHYNODIOL DIACETATE	NORETHYNODREL
COMBINATIONS									
Norlestrin 21/2.5 (Parke, Davis)	21	In lavender compact; pink tablets with "901" on one side		0.05			2.5		
Norlestrin-Fe 1 (Parke, Davis)	28	In green compact; 21 yellow tablets with "904" on one side, 7 brown 75-milligram ferrous fumarate tablets		0.05			1.0		
Norlestrin-Fe 2.5 (Parke, Davis)	28	In lavender compact; 21 pink tablets with "901" on one side, 7 brown 75-milligram ferrous fumarate tablets		0.05			2.5		
Modicon	21	In white dial pack; aqua foil cover; 21 white tablets with "Ortho" on each side		0.035		0.5			
Ortho-Novum 1/50 (Ortho)	21	In white dial pack; yellow tablets with "1" on each side	0.05			1.0			
Ortho-Novum 1/50 (Ortho)	28	In white dial pack; 21 yellow tablets with "1" on each side, 7 green placebos	0.05			1.0			
Ortho-Novum 1/80 (Ortho)	21	In white dial pack; lavender (white after 1/7/76) tablets with "1" on each side	0.08			1.0			
Ortho-Novum 1/80 (Ortho)	28	In white dial pack; 21 lavender (white after 1/7/76) tablets with "1" on each side, 7 green placebos	0.08			1.0			
Ortho-Novum 2 (Ortho)	21	In lavender dial pack; white tablets with "2" on each side	0.1			2.0			

TABLE 2-1 — THE PILLS: WHAT'S IN THEM (CONTINUED)

BRAND NAME	NUMBER OF TABLETS	DESCRIPTION	ESTROGENS (MILLIGRAMS)		PROGESTOGENS (MILLIGRAMS)				
			MESTRANOL	ETHINYL ESTRADIOL	NORGESTREL	NORETHINDRONE	NORETHINDRONE ACETATE	ETHYNODIOL DIACETATE	NORETHYNODREL
COMBINATIONS									
Ortho-Novum 10 (Ortho)	20	In blue dial pack; white tablets with "10" on each side	0.06			10.0			
Ovcon-35 (Mead Johnson)	28	In pink cardboard package; 21 peach tablets, 7 green placebos		0.035		0.4			
Ovcon-50 (Mead Johnson)	28	In yellow cardboard package; 21 yellow tablets, 7 green placebos		0.05		1.0			
Ovral (Wyeth)	21	In comb case; white tablets		0.05	0.5				
Ovral-28 (Wyeth)	28	In comb case; 21 white tablets, 7 pink placebos		0.05	0.5				
Ovulen (Searle)	20	In white compact; white pentagonal tablets with "401" on one side	0.1					1.0	
Ovulen-21 (Searle)	21	In white compact; white pentagonal tablets with "401" on one side	0.1					1.0	
Ovulen-28 (Searle)	28	In white compact; 21 white pentagonal tablets with "401" on one side, 7 pink placebos	0.1					1.0	
Zorane 1/20 (Lederle)	28	In pink compact; 21 pink tablets, 7 white placebos		0.02			1.0		

TABLE 2-1 — THE PILLS: WHAT'S IN THEM (CONTINUED)

BRAND NAME	NUMBER OF TABLETS	DESCRIPTION	ESTROGENS (MILLI-GRAMS)		PROGESTOGENS (MILLIGRAMS)					
			MESTRANOL	ETHINYL ESTRADIOL	NORGESTREL	NORETHINDRONE	NORETHINDRONE ACETATE	ETHYNODIOL DIACETATE	NORETHYNODREL
COMBINATIONS										
Zorane 1.5/30 (Lederle)	28	In blue compact; 21 blue tablets, 7 white placebos		0.03	–			1.5		
Zorane 1/50 (Lederle)	28	In green compact; 21 green tablets, 7 white placebos		0.05				1.0		
PROGESTOGENS ONLY (Minipills)										
Micronor (Ortho)	35	In white dial pack, green tablets with "0.35" on side				0.35			
Nor-Q.D. (Syntex)	42	In cardboard package; yellow tablets				0.35			
Orvette (Wyeth)	28	In blue compact; yellow tablets			0.075				

deluding themselves if they believe that this is a significant reduction in the estrogen potency of their pill.

Is it true that the undesirable side effects and complications of the Pill are due to the estrogen in them?
Many, but not all, of the Pill side effects and complications listed in Table 2–2 may be due to the estrogens the Pill contains.

Do the progestogens have any undesirable side effects?
The progestogens may produce undesirable and distressing side effects. They are listed in Table 2–3.

Why does progestogen cause such miserable side effects?
Progestogens, or *progestins*, as they are called, are more closely related to the male hormone testosterone than they are to the female hormone progesterone. The male-hormone effect of progestins has been demonstrated by several reports of female offspring born of women who inadvertently took the pill before they knew they were pregnant. The formation of a grossly enlarged clitoris resembling a male penis, and labia majora resembling a male scrotum, is believed to be due to the passage of progestins across the placenta at the time these organs were being formed.

To avoid the complications of the progestogens, why not use progesterone in the birth control pill?
Progesterone is relatively ineffective when given in the form of a pill. One birth control pill, Provest, contained medroxyprogesterone acetate, which is very similar to progesterone. Provest avoided many of the undesirable side effects of the

---

TABLE 2-2 — PROBABLE ESTROGEN SIDE EFFECTS OF ORAL CONTRACEPTION

1. Nausea, bloating, vomiting
2. Fluid retention
3. Breast tenderness
4. Increased skin pigmentation (*cloasma*), or "mask of pregnancy," on face
5. Increased mucous discharge from glands of cervix, cervical eversion
6. Headaches during days both on and off the Pill
7. Worsening of migraine headaches
8. Increase in blood pressure
9. Change in sugar tolerance and insulin requirements in both diabetics and non-diabetics
10. Abnormalities in blood clotting tests
11. Thrombophlebitis (presence of inflamed blood clot in a vein)
12. Pulmonary embolism (passage of blood clot to lung)
13. Cerebral thrombosis (presence of clot in blood vessel in the brain)
14. Myocardial infarction (heart attack due to blood clot in artery of heart)
15. Visual changes, altered contour of the eye and cornea, with contact lens discomfort
16. Changes in certain metabolism tests: thyroid, liver, and fat metabolism
17. Increased growth of benign (noncancerous) fibroid tumors of the uterus
18. Increased growth rate of estrogen-dependent cancers of the breast and uterus (however, estrogen doesn't create new ones)
19. Vitamin deficiencies
20. Possible lowering of the convulsive threshold in sensitive epileptics
21. Urinary tract changes and infection
22. Increased incidence of benign liver tumors and gall bladder disease

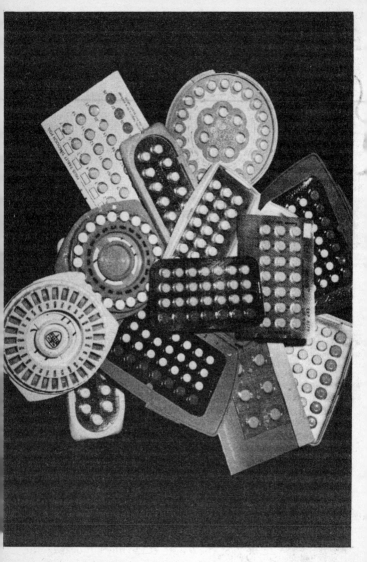

Figure 2-1.   Various Brands of Birth Control Pills

TABLE 2-3—PROBABLE PROGESTOGEN SIDE EFFECTS

1. Absent or very scanty periods
2. Acne, oily skin
3. Increase in facial hair, thinning or loss of hair on head*
4. Increased appetite and weight gain
5. Smaller breasts
6. Increased predisposition to monilia (yeast) infections*
7. Change in sugar tolerance and insulin requirements in
    both diabetics and nondiabetics
8. Fatigue,* diminished sex drive,* depression*
9. Breakthrough bleeding
10. May alter liver function and cholesterol concentration in the bile
11. May cause liver tumors
12. Altered lipid or fat metabolism

*Effect mentioned is questionable.

progestogens. However, it was taken off the market because it was found that large doses were associated with an increase in both benign and malignant breast tumors in beagles given this medication experimentally.

Are the five progestogens of equal strength?
The relative strengths of the progestogens is based on how long the least amount of a given progestogen, combined with a fixed amount of estrogen, can delay the start of a healthy woman's period for two weeks. Table 2–4 shows the relative potency of the five progestogens according to that standard. Norgestrel is by far the most potent.

How do I know if I am receiving the best pill for me?
Dr. James H. Nelson has charted the spectrum of relative *estrogen dominance* of the most commonly used oral contraceptives (Table 2–5). Though he calls the chart "educated guesswork based on biological and clinical evidence available," it does help physicians select the correct brand of the Pill for a specific type of woman.

    Results of the most recent study of the relative potencies of some of the most commonly available oral contraceptives are shown in Table 2–6. The length of the black blocks on the left reflects the relative strength of the progestogens, as shown in Table 2–4. Note that the length of the black box for

TABLE 2-4 — RELATIVE POTENCY OF PROGESTOGENS (AS MEASURED BY DELAY OF MENSES)

	Relative Potency of 1 mg
Ethynodiol diacetate	15
Norethindrone	1
Norethindrone acetate	2
Norethynodrel	1
Norgestrel	30

TABLE 2-5 — HYPOTHETICAL SPECTRUM OF BIRTH CONTROL PILLS LISTED B[Y] RELATIVE ESTROGEN DOMINANCE

	MOST ESTROGEN-DOMINANT	PROGESTOGEN ONLY
COMBINED	Enovid-E Enovid 10 Enovid 5 Ovulen Norinyl 2 Ortho-Novum 2 Demulen Norinyl 1/80 Ortho-Novum 1/80 Norlestrin 1 Norinyl Ortho-Novum 1 Ovral Norlestrin 2.5 Ortho-Novum 10 Loestrin	
SEQUENTIAL*	Oracon (throughout cycle) Norquen (Days 1-14) Ortho SQ (Days 1-14)	Norquen (Days 15-20) Ortho SQ (Days 15-20)
MINI	(Progestogen only)	Nor-Q.D. Micronor Ovrette

* Sequentials withdrawn from market - Feb, 1976

28

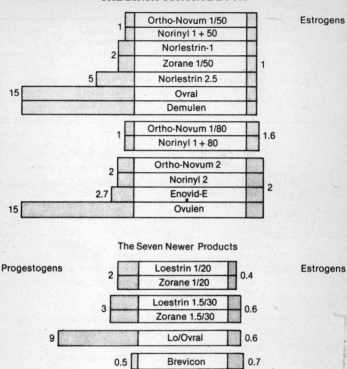

| | Progestogens | | Estrogens |

The Seven Newer Products

TABLE 2-6

the progestogen in Demulen is equal to that of Ovral; Demulen has 1 milligram ethynodiol diacetate, with a relative potency of 15 (Table 2–4), while Ovral has only .5 milligram norgestrel, but its relative potency of 30 is for each milligram. The black boxes on the right show the relative strength of the estrogen in each pill. In this table, the strength of ethinyl estradiol and mestranol are considered as being equal.

Based on the preceding discussion, I would think that a doctor was not too sharp if he or she prescribed Ovral or

Norlestrin 2.5 as contraception for a woman with acne and facial hair, as progestins of that strength would only worsen these existing conditions. If breakthrough bleeding is a problem, a pill with less estrogen will certainly not be the answer.

Table 2–7 helps you tell if you are receiving the best contraceptive for your specific needs. In Table 2–7 I have again listed all the known side effects of oral contraceptives and the recommended measures doctors should take in correcting them.

From the preceding chart it appears that the minipill, which contains only progestogen, has many advantages over the combined pill. Are there any disadvantages?

If 100 women use the minipill for one year there will be approximately 1.5 to 3 unwanted pregnancies, or a success rate of 97 to 98.5 percent. The combination pill, on the other hand, is 99.3 percent effective. Unlike other birth control pills, the minipills must be taken every day without interruption, and if one is forgotten the chances of pregnancy are much greater than if one combination pill is missed. Because the minipill contains no estrogen, at least half the women using it will experience annoying, unpredictable bleeding.

There is data available from 18 separate studies which strongly suggests a higher incidence of ectopic pregnancy among women who accidentally conceive while using the minipill (see ectopic pregnancy, Page 90).One group of researchers suggested that the progestin norgestrel, the type found in Ovrette, was more likely to be the culprit than other progestins. From the information available, it is clear that a doctor should always consider the possibility of an ectopic pregnancy in a woman who develops lower abdominal pain while she is on a progestin-only oral contraceptive.

The mechanism by which a minipill makes one more susceptible to an ectopic pregnancy is unknown. However, it is theorized that the progestin slows down the transport of the fertilized egg by the Fallopian tube. As a result, it attaches itself within the tube rather than its normal location in the endometrium of the uterus.

The estrogen contained in the combination birth control pills is capable of reducing the quantity of breast milk in nursing women. The progestin-only minipill, on the other

TABLE 2-7 — MANAGING SIDE EFFECTS OF ORAL CONTRACEPTIVES

↓—DECREASE DOSE   ⟶—NO CHANGE IN DOSE   ↑—INCREASE DOSE

SIDE EFFECT	RECOMMENDED CORRECTION OF SIDE EFFECT		OTHER SUGGESTIONS
	ESTROGEN CORRECTION	PROGESTIN CORRECTION	
1. Nausea, vomiting, bloating	↓	⟶	Minipill
2. Fluid retention	↓	⟶	Minipill
3. Breast tenderness	↓	⟶ or ↑	Minipill
4. Increased skin pigmentation	↓ or Stop	⟶	Minipill
5. Increased mucus discharge	↓	⟶	
6. Headache, migraine	↓ or Stop	↓ or Stop	
7. Increased blood pressure	↓ or Stop	⟶	
8 Thrombophlebitis	Stop	Stop	
9. Varicose veins	↓ or Stop	⟶	
10. Change in contact lens discomfort	↓ or Stop	⟶	Minipill
11. Blind spots	Stop	Stop	
12. Increased growth of benign fibroids	↓ or Stop	⟶ or ↑	Minipill
13. Breast or uterine cancer	Stop	Stop	
14. Change in thyroid	⟶	⟶	
15. Heart attack	Stop	Stop	
16. Pulmonary embolus	Stop	Stop	
17. Liver disease	Stop	Stop	
18. Gall bladder disease	Stop	Stop	
19. Decreased breast milk in nursing mothers	Stop	⟶ or ↑	Minipill
20. Increased sensitivity to light	↓ or Stop	⟶	Minipill
21. Menstrual flow too heavy	↓	↑	
22. Cervical eversion	↓	⟶	
23. Urinary tract infection	↓	⟶	
24. Light or absent periods	↑	⟶ or ↓	
25. Acne	↑	↑	High-estrogen pill
26. Increased facial hair, thinning of hair of head	↑	↑	
27. Decreased size of breasts	↑	↑	

31

TABLE 2-7 — MANAGING SIDE EFFECTS OF ORAL CONTRACEPTIVES (CONTINUED)

↓ —DECREASE DOSE   ⟷ —NO CHANGE IN DOSE   ↑ —INCREASE DOSE

SIDE EFFECT	RECOMMENDED CORRECTION OF SIDE EFFECT		OTHER SUGGESTIONS
	ESTROGEN CORRECTION	PROGESTIN CORRECTION	
28. Increased weight gain and appetite	↓	↓	
29. Yeast infections	⟷	↓	
30. Decreased sex drive	↑	↓	High-estrogen pill
31. Depression	↑	↑	
32. Breakthrough bleeding	↑	⟷ or ↓	
33. Decreased vaginal secretion (dry vagina)	↑	↓	
34. Worsening of diabetes	↓ or Stop	↓ or Stop	
35. Elevated blood lipids	↓ or Stop	↓ or Stop	Norgestrel

hand, does not appear to adversely affect the quantity of milk produced. As a result, many obstetricians prescribe the minipill as contraception for nursing women. Other doctors are reluctant to do this because no large-scale studies have been conducted to prove that small amounts of progestins ingested in the milk over a prolonged period of time are harmless to a nursing infant. While minipills do not appear to decrease milk quantity, there are statistics available which show that they do alter the basic composition of breast milk. These changes include a decrease in total protein content, milk fats, lactose, phosphorous, calcium, magnesium, and zinc. It is for these reasons that minipills are not usually a doctor's first choice of contraception for the nursing woman.

Theoretically, it would be nice to be able to prescribe minipills for women whose medical problems absolutely preclude the use of pills containing estrogen. However, this is not possible, since chemists have found that a small percentage of the norethindrone in Micronor and Nor-Q.D. is converted to estrogen in the body. Though the makers of Ovrette claim that the norgestrel in their product is less likely to do this, they do not recommend using it under circumstances in which other birth control pills are contraindicated or forbidden.

Doesn't Modicon, a combination pill, contain the lowest dose of estrogen of all combination pills?

Actually, all Modicon tablets were recalled in October, 1975, because it was found that they contained less estrogen than even the manufacturers thought they had. Each tablet of the new wonder drug was supposed to contain .035 milligram ethinyl estradiol and .5 milligram norethindrone. However, because the dye used to color the Modicon tablets faded when it was exposed to light, an undetermined number of pills had levels of estrogen below the .035 milligram originally quoted, and the 150,000 women who were using this Pill in 1975 had an increased risk of pregnancy.

Modicon is now available again. The newest product is a pure white pill that contains no dye and that is protected from all elements by a special foil package.

What were the sequential birth control pills, and why were they withdrawn from the market?

In February, 1975, under orders from the FDA, the manufacturers of sequential contraceptives stopped the sale of these pills. This came as a shock to the millions of American women using the brands Oracon, Ortho-Novum SQ, and Norquen, which all provided for fourteen to sixteen days on estrogen only, followed by five to seven days on estrogen combined with progestin.

Many gynecologists were disenchanted with sequential preparations prior to their withdrawal from the market. One reason was that the pregnancy rate, though lower than that of the minipill, was at least 1 percent higher than that of the combination pill. Missing a sequential pill in mid-cycle was more likely to result in ovulation and pregnancy.

Each of the sequentials contained more estrogen than the normally acceptable .05 milligram limit of most of the newer birth control pills. Prior to the ban, it was noted that the increased amount of estrogen heightened the risk of thrombosis, or blood clot formation (see Page 36).

The last and most disturbing finding, which precipitated the removal of these drugs from the market, was the probable relationship between sequential contraceptives and the development of endometrial cancer in women using them.

If I use birth control pills and don't want my period to come on the expected date, how can I alter that situation?
This can easily be done with combined pills by stopping them seven days or less before the full supply is finished, and discarding the remainder of the pills in the pack. A normal period will follow, and then the next new box of pills may be started as usual. An alternative method is to to prolong the cycle by using additional pills from another pack for up to 21 days.

When I begin taking birth control pills, how long does it take to be safe from pregnancy?
Contrary to the popular belief that the Pill must be taken for one or even two months before it becomes effective, the Pill is safe after taking ten pills from the first pack.

If I forget to take a pill, what should I do?
The best advice is to take the Pill when you remember it has been forgotten. Though this may mean you are taking two pills at one time, it is not harmful. Missing one combined pill during the cycle will rarely result in pregnancy. However, missing a minipill at any time during the month can be dangerous. Pregnancy rates are lowest and episodes of breakthrough bleeding are lessened when the pills are taken at approximately the same time each day. If two consecutive pills are missed, double the dosage for the next two days. Then resume the regular schedule, but use another method of contraception for the remainder of that cycle. Menstrual-like bleeding often takes place soon after two pills are missed, and occasionally after one pill is missed. If not heavy, it is best ignored until all the pills are taken.

What is the relationship between birth control pills and diseases of the liver?
There is no doubt that the estrogen in the pill is capable of altering the results of certain laboratory tests which measure liver function. These test results revert to normal when the Pill is stopped, and this phenomenon appears to be harmless.

If you have liver disease, never take any form of the Pill.

This warning applies to the minipill as well since it may also activate certain enzymes or chemicals in the liver.

A small percentage of women suffer from a condition known as *recurrent cholestasis of pregnancy*, a condition which develops when the increased estrogen and progesterone during pregnancy makes it difficult for the liver to rid itself of the bile it produces. As a result, the bile backs up into the circulation and causes severe itching of the skin, and occasionally jaundice, or yellowing of the skin. Since birth control pills produce the same effect, these susceptible women should never use them.

Hepatitis is a disease caused by a virus; its symptoms include jaundice, loss of appetite, and pain under the right rib cage due to enlargement of and infection within the liver. Recovery is slow but complete in practically all cases. Should a woman take birth control pills while she has hepatitis? A favorable report of thirty-four women who did take birth control pills throughout the attack of hepatitis was recently presented to the *Journal of the American Medical Association (JAMA)*. The small number of patients in the study makes any favorable conclusions suspect until more impressive data is available. Until then, most doctors would not prescribe the Pill until recovery, as measured by normal blood tests, is complete. I have seen women who have been denied birth control pills because of a history of hepatitis years before, but if the liver function studies are now normal, there is no reason to withhold the Pill.

In 1973, Dr. Janet Baum suggested a possible relationship between Pill use and an increased incidence of liver tumors called *hepatomas*. Since then, almost two hundred pill users with that once-rare tumor and another tumor called focal nodular hyperplasia have been reported: some of them died from intraabdominal hemorrhage despite normal liver function tests.

Hepatoma and focal nodular hyperplasia appears to be more common in women whose birth control pills contain mestranol rather than ethinyl estradiol. That may be due to the fact that mestranol has been on the market longer, so more women have used it. Some investigators doubt that the estrogen component is solely to blame for liver hepatoma; they believe it is the combined effect of progestogen and estrogen which creates this disease. (However, a small percentage of women with liver tumors used progestin-only mini pills, which contain no estrogen.) There also appears to be a time factor involved, since hepatoma is more prevalent among women who have used birth control pills for more than four years.

Hepatoma is diagnosed by X-ray scan of the liver. Though the extent of this complication has yet to be made clear, women on the Pill who feel a mass (enlargement) or pain under the right rib cage or on the upper right side of the abdomen should stop the Pill and seek medical evaluation.

Do birth control pills affect the gall bladder?

Bile passes from the liver to the gall bladder. Gallstones may form within the bile when it contains increased amounts of cholesterol. In one recent investigation of twenty-two healthy women using oral contraceptives, it was noted that the concentration of cholesterol in the bile was increased significantly. Studies have confirmed that women using the Pill are much more likely to develop gallstones which require surgery. This risk appears to be greater if the Pill has been used for more than a year.

Whether it is the estrogen or progestin which causes gallstones remains controversial. In experimental studies on laboratory animals, both have been found to increase the cholesterol concentration of bile. Studies of women using only estrogen for menopausal symptoms have confirmed a significantly higher incidence of gall bladder disease requiring surgery. Two studies reported in the British Medical Journal have noted that when women use only the progestin, liver-function and bile-excretion tests are not abnormal. However, when combined with estrogen, progestins will exaggerate the effects that estrogen produces. The point of these studies is that both estrogens and progestins have the potential to adversely alter liver function, bile excretion, and gall bladder disease.

When people say that birth control pills cause blood clots, what do they mean?

Let's first define some essential terms. A *thrombus* is a plug, clot, or solid piece of blood attached to the wall of an artery or vein. When in a vein *(phleb-)*, it is often accompanied by inflammation *(-itis)*. *Thrombophlebitis* is most common in the veins of the legs and pelvis, and may be either superficial or deep. The superficial variety is located just beneath the surface of the skin in the varicose veins which may develop with childbirth. Few women have serious complications from superficial thrombophlebitis, but thrombophlebitis of the veins deep in the legs and pelvis often present a real threat to a woman's life. Unfortunately, deep thrombophlebitis may occur without any warning symptoms at all. When one of these deep clots becomes dislodged from the wall of the vein, it travels through the circulation and is called an *embolus*. If this embolus reaches the lung, it is then called a *pulmonary embolus*. There, it may block the opening of a large oxygen-carrying blood vessel, causing instant death.

The formation of a thrombus in a small blood vessel of the heart prevents oxygen from reaching areas of that vital organ. As a result the heart muscle, or *myocardium*, dies or becomes *infarcted*. Survival from *myocardial infarction*, or "heart attack", will depend upon how great an area of myocardium is destroyed due to the lack of oxygen.

Cerebral thrombosis, or "stroke", takes place when a clot obstructs a blood vessel in the brain. That may result in paralysis, loss of consciousness, and death. Again, the degree of disability depends on how great an area has been deprived of oxygen by the thrombus. Occasionally, thrombi (plural for thrombus) in the small blood vessels will produce subtle changes, such as tiny blind spots in the field of vision of one eye. Thrombi may also form in certain intestinal blood vessels, causing what is called *mesenteric thrombosis*, which may also prove fatal.

The common bond between all these conditions is that they have a greater likelihood of occurring in women who use birth control pills. Many investigators have proven beyond a doubt that the estrogen in the Pill is responsible for an increase in certain blood substances called *clotting factors*, which enhance the formation of thrombi in the circulation.

What are the risks of thrombophlebitis or pulmonary embolus if I use birth control pills?

The initial optimism about the Pill ended abruptly in 1968 when a study from Britain demonstrated the relationship between the Pill, thrombus formation, and embolus. Of the many studies conducted since then, the vast majority have demonstrated that women using birth control pills are six

times as likely to develop thrombophlebitis as nonusers. In
1974, the Royal College of General Practitioners in England
reported that the incidence of thrombophlebitis was related
to the dose of estrogen contained in the Pill. Among women
using the .05 milligram estrogen pill, deep thrombophlebitis
was noted in 81 per 100,000 users per year compared to 112
per 100,000 users per year among women using pills containing more than .05 milligrams of estrogen. This comparison shows clearly that the risk of thromboembophlebitis was
reduced by almost 28 percent in those women on the .05 milligram dose. It has been estimated that the risk of dying
from a pulmonary embolus ranges between 1.5 to 4 women
out of every 100,000 using the pill, with the higher frequency
being noted mostly in women over forty years of age.

Is there any way to reduce the incidence of thrombus formation and fatal emboli?

The incidence of these problems can be reduced if doctors
would prescribe the .05 milligram or lower doses of estrogen
more often and discontinue birth control pills in most
women over forty and all women over forty-five. Women
with a history of superficial phlebitis, deep phlebitis, or previous embolus should never be given the Pill. The Pill should
be used with caution by women with strong family histories
of such conditions. Most women will develop varicose veins
following childbirth, and in the absence of inflammation
there is no reason to withhold the Pill. However, individuals
with extensive or painful varicose veins are more prone to
phlebitis, and because of this the Pill is best avoided.

Stop the Pill immediately and see your doctor if you experience vague pains or swelling in one or both legs, lower
abdominal pain, chest pain, shortness of breath, unexplained cough especially if blood-tinged, blurred vision, severe headaches, or partial loss of vision.

What is the risk of heart attack in Pill users?

The same group from England that first noted the relationship between oral contraceptives and thrombophlebitis recently reported that oral contraceptive use increases the risk
of myocardial infarction. They noted that users of birth control pills between the ages of thirty and thirty-nine were almost three times as likely to suffer both fatal and nonfatal heart attacks as were nonusers. In the forty- to forty-

four-year-old age group, the risk increased to 5.7 times for nonfatal and 4.7 times for fatal, heart attacks. When translated into actual women affected by both fatal and nonfatal heart attacks, oral contraceptive users between the ages of thirty and thirty-nine had an incidence of 11 per 100,000, compared to 4 per 100,000 in the group not using birth control pills. In the forty- to forty-year-old age group the respective figures were an alarming 112 per 100,000 and 22 per 100,000. The investigators also found that when other risk factors of heart disease were present, such as smoking, obesity, diabetes, and high blood pressure, the combined effect was far greater than the sum of the individual risks.

In October, 1977, *The Lancet*, a leading British medical journal, reported the latest information in a continuing study of 46,000 women using oral contraceptives. This report showed that the increased death rate among women using birth control pills was due not only to heart attacks, but also to a wide variety of other circulatory diseases such as elevated blood pressure, strokes, and heart disease resulting from rheumatic fever. The authors of this study concluded that pill users faced a 40 percent higher death rate than women of the same age who never used the Pill. In addition, women on the Pill for five years or longer had a death rate nearly ten times higher than women who never used the Pill and four times higher than those using the Pill for less than five years.

What is the risk of heart attack among women who smoke?
In a recent analysis of statistics from England, Dr. Anrudh K. Jain of the Population Council noted that smoking among oral contraceptive users was the main factor responsible for significantly increasing the risk of both fatal and nonfatal heart attacks. Dr. Jain has convincingly demonstrated that the effect of the Pill and cigarette smoking is "synergistic," meaning that the total death rate associated with the combination of these two factors is many times higher than would result from each factor acting independently. Women between the ages of forty and forty-four who neither smoke nor take the Pill, have a 7 per 100,000 chance of experiencing a fatal heart attack. For nonsmokers on the Pill the risk rises to 10 per 100,000, while smokers not on the Pill demonstrate a fatal heart attack rate of 16 per 100,000 (Table 2–8). When smokers in this age group use the Pill, the death risk

Annual Mortality from Myocardial Infarction for Pill Users and Nonusers

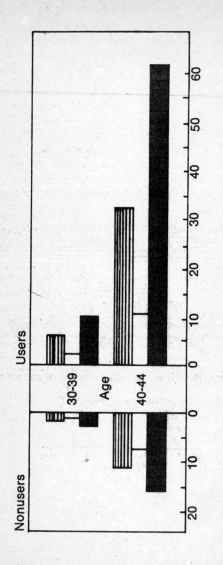

■ Smokers and nonsmokers combined   □ Nonsmokers only   ■ Smokers only

Deaths per 100,000

TABLE 2-8

40

climbs to a very dangerous 59 per 100,000 for all smokers and 83 per 100,000 for those women classified as being heavy smokers. Dr. Jain defines a heavy smoker as one who smokes 15 cigarettes per day or more. Nonsmoking women between the ages of thirty-five and thirty-nine experience only 4 deaths per 100,000, but heavy smokers in this age group have a myocardial infarction mortality of 24 per 100,000. In the thirty to thirty-five year age group, the comparative figures are 2 and 16 per 100,000 women.

Dr. Jain's conclusions are worth noting: "Those women who smoke as well as use oral contraceptives and want to reduce the risk of myocardial infarction should be encouraged to give up smoking. Smoking, in other words, should be considered as another contraindication for the prescription of oral contraceptives."

Do oral contraceptives alter the lipid content (cholesterol, fatty acids, etc.) in the blood, believed to be associated with a higher risk of heart attack?

Lipids refer to a wide variety of potentially harmful chemical substances in the blood, including *fatty acids*, *cholesterol*, *phospholipids*, and *triglycerides*. It has been theorized that high concentrations of these substances in the blood help to accelerate *atherosclerosis*, which is the formation of lipid plaques lining the walls of blood vessels. The effect of this is a narrowing of the blood vessel, thereby making it more prone to blockage by a thrombus, or clot.

Some studies have demonstrated that estrogens given to postmenopausal women lower blood cholesterol levels, while other studies testing the estrogen component of oral contraceptives have shown either no change or a minimal increase in blood cholesterol concentration. Progestins, on the other hand, have in most studies increased blood cholesterol levels. (The one very important exception to this was a 1975 report in which it was found that norgestrel [Ovrette] given daily without any estrogen significantly lowered the blood levels of cholesterol, triglycerides, fatty acids, and phospholipids. If these findings are substantiated by other research groups, a pill such as Ovrette would become the desirable oral contraceptive for women having elevated blood lipids or a strong family history of heart disease.)

Though many of the findings linking birth control pills with changes in phospholipid and fatty acid metabolism are inconsistent, it has been clearly established that elevation of blood triglycerides may be attributed to the estrogen component of the Pill. Progestins have been found to either lower triglyceride levels or not affect them.

The above studies demonstrate that estrogens and progestins do alter lipid concentrations in the blood. For this reason, the birth control pill with the lowest dose of both components should be used. If you have a strong family history of high cholesterol and heart disease, you should have your blood lipids analyzed before starting the Pill, use a Pill with a low dose of both estrogen and progestin, and have your blood lipids checked annually if prolonged use of oral contraception is anticipated. Based on this report, the patient with a strong family history of heart disease would be best treated with a birth control pill with very little estrogen, and norgestrel as the progestogen.

Are certain blood types more prone to thromboembolism?
For some unknown reason women with blood type A appear to be more susceptible to thromboembolism, whereas those with blood group O are more resistant. The significance of these findings is minimal at best and should not deter a woman of blood group A from using birth control pills. However, the lowest possible dose of estrogen, or the minipill, should be used by these individuals.

Can the Pill cause high blood pressure?
Many large studies involving thousands of women have demonstrated that the estrogen in the Pill is capable of causing abnormal elevation of blood pressure, or *hypertension*. This problem develops in approximately 5 to 7 percent of all women who use the Pill. It must not be taken lightly, since it subjects 600,000 women in this country to a greater risk of both myocardial infarction and a type of stroke caused by bursting of blood vessels in the brain. Hypertension produced by the Pill usually occurs within the first six months of use, though exceptions to this rule occur only too often.

When a blood pressure reading is taken, it is recorded as two numbers. The first, higher, number is called the *systolic* pressure, while the second, lower, number is termed the *diastolic* pressure. A normal reading for a young, healthy woman may range from 90 (systolic)/ 60 (diastolic) to 130/80. Many doctors consider the reading of 140/90 as the borderline between normal and hypertensive. Oral contraception should not be taken when the blood pressure is at this level or above. If your once-normal blood pressure rises to 140/90 while you are taking the Pill, stop the pill immediately and use other contraception. Your blood pressure will revert to normal within six months after you stop the Pill. Occasionally when the blood pressure is borderline as a result of a combination pill, the minipill can become a logical alternative, provided the blood pressure is carefully monitored every three months.

Though hypertension is defined as a blood pressure above 140/90, it is disturbing that oral contraceptives raise the blood pressures to some degree in almost every woman who uses them. In one survey, after four years of oral contraceptive use the systolic pressure was elevated an average of 14 points and the diastolic 8.5 points. Though the blood pressures of all these patients were still in the normal range, the adverse effects of these small changes, though unknown at the present time, may be potentially dangerous. Referring to these changes, Dr. Myron Weinberger of Indiana University, an expert on the subject, states, "It is clear that definite blood pressure changes invariably accompany oral contraceptive usage. We must therefore ask what may be their clinical importance. From actuarial data we have learned that the 'best' blood pressure is the lowest compatible with normal functioning; increases such as those described (elevated but not hypertensive) have been associated with increased morbidity and decreased longevity. By extrapolation, prolonged use of oral contraceptives may influence both health and life-span unfavorably."

Are some women more susceptible to Pill hypertension than others?

Women with a family history of hypertension have an increased tendency to develop hypertension on the Pill. Hypertension in this country is also more common among blacks, and studies are presently being conducted to determine if black women without hypertension are more prone to this Pill complication. Patients with preexisting kidney diseases accompanied by hypertension are especially at risk and should not take the Pill. Findings are controversial as to whether or not women with a history of *toxemia*, or hypertension found only during pregnancy, are more prone to develop a rise in blood pressure on the Pill. If such women take the Pill, they should use the lowest estrogen dose or a minipill, and record their blood pressures frequently. Other susceptible women are those over forty, and those who are obese. To date there is no evidence linking Pill hypertension with smoking habits, number of children, or social class of the woman using the Pill.

Other than an elevation of blood pressure, are there any warning symptoms of hypertension?

Though hypertension is often without symptoms, the presence of a headache, dizziness, blurred vision, nose bleeds, and a sensation of ringing noises in the ears should alert a woman on the Pill to have her blood pressure checked.

Is it true that certain black women can't take birth control pills?

Sickle cell anemia is an extremely serious disease which a small percentage of blacks are born with. *Sickle cell trait*, on the other hand, is present in 10 percent of all blacks and is without symptoms other than a mild anemia. Sickle cell trait is a significant condition because two people with the trait will produce a baby with sickle cell disease 25 percent of the time.

Both pregnancy and birth control pills may cause a life-threatening crisis in patients with sickle cell disease; these women must never take the Pill. However, women with sickle cell trait can use oral contraceptives.

Can birth control pills cause the thyroid gland to become overactive?

Oral contraceptives cause characteristic changes in some tests which measure thyroid function. These changes are also noted during pregnancy and are believed to be due to the elevated estrogen levels present in the body at this time. Though the thyroid tests become somewhat altered, the actual working of the thyroid gland remains unchanged. If a doctor is not aware that a woman is taking birth control pills, the test results may initially confuse him into thinking her thyroid gland is overactive. However, other, more specific, tests easily confirm the fact that the thyroid is functioning normally, and this should not present a problem either in diagnosis or treatment. When a woman stops using birth control pills, the altered tests will return to normal within a few days. The minipill will not cause these changes.

What is the relationship between diabetes and birth control pills?

Most studies agree that oral contraceptives have a detrimental effect on the blood sugar and blood insulin tests taken by both healthy and diabetic women. The estrogen and progestogen components have both been held responsible for these changes. For women with normal glucose or sugar tolerance tests prior to using the Pill, it has been estimated that anywhere from 12 to 39 percent will develop an abnormal test while using the Pill. This "chemical diabetes" produces no symptoms, and reverts to normal when the birth control pill is no longer used. However, no one knows the long-term effect of this stress to the body. The elevation of blood insulin levels in these individuals means that the pancreas, which produces insulin, is being stressed to turn out more and more insulin in its attempt to remove the excess sugar from the blood. Even when the blood sugar is normal in Pill-users, this exaggerated insulin response is still present.

It has convincingly been proven that the progestogen, even in the lower amounts found in the minipill, exerts its own very definite effects. In a study of thirty-one women with normal sugar tolerance tests, .35 milligram norethindrone was given on a daily basis. The results showed that there was no change in blood glucose, but there was a definite rise in all the blood insulin values. William Spellacy and his colleagues noted a significant elevation of both the blood glucose and plasma insulin levels after treating seventy-one women with .075 milligram norgestrel daily for one year. Before treatment, all seventy-one women had normal glucose tolerance tests, but after a year almost 16 percent demonstrated at least a borderline abnormality in their glucose tolerance tests.

For the woman with a borderline blood sugar level, oral contraceptives often provide the stress needed to make it definitely abnormal. Though stopping the Pill usually brings all these values back to normal, in a few disturbing reports the diabetic changes have persisted even after stopping the Pill. Because of this, most doctors would not prescribe oral contraceptives to these borderline individuals.

Surprisingly, the diabetic who takes insulin will have less

difficulty obtaining a prescription for the Pill from her doctor than the woman with a borderline test. The reason for this is that once a person is on insulin, the extra amounts needed for Pill-users is usually very little, and it is easily tolerated without apparent ill effect to the patient.

However, since diabetics are more prone to atherosclerosis, heart attack, and hypertension, birth control pills, which may worsen all these conditions, still appear to be a poor method of contraception for diabetic women.

Do birth control pills alter my vitamin and mineral needs?
Several studies have indicated that the estrogen in oral contraceptives prevents the body from absorbing certain important vitamins and minerals. Included among these are Vitamin B6 (pyridoxine), riboflavin, folic acid, Vitamin B12, zinc, and possibly Vitamin C.

No less than six different investigators have shown a relationship between B6 deficiency and use of birth control pills. The estrogen is the factor to blame, since a healthy male volunteer who was given estrogen (ethinyl estradiol) for a period of five weeks developed the deficiency.

Though adverse psychological effects of the Pill such as depression have been associated with the progestogens, some authors have attributed this symptom to the deficiency of Vitamin B6. In one report of fifty-eight Pill-users suffering from depression, administration of a high daily dose of B6 resulted in a marked improvement of symptoms in forty-four of these women.

Several workers in the field have suggested that all women using oral contraceptives receive a Vitamin B6 supplement daily. The RDA, or Recommended Dietary Allowance, is 2 milligrams B6 for adult women not using birth control pills. A daily dose of ten times that, or twenty-five milligrams, is recommended for women who use birth control pills. Foods rich in B6 are wheat germ, liver, meats, fish, kidney, whole grain cereals, milk, soy beans, bananas, peanuts, and corn.

The need for riboflavin is often closely related to the need for B6, since both vitamins are used by the body in a similar fashion. Foods rich in riboflavin are milk, eggs, cheese, green leafy vegetables, liver, kidney, and beef heart.

Folic acid deficiency, though not uncommon, rarely reaches the point where it produces its characteristic anemia. The possible association between folic acid deficiency and oral contraceptive use has been studied since 1969. Some investigators have reported deficiencies in Pill users, while others have not. The RDA of folic acid is 400 micrograms a day, and in pregnancy it is double this amount. The average nonprescription multivitamin contains a maximum of 300 micrograms per tablet, but any amount greater than this requires a prescription. Excellent food sources of folic acid are raw green leafy vegetables, citrus fruit juices, lean meats, veal, liver, kidney, and yeast.

Keeping adequate stores of folic acid should be of more than academic interest to women for two reasons. Firstly, many women conceive soon after stopping the birth control pill, (though it is unwise to do so—see Page 48) and if a slight folic acid deficiency exists, the hormonal effect of the pregnancy may actually make it worse. Secondly, it is well known that a folic acid deficiency in the first three months of pregnancy may be associated with birth deformities in the fetus. Recent reports have shown a higher rate of anomalies in babies conceived within three months of stopping the Pill. Might these subtle folic acid deficiencies be at least partially responsible? The answer is not now known.

The type of anemia produced by a lack of Vitamin B12 is similar to, but far less common than, that caused by insufficient folic acid.

Some women who use birth control pills and some pregnant women have subnormal and even drastically lowered B12 levels. The RDA for pregnancy and birth-control-pill users is 8 micrograms a day; liver, kidney, muscle meats, eggs, and cheese are all excellent sources of B12.

Thiamine is another B vitamin. Initial findings of two studies suggest that oral contraceptives may cause a very mild thiamine depletion which should not require thiamine replacement.

Zinc is a necessary body mineral whose levels are significantly lower in women using oral contraceptives. Adequate replacement is found in oysters and other seafood, liver, wheat germ, and yeast.

Opinions differ as to the effect of birth control pills on Vitamin E levels. Increases and decreases have both been reported, and it is generally concluded that supplements of Vitamin E are of little value, if any.

Though Vitamin C (ascorbic acid) requirements for

women using the Pill have not been thoroughly investigated, it would appear that they are increased. Supplemental Vitamin C is best obtained in citrus fruits.

On the positive side, the dietary requirements for iron may be diminished in women using birth control pills since periods are usually lighter and less iron-containing blood is lost. The absorption of calcium from the intestine into the body tissues is enhanced because of the estrogen in the Pill, so the requirement for this mineral is reduced among Pill users. It has also been reported that the needs for Vitamin K, Vitamin A, niacin, and copper may be less for women on the Pill, but further studies are needed to confirm this. (It is fortunate that the occasional increase of Vitamin A levels among Pill users is only minimal, since excessive amounts, called *hypervitaminosis A*, may be responsible for fetal defects if pregnancy occurs.)

Of interest is the fact that certain clotting factors in the blood are dependent upon the presence of Vitamin K. Since Vitamin K levels will be increased among some Pill users, researchers have suggested that it is this phenomenon which may be responsible for the increased incidence of thrombus formation (see thrombus and emboli) among oral contraceptive users.

What evidence exists that fetal anomalies are more frequent when birth control pills are taken within three months before or as late as two months after conception?

The potential of the progestogens for producing masculinization of the female fetus has already been discussed. Two recent reports have noted that women accidentally taking birth control pills early in pregnancy, or given these and other hormones immediately before conception, were at a five times greater risk of giving birth to deformed babies. In some cases the hormones were prescribed as pills or as an intramuscular injection to "bring on" a late period. In other women the hormones were prescribed in an effort to maintain and support pregnancies threatening to end in miscarriage.

The characteristic pattern of anomalies in the affected offspring have been given the acronym VACTERL (Vertebral, Anal, Cardiac, Tracheoesophageal [*trachea*, "windpipe", and *esophagus*], Renal [kidney], and Limb). When the hormone preparations were taken after pregnancy had begun, the great majority of affected offspring were boys, but the distribution of males and females was equal when the women stopped the Pill in the menstrual cycle just prior to conception.

In the January 13, 1977, issue of the New England Journal of Medicine, researchers presented further evidence linking fetal exposure to female hormones with cardiac birth defects. In this study, 1,042 women who had received a variety of female hormones during the first four months of pregnancy were compared to a control group of women who received no medications. Among the group receiving hormones, the incidence of cardiac defects was 18.2 per 1000 births compared to 7.8 per 1,000 births in the control group. Of the 1,042 women who ingested hormones during their pregnancies, a subgroup of 278 specifically used birth control pills. There were 6 children born with cardiac birth defects in this group, equal to an incidence of 21.5 per 1,000 births.

The very vital lesson to be learned from these preliminary studies is that the absence of pregnancy must first be confirmed before oral contraceptives are given. In addition, hormones should no longer be used as a pregnancy test or to bring on periods, and should rarely, if ever, be used to support a pregnancy in jeopardy. In the rare cases where the latter is necessary, pure progesterone preparations given intramuscularly appear to be safest for the developing fetus. If you miss one or more pills during a cycle, followed by no period after the last pill is taken, get a pregnancy test before starting a new box of pills. By restarting the pills in the presence of an undiagnosed pregnancy, the risk to the fetus is greatest, since VACTERL anomalies are most likely to occur between the fifteenth and sixtieth day of embryo development.

Though most authorities agree that hormones taken early in pregnancy may be harmful to the fetus, recent evidence from England and Harvard University emphatically refute the claim that hormones taken prior to conception can adversely affect the fetus. In fact, both studies demonstrated a significantly lower miscarriage and stillbirth rate among former Pill users when compared with a group of women who had not taken the Pill prior to conception. Despite these favorable reports, most doctors still suggest that if you stop using the Pill, you should continue with another form of contraception for three months before trying to become pregnant. The reason for this is not a fear of fetal anomalies, but a desire on the part of the doctor to determine the exact date of conception since periods tend to be irregular for the first three months after stopping the Pill. If pregnancy should inadvertently occur during this time, elective abortion because of fear of a fetal anomaly would appear to be ill-advised.

What harmful effects can the Pill have on the breasts?
Based on the results of several large studies, there is no evidence to suggest that oral contraceptives cause breast cysts or cancer. The estrogen in the Pill may be responsible for some breast tenderness and increased fullness, but these symptoms can usually be avoided by using a Pill with a low estrogen content. It should be noted that experimental cancers of the breast have been produced in rodents and dogs by giving the animals extremely high doses of estrogen without interruption over prolonged periods of time. The imbalance caused by giving only estrogen can't be equated with the combined effect of a progestogen and estrogen in low doses followed by a week of rest, as is the case with birth control pills.

Is it true that some cases of breast cancer worsen if estrogen is given?
Approximately 40 to 50 percent of breast cancers appear to be estrogen-dependent. This means that once the cancer is present, estrogen will worsen the condition, making the cancer grow faster. Proof of this is the marked improvement many women experience when their estrogen-producing ovaries are removed as treatment for advanced breast cancer. Because of this, birth control pills (or any estrogen for that matter) should never be taken by a woman who has had breast cancer.

If my mother had breast cancer, is it safe for me to take birth control pills?
A woman with a strong family history of breast cancer has a much greater chance of developing breast cancer than does a woman without such a history. Since the Pill does not cause cancer, many doctors prescribe it for such a woman with a family cancer history provided that she has a breast exam every six months and a breast X-ray, *mammography*, at least

every two years after the age of thirty-five. Other physicians don't prescribe Pills for such a woman at all, for fear of accelerating the growth of a small, undiagnosed breast cancer.

Should women with benign fibrocystic disease of the breasts use birth control pills?

Most studies suggest that women with fibrocystic breasts are at greater risk of developing breast cancer than women in the general population. With the exception of one study, it appears that oral contraceptives may actually be beneficial to women with this condition. This exception, reported in the *Journal of the National Cancer Institute* in 1975, involved 452 women with breast cancer. Of this group, the authors noted a six- to eleven-fold risk of breast cancer among oral contraceptive users with a history of prior breast biopsy showing benign disease.

Completely contrary to these results was another study of 110 patients with fibrocystic disease treated with high doses of Enovid over a long period of time. Objective improvement was noted in 76, meaning that the size of the cysts actually got smaller. In no case did malignancy develop. Based on these findings, doctors have theorized that using birth control pills to treat women with fibrocystic disease may actually reduce the risk of a malignancy developing. Obviously, much more data is needed to determine the validity of this hypothesis.

Does eversion of the cervix in women using birth control pills have to be treated?

Women using birth control pills tend to have a greater incidence of cervical eversion than nonusers (Chapter 1), probably because of the estrogen component in the Pill. It is also not unusual for these everted cervical glands to be covered over by the cells from the outer surface of the cervix. When this happens, the mucus in the gland can't be released, and small yellow *Nabothian* cysts are formed. They produce no symptoms, are harmless, and need not be treated. Too many doctors spend too much time cauterizing (burning), freezing, and cutting out Nabothian cysts and everted glands that should be left alone.

Erosion of the cervix is an actual defect or sore often associated with inflammation on the surface of the cervix. They should not be confused with eversion, though they often are. An erosion will usually bleed following direct contact, as in intercourse. A doctor should be able to demonstrate the bleeding from an erosion by touching a cotton-tipped applicator to the eroded spot. Cervical erosion is more annoying than serious, and is easily treated in the office by either cauterization or cryosurgery (freezing) of the involved area.

Are the birth control pills ever responsible for an abnormal pap smear or cancer of the cervix?

Investigations to date have failed to demonstrate a relationship between use of birth control pills and the incidence of abnormal Pap smears, cancer of the cervix, and precancerous conditions of the cervix called *dysplasia*.

Cancer of the cervix is truly a venereal disease related to a woman's age of first coitus as well as coitus with multiple sexual partners. Today's sexual revolution has brought with it an epidemic among young women of dysplasia and *carcinoma-in-situ*, or cancer limited to the upper surface of cells on the cervix. This condition, if left untreated, may progress over a period of years to the invasive and dangerous stage of this disease.

Many gynecologists believe that the use of birth control pills happens to coexist with, but is not the cause of, these changes to the cervix. For this reason, they do not restrict the use of birth control pills in the presence of dysplasia or carcinoma-in-situ. There have been several studies carried out to support this position.

In June, 1977, a much-publicized ten-year study was presented by researchers at the University of California at Los Angeles. Of 600 women started on the Pill, 300 had no abnormality of the cervix while 300 had dysplasia. Those women free of dysplasia at the start of the study showed no increased tendency to develop it within the first 7 years on the Pill. However, women with dysplasia who selected the Pill were 6 times more likely to develop a more severe form of dysplasia or even carcinoma-in-situ than those with dysplasia who selected the IUD or diaphragm. If these findings are substantiated, doctors in the future will be more reluctant to prescribe oral contraceptives for women with precancerous or cancerous changes of the cervix. At the present time, the best advice for all Pill-users with a history of dysplasia is to have a Pap smear at least every six months.

Are birth control pills a good treatment for irregular periods?

The term *irregular periods* encompasses a wide range of menstrual patterns from frequent, prolonged, and heavy, to infrequent, short, and light. The cause of the irregularity must be determined before any medication is taken.

For the woman over forty with heavy and frequent periods or vaginal staining, a sampling of the endometrium must be obtained to be sure that there is no evidence of a cancerous or precancerous condition. This may be done by having a D & C (*dilatation*, or opening of the cervix, and *curettage*, or scraping of the endometrium) performed in a hospital (Figure 2–2). Two less expensive office procedures of almost equal accuracy and not requiring anesthesia are performed by means of the Gravelee Jet Wash and Vabra Aspirator, which are two types of suction devices used to obtain samples of endometrial cells and tissue. Some women find these procedures to be almost painless; other women experience a great deal of discomfort. A paracervical block may be helpful in relieving severe degrees of pain.

As previously mentioned, birth control pills taken by women over forty present very definite hazards, and are best avoided if possible.

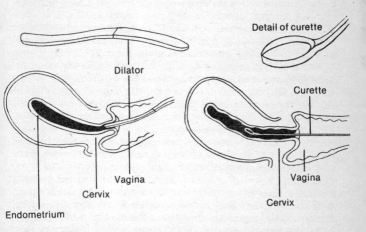

Figure 2-2.   Dilator and Curette Used for D & C

In younger women, especially teenagers who experience heavy or frequent menstruation, a D & C is rarely necessary. The usual cause of such bleeding is the immaturity or malfunctioning of the hypothalamus (see Chapter 1). Unpredictable release of FRF causes production of estrogen by the follicle. However, since LRF is not released, neither is pituitary LH. In the absence of this hormone, ovulation can't take place. Characteristically, these young women may go for months without a period, and then suddenly, without premenstrual symptoms, a tremendously heavy flow with blood clots may appear and last for many days. The heavy bleeding takes place because the endometrium, which is stimulated only by estrogen and not progesterone, sheds its lining unpredictably. These periods are practically always painless.

A complete gynecological exam must be performed on these young women to be sure that no serious abnormality is present. A test measuring thyroid function is often helpful, since occasionally an underactive thyroid gland may be responsible for this type of bleeding problem. In addition, if there is heavy bleeding, blood coagulation studies should be done to be sure that a clotting or platelet deficiency is not the source of the problem. If all these tests are normal, birth control pills may be given for several months simply for the sake of allowing lighter, more predictable periods, and preventing severe anemia from developing. Since many of these women have some degree of anemia, iron tablets are often helpful in building up the hemoglobin levels. However, the fact must be emphasized that the Pill will in no way correct the hypothalamus problem. After approximately three to four oral contraceptive cycles, the Pill may be stopped and future menses observed. If the hemorrhage recurs, the Pill should be started again. In time, the hypothalamus of these young women will eventually function more efficiently and more predictably. Often the first sign of this maturity is a surprisingly painful period lasting less than one week and indicating that ovulation probably had taken place two weeks earlier.

When a young woman with previously normal periods notes that they are now several months apart and very light, the hypothalamus is usually the culprit again. In stressful situations this structure fails to release any of its factors, including LRF. Women in college dormitories, prisoners, dieters, heroin addicts, and thousands of other women under pressure have this hypothalamus defect in common. Menses usually return to normal when the lifestyle changes for the better. The use of birth control pills solely to regulate menses on a monthly basis is not advised, since the Pill will only further limit the hypothalamus's already inadequate functioning.

Don't some doctors believe that a woman with an infertility problem has a better chance for pregnancy immediately after using birth control pills?

If your doctor believes that, change doctors. The weird idea of using the pill to enhance fertility is without factual basis. Because of its hypothalamus suppression, along with the greater probability of fetal anomalies in the event that conception does take place, the Pill must never be used in this manner.

Why do some doctors advise their patients to stop using the Pill for two or three months every three years?

Many doctors do this because they want to be sure that ovulation and menses will return to normal following prolonged suppression of the hypothalamus by the Pill. This is certainly a valid argument, especially for young women with unproven fertility. However, the opposing view—that the unproven fertility may, unhappily, become proven during these three months—is also valid. Since 98 percent of all women on the Pill ovulate within three months after the Pill is stopped, pregnancy becomes a threat during this period of time. For the 2 percent of women with a suppressed hypothalamus, a prolonged absence of ovulation and menstruation may take place after the Pill is stopped. This condition, termed *post-Pill amenorrhea*, is usually related not to how many months the Pill is taken, but more to the menstrual pattern of the individual prior to starting the Pill. Because of this, it is probably wiser to insist you are carefully screened before taking the Pill, rather than arbitrarily stopping it every two or three years. If you are a young woman with a history of very irregular periods, another form of contraception should be considered. If you decide to use birth control pills, the minipill is your best choice. Certainly, for the woman who is not interested in future childbearing, there is no logical reason for temporarily stopping the Pill.

Some 20 to 40 percent of all women with post-Pill

amenorrhea also experience *galactorrhea*, the presence of a thin, clear-to-milky discharge from one or both nipples, which results from suppression of a hypothalamus-releasing factor responsible for preventing lactation. This factor is called *PIF*, or *prolactin inhibitory factor*. In the absence of PIF, the hormone *prolactin* is released in excess from the pituitary gland, and galactorrhea or inappropriate lactation occurs.

Usually the galactorrhea subsides with the return of ovulation. Ergocryptine is a new drug which has been used with great success in inhibiting prolactin release, and consequently suppressing lactation. Ovulation and menstruation may also be restored when this drug is administered.

The idea that the Pill may cause permanent sterility just isn't true, and the absence of ovulation accompanying post-Pill amenorrhea may be successfully treated with one of the newer ovulation-inducing drugs. However, you must realize that these agents are not innocuous. Complications of their use may include multiple births, a higher miscarriage rate, and overstimulation of the ovary, with production of large cysts. On rare occasions, the ovarian cysts may be associated with the presence of fluid or blood in the abdominal cavity.

Is it true that some women experience loss of scalp hair, acne, weight gain, or an increase in facial hair after the birth control pill is stopped?
Hair follicles go through various phases of growth in all individuals. Usually, 85 percent of scalp hairs are in an active growing phase, termed the *anagen* phase, and 15 percent are in the resting, or *telogen*, phase. Hair loss takes place during the telogen phase. For unknown hormonal reasons, some women note an alarming increase in scalp hair loss for two to three months following pregnancy or use of birth control pills. Microscopic study of hair follicles at this time indicates that 50 percent are in the telogen phase. The extra 35 percent of telogen phase hairs represents a total of millions of hairs lost during this time. That sometimes frightening condition corrects itself within 3 to 6 months with 85 percent of the hairs returning to the anagen phase. Improvement may not be noted immediately, since it will take approximately one year for a hair to achieve a respectable length.

Occasionally a woman notes an increase in facial hair,

acne, and weight gain after she stops using oral contraceptives. The condition is believed to be due to a sudden, though temporary, increase of male hormone secretion from the adrenal gland, and it appears to be more common among women with a preexisting tendency toward acne and facial hair.

Though the mechanism is unknown, the estrogen in the Pill is believed responsible for decreasing the concentration and accumulation of ear wax among women using oral contraceptives. That beneficial effect is lost shortly after the Pill is stopped. Some women actually report greater amounts of ear wax than ever before during the first two post-Pill months.

Can birth control pills stunt the growth of a young girl?
Theoretically, if a girl is given estrogen prior to achieving her full adolescent growth, premature closure of the long bones of the legs may occur. This can result in the reduction of final height by about one inch, but occasionally by as much as three inches. Hormones taken after the onset of periods don't affect a woman's final height.

Can a woman who is breast feeding use birth control pills?
A significant number of nursing women will notice a decrease in milk supply due to the effect of the estrogen in the Pill. In addition, minute quantities of estrogen are transmitted to the baby in the milk. Though the effect of such a small dose of estrogen is unlikely to cause any harmful side effects, a minipill would appear to be the wisest choice for the nursing woman who wants to use oral contraceptives.

Is the Pill effective in treating young women who experience severe menstrual cramps?
Dysmenorrhea is defined as pelvic pain occuring prior to, or with the onset of, the period. It is the most common menstrual disorder of women in their teens, accounting for millions of hours lost from school and work each year.

Sufferers of this condition are perfectly normal on gynecological examination. However, it has been demonstrated that the uterine contractions in these women are of greater intensity and duration at the time of the period than those of individuals not suffering from dysmenorrhea. It is theorized that this may be due to greater sensitivity of their uterine muscles to the contractions caused by circulating prostaglandins at the time of the period. (See Chapters 7 and 11.)

Though psychiatrists have suggested for years that severe dysmenorrhea probably represents a manifestation of deeper emotional disturbances, the fact remains that the condition is relieved completely when ovulation is suppressed by a combination birth control pill. Use of the pill for a period of three or four months helps to break the miserable cycle of pain, and when the Pill is stopped, periods occasionally are permanently improved. If the pain recurs, the Pill may be restarted and continued for a longer period of time.

What is endometriosis and how effective are birth control pills in treating it?

Endometriosis is a fairly common, often painful condition of young, menstruating women caused by the presence of pieces of endometrium in areas other than their normal location within the uterus. The average age at the time of diagnosis is thirty-five, though 15 percent of patients are under thirty. The disease is very rare in women who give birth to the first child before the age of twenty, but fairly common in those who delay childbearing until after the age of thirty.

It is not known why certain individuals are susceptible to endometriosis and others aren't. The method by which the fragments of endometrium spread to other areas within the pelvis is also not known. The most popular theory is that they are passed backward from the endometrial cavity into the Fallopian tubes, and then out through the fimbria into the abdomen at the time of menstruation. There, the endometrial tissue continues to function and responds to hormones as does normal endometrium. Unfortunately, when menstruation takes place the blood passes into the pelvic organs which are involved, instead of out of the body.

Over a period of months and years, large cysts filled with old dark blood and termed *chocolate cysts* may form. The bursting of these cysts often requires emergency surgery. Scar tissue develops throughout the entire pelvis as the disease process continues. The ovary is most commonly involved, though other pelvic structures—such as the ligaments supporting the uterus, the intestinal lining, and the urinary bladder—may also be diseased. It is not uncommon for the back of the uterus to become firmly attached to the wall of the bowel, thereby assuming a *retroflexed*, or backward, tilt from which it can't be moved except through surgery. Infertility is very common in women suffering from endometriosis, due to scarring around the tube, which prevents its normal movement, as well as poor functioning of the ovary involved in the disease process.

Another enigma of the disease is that the symptoms are not often related to the amount of endometriosis that is present. I have seen several patients in my own practice with chocolate cysts filling the entire pelvis, diagnosed only because they came in for a routine checkup. Others with severe pain have been noted to have only one or two tiny fragments of endometrium in the pelvis. The most common symptoms of endometriosis are severe dysmenorrhea (painful periods), lower abdominal soreness, and low back pain which persists throughout the month. Pain with intercourse is also very common.

Pregnancy appears to have a beneficial effect on most women suffering from endometriosis. Those who previously had severe pelvic pain often experience nine blissful months. The reason for this is believed to be the reaction created in the endometriosis sites by the high progesterone levels of pregnancy. Endometriosis fragments actually change appearance and become smaller. Since no menstrual bleeding takes place in the nine months of pregnancy, no further bleeding is noted in the pelvis.

Dr. Robert Kistner suggested more than ten years ago that progesterone intramuscularly, or progestogens as birth control pills, could create "pseudopregnancy" in sufferers of endometriosis. By giving four Enovid tablets per day for at least nine months without stopping to allow a period, he claimed that 85 percent of his patients noted significant relief of symptoms. Subsequent reports by other doctors have not been nearly as optimistic. Today, most authorities believe that surgery is the one and only method of treating extensive endometriosis. When infertility is a problem, surgical removal of as much endometriosis as possible will achieve a far greater chance for conception.

The most disturbing thing about both surgical and hormonal treatment is that the disease tends to come back after treatment regardless of which is used, though it is far more likely to happen following the latter method. Unfortunately, the only permanent cure is hysterectomy, with removal of the ovaries if they are involved with extensive disease. The chance that remaining endometriosis fragments will grow again is enhanced if the ovaries are not removed. Occasionally, after the ovaries are removed, the disease may still flare up if replacement estrogen is given in pill form.

Pseudopregnancy should be used to treat only young women with minimal degrees of endometriosis—women who are not attempting to become pregnant but who suffer from abdominal discomfort, painful menses, and pain with intercourse. Today's pseudopregnancy treatment consists of taking every day for at least nine months one tablet of a progestin-dominant birth control pill. (Enovid is no longer used to create pseudopregnancy, as such high doses of this estrogen-dominant pill could produce extremely serious complications.) Danazol is a newer medication which has been used with great success in the treatment of endometriosis; it is discussed in Chapter 10.

How do I distinguish between dysmenorrhea due to a small amount of endometriosis, and dysmenorrhea of unknown cause?
Often it is difficult, if not impossible, for your doctor to make this distinction. However, certain clues in your history, such as pain throughout the month, are more likely to indicate endometriosis. On a pelvic exam it is sometimes possible for your doctor to feel the scarring and nodules of endometriosis in the ligaments supporting the uterus, and a fixed retroflexed, or backward, uterus often suggests the condition. If birth control pills are taken in the usual manner with one week of rest to allow menses, the woman with endometriosis may be more likely to experience pain at the time of the bleeding. If your doctor is in doubt, viewing the pelvis with a laparoscope (see Chapter 9) demonstrates to him or her the characteristic bluish or brown deposits of endometriosis on the ovary or other pelvic structures.

Do oral contraceptives affect the urinary tract?
The *ureters* are two tubes which carry urine from the kidney to the urinary bladder. At least three different studies have demonstrated a dilatation or widening of the ureter in a small percentage of women using oral contraceptives. In addition, growth of bacteria in the urine as well as actual in-

fection is significantly more common in Pill users. It is the estrogen fraction which seems to be responsible for these changes. In one investigation it was found that pills containing ethinyl estradiol were more likely to increase bacterial infection than those which contained mestranol. Furthermore, users of sequential pills appeared to have a higher incidence of urinary infection, probably because of the continued doses of pure estrogen without progestogen.

The findings of Doctors Martin Vessey and Richard Doll reported in 1976 are contrary to all of the above reports. In their extensive study they found no evidence of an association between oral contraceptive use and hospital treatment for infections of the urinary tract. On the contrary, they noted an excess of cystitis (urinary bladder inflammation) and other urinary infections among diaphragm users. They theorize that this may be due to the pressure of the diaphragm rim on the urethra.

Are users of birth control pills more susceptible to infections than nonusers?
Certain bacterial and viral infectious diseases have been found to be significantly more common among women using oral contraceptives. These diseases include laryngitis, *tracheitis* (inflammation of the trachea, or windpipe), chronic *nasopharyngitis* (inflammation of the nose and throat), influenza, *bronchitis* (inflammation of the respiratory tubes into which the trachea divides), pleurisy (inflammation of the membrane surrounding the lung), and mouth ulcers.

In trying to find a scientific explanation for this higher rate of infection, researchers in California have studied the levels of certain blood proteins called *gamma globulins*. These substances, because they provide immunity against infections and diseases, belong to a group of proteins known as *immunoglobulins*. Oral contraceptive users were found to have significantly lower levels of gamma globulin than nonusers. Furthermore, as the dose of estrogen in the Pill was increased, the gamma globulin concentration decreased even further. As a result, it was theorized that this decrease of gamma globulin may play a role in the increased prevalence of viral infections among Pill-users. Further investigation will be needed to confirm or deny this relationship.

One very recent study, presented at the Interscience Conference on Antimicrobial Agents and Chemotherapeutics in Chicago, has shown that oral contraceptives may offer some protection against recurrence of one type of virus. This virus, named genital herpes simplex or HSV–2, is known to be sexually transmitted and responsible for causing painful blisters of the outer genitals which tend to recur over a period of months or even years. Investigators noted that the recurrence rate for HSV2 among women not using oral contraceptives was 1.6 times that of those using the Pill, with one recurrence every 51 days as opposed to a recurrence every 82 days among Pill-users.

If I have had intestinal bypass surgery, should I use the Pill?
Intestinal bypass is the name of an operation performed as treatment of massive obesity. In this procedure, the surgeon detaches a segment of the intestine and then unites the two ends above and below the detached segment. Following surgery, weight loss is dramatic because nutrients and food breakdown products are no longer readily absorbed into the body through the shortened intestine. During the past 5 years this operation has gained great popularity in the United States.

However, a recent study has demonstrated that following bypass surgery oral contraceptives are not adequately absorbed into the blood stream from the intestine. For this reason oral contraceptives are an unreliable method of contraception for women who have had this operation.

What is the effect of birth control pills on women suffering from intestinal ailments such as colitis, food poisoning, nervous stomach, and ulcers?
Oral contraceptives do not appear to have a detrimental effect on these conditions. (The Pill actually decreases the incidence of duodenal ulcers.) However, women with these problems should take a Pill that has as low a dose of estrogen as possible in order to avoid nausea or vomiting.

Can vomiting prevent the Pill from working properly?
If you vomit within four hours after having taken a birth control pill, take another pill, since there is a good chance that all the hormones will not have been absorbed into the body. If frequent vomiting occurs during the Pill cycle, other contraception should be used.

Does diarrhea interfere with the Pill's effectiveness?
In instances of severe diarrhea, the intestinal tract will not have time to adequately absorb the full hormone content of the Pill. This may happen in a perfectly healthy woman who has an attack of stomach flu or food poisoning while using the Pill. In one report, eight healthy women using oral contraceptives for periods ranging from two to thirty-six months became pregnant after experiencing diarrhea lasting from one to five days. The symptoms were present between Days 3 and 16 of the cycle, and no pills had been missed. Therefore, if you have an attack of severe diarrhea during the Pill cycle, use a different method of contraception until after your next period, when a new cycle of pills can be started.

Are headaches related to use of the Pill?
Headaches are occasionally a complication of Pill use, and seem to occur most frequently during the week that the Pill is not being taken. Investigators are uncertain as to whether it is the progestogen or the estrogen component that is responsible for these headaches. Though the cause of most headaches is either unknown or the result of nervous tension, on rare occasions headaches may represent a symptom of a more serious condition such as hypertension or an impending stroke (see cerebral thrombosis). Headaches that are severe, that occur frequently, and that begin or intensify after using the Pill, require immediate attention and thorough evaluation by a physician, preferably a neurologist. If the cause of the headache remains in doubt, it is probably best to discontinue the Pill permanently.

Should women who get migraine headaches use oral contraceptives?
Migraine is a special type of severe recurrent headache. It is often preceded by visual disturbances such as blind spots and double vision, dizziness, numbness of the face, or even temporary paralysis that may strongly resemble symptoms of a stroke. The actual headache may be one-sided or generalized over the entire head, and is often accompanied by nausea, vomiting, and intolerance to light. The headache may last from a few hours to several days; the average length is six to eighteen hours. For some unknown reason, migraine appears to be more common in women than in men.

Though the cause of migraine remains unknown, it is strongly suggested that the pre-headache symptoms are due to a disturbance in the circulation and blood flow within the smaller blood vessels in the brain. The headache is produced by a dilation or expansion of blood vessels outside the brain which causes pressure on surrounding nerves. Investigators have only recently become aware that migraine may actually be a potentially dangerous condition. Ample evidence is available to show that some migraine patients have a decrease in blood flow to the brain as severe as that of a patient suffering from a stroke. Furthermore, permanent neurological damage following a migraine has been reported on rare occasions.

Since oral contraceptives may alter blood coagulation factors and produce circulatory changes, they are best avoided in individuals with a recent or past history of migraine headache. In a report given at the International Headache Symposium in Denmark in 1971, it was reported that 50 percent of migraine sufferers found that their attacks worsened while they were on the Pill, 40 percent found that they were not affected, and 10 percent reported their migraine improved. Factors likely to characterize women whose migraine became worse while they were on the Pill were an age of 30 and over, previous childbirth, a menstrual cycle longer than thirty-three days or shorter than twenty-seven days, and a tendency to experience headaches at the time of menstruation. One study reported on at the symposium revealed that some women with no previous history of migraine developed it while on the pill, and 70 percent of this group found that their headaches disappeared after they stopped using it.

Do birth control pills alter the effects of other drugs taken at the same time?
As previously mentioned (see Page 45), birth control pills may adversely affect your glucose tolerance by causing an increase in the daily dose of insulin or pills that lower blood sugar such as Orinase, Diabinese, Dymelor, and Tolinase.

If you need anticoagulation drugs such as heparin, Coumadin, Dicumarol, and Panwarfin, the dosages of these medications will be greater if birth control pills are also being used. This is due to the fact that birth control pills have the antagonistic effect of increasing certain clotting factors in the blood (see Page 36). However, I can't envision a situation in which you would be using anticoagulants and birth control pills at the same time. The same may be said for the variety of medications used in the treatment of hypertension, or high blood pressure. Since the birth control pills may, in susceptible individuals, cause a significant rise in blood pressure, a greater amount of the antihypertensive drug would then be needed to lower the blood pressure to a safe level. However, hypertension is a contraindication to oral contraceptive use (see Page 42), and it would be most unusual for a woman to be using that combination of drugs.

Cholestyramine is a popular medication used in reducing blood cholesterol levels. Greater amounts of it are needed if you are using birth control pills, because oral contraceptives increase blood cholesterol levels (see Page 41).

As previously mentioned (see Page 46), prolonged use of birth control pills may be responsible for a deficiency of Vitamin B6 (pyridoxine), riboflavin, folic acid, Vitamin B12, zinc, and Vitamin C. Whether or not these losses require additional intake of these substances remains controversial. Since birth control pills may actually increase the body's supply of copper, calcium, niacin, Vitamin K, and Vitamin A, the dietary intake of those elements may be reduced.

Finally, a recent project at the Oklahoma Center for Alcohol has demonstrated that women using birth control pills were more likely to feel the effects of a drink for a longer period of time than women who did not use birth control pills. Blood alcohol levels of twenty-two women were measured following a stiff drink, and it was demonstrated that eleven of these women who were not on the Pill had no alcohol in their blood after an average of four hours and fifteen minutes. The eleven women on the Pill took five hours and thirty minutes to eliminate all the alcohol in their blood.

Do other drugs alter the effectiveness of birth control pills?
There are several commonly used drugs which alter the body's metabolism of estrogen to such a degree that the effectiveness of an oral contraceptive may be diminished. The potential for an unwanted pregnancy, though unlikely, is then theoretically possible, especially when pills with the lowest amounts of estrogen are used. Barbiturates, used as sleeping pills, are examples of drugs which alter estrogen metabolism. Butazolidin, a medication often used in the

treatment of arthritis, phlebitis, and traumatic joint injuries, may also reduce oral contraceptive efficacy. Miltown and Equanil are two popular brands of meprobamate, a drug used in the treatment of anxiety and nervous tension, which may also exert this type of effect. Dilantin, a medication used to treat epilepsy, and rifampin, a new drug in the treatment of tuberculosis, both appear capable of altering estrogen metabolism. To date, there are reports of eight women who have become pregnant while taking a combination of rifampin and oral contraceptives. It has also been noted that ampicillin, probably the most commonly used of all antibiotics, diminishes the excretion of estrogen in the urine. I know of no studies, however, that have demonstrated a higher pregnancy rate among women using oral contraceptives and ampicillin at the same time.

How do birth control pills influence a woman's sexual response?

Over 40 different medical publications have attempted to evaluate the effect of oral contraceptives on a woman's sexual responses. The difficulties encountered in trying to study such an emotional subject are readily apparent. For example, how does one determine if a woman's increased libido is due to the specific ingredients of a birth control pill or to the security in knowing that an unwanted pregnancy is unlikely to occur? To date, the vast majority of these investigations have suffered from a lack of scientific objectivity and skill on the part of the researchers. Despite these deficiencies, some meaningful conclusions do emerge from all of these studies. The most important statistic is that the majority of women using oral contraceptives will experience no major psychosexual changes. Approximately 70 percent of all Pill-users, regardless of age or marital status, will note no change in libido. Of those 30 percent noting a change in libido, that change is usually for the better. Several studies have demonstrated an increase in coital frequency among women using the Pill over a prolonged period of time, but other studies have failed to confirm these findings. One group of researchers noted that birth control pills did not influence the total frequency of intercourse, but they did influence the time of the menstrual cycle in which intercourse took place. Since birth control pills eliminate ovulation and uncomfortable premenstrual symptoms associated with the release of progesterone by the corpus luteum (see Chapter 1), Pill users are more likely to enjoy coitus during the premenstrual phase of the cycle.

Most researchers believe that loss of libido experienced by a small percentage of women using oral contraceptives is unrelated to the specific type and amount of estrogen or progestin that they contain. Others, however, believe that estrogen-dominant pills are less likely to decrease libido than progestin-dominant pills. If sexuality is adversely affected while a woman is using a progestin-dominant pill, switching to one having a greater relative amount of estrogen (see Tables 2–5 and 2–6) may occasionally be helpful.

How do oral contraceptives alter the white blood cell count?
The white blood cell count (WBC) is one of the most commonly ordered tests in clinical medicine. An elevation of this count is often essential to your doctor's diagnosis of common surgical conditions, such as acute appendicitis. The normal range of a WBC count is usually between four thousand and ten thousand. However, in both pregnant women and in women using the Pill, the count is often higher than ten thousand. The degree of elevation appears to be related to the amount of estrogen in the Pill and the length of time the woman has used the Pill. For the Pill user who is both obese and a heavy smoker, these combined effects will often elevate the WBC count over fourteen thousand. (Reminding your surgeon of these facts may occasionally save a normal appendix from extinction.)

Are there any dangers from surgery in women using birth control pills?
Your immobility immediately following a major surgical operation, combined with detrimental effects of the Pill on blood clotting, will increase the risk of fatal pulmonary embolus following the surgery. For this reason, if surgery is elective or nonemergency, it is best to stop the pills for four weeks before the operation is performed.

Does the Pill in any way prevent VD?
This misconception is strange, but common. To dispel this dangerous notion, the FDA has required that the following statement be added to the labeling of birth control pills:

"Caution: Oral contraceptives are of no value in the prevention or treatment of venereal disease."

What effect do birth control pills have on the menopause?

Birth control pills can't accelerate or postpone the onset of
the menopause. However, because of the estrogen they contain, oral contraceptives usually mask the symptoms which
accompany the menopause, such as the characteristic hot
flashes. It is not unusual for a woman in her late forties to
suddenly experience these symptoms within days after she
stops using the Pill.

Is there a law prohibiting doctors from prescribing contraception for sexually active teenagers without parental consent?

Though several states have strict laws forbidding this practice, no case has ever been reported where a physician was
taken to court for providing contraception to a minor.
Furthermore, the American Medical Association, the American Academy of Pediatrics, and the American College of Obstetrics and Gynecology have all publicly supported the position that sexually active teenagers be provided with contraception. In addition, the American College of Obstetrics
and Gynecology has stated that the confidentiality of the
teenager in such matters must be respected and given pre-
cedence of the demands of angered or inquisitive parents attempting to breach confidentiality. One of the most common
fears of teenagers is that the doctor will report her to her
parents. My advice to teenagers with this problem is to call
the doctor's office and use an alias if necessary to determine
his or her attitude about contraception. If he or she appears
hostile, uncooperative, or morally outraged, find another,
more sympathetic, doctor or consult a local family planning
clinic.

How much do birth control pills cost?

At most retail pharmacies the cost is approximately $4.50
per pack for all standard brands. A box of minipills sells for
about $4.00. There is a significant difference in price when
the pills are purchased at a discount pharmacy, where the
average price quoted to me was $3.50 for the standard
brands and $3.20 for one pack of minipills. Family planning

clinics are often the least expensive source. Doctors usually have an abundant supply of free pill samples, and you should not be embarrassed to ask for them when you go for your checkup.

Which is safer, the Pill or the IUD?

A federal survey taken during the first six months of 1973 concludes that more women died from using the Pill than from using the IUD (intrauterine device), but the IUD was responsible for more hospitalizations. It was estimated that the death rate from IUD use was somewhere between 1 and 7.3 of every 1,000,000 women using it for a period of one year. The death rate for the Pill was between 22 and 45 per 1,000,000 users per year. The hospitalization rate associated with IUD complications was 7 of every 1,000 women per year, compared to 1 per 1,000 women for the birth control pills.

Dr. Christopher Tietze and his coworkers at The Population Council have tried to analyze mortality rates associated with the six different regimens of fertility control among different age groups in the general population. Their findings are expressed in Table 2–9.

The regimens of control are defined as follows:

1. No method—Deaths expected if no method of contraception is used and there is no recourse to induced abortion

2. IUDs only—Deaths expected from a population using IUDs without recourse to abortion

3. Abortion only—Deaths expected from a population using early induced abortion as the only method of fertility control

4. Traditional contraception only—Deaths expected from a population of women using diaphragm and condom contraception without recourse to abortion

5. Orals only—Deaths expected from a population of women using oral contraceptives without recourse to abortion in case of failure

6. Traditional contraception and abortion—Deaths expected from a population of women using diaphragm and condom contraception with recourse to abortion

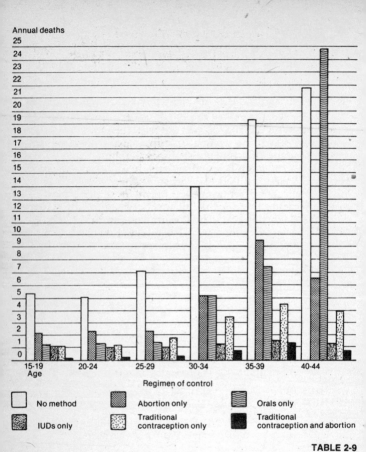

Annual deaths

No method		Abortion only
IUDs only		Traditional contraception only
Orals only		Traditional contraception and abortion

Age

Regimen of control

TABLE 2-9

70

Some interesting conclusions may be drawn from Table 2–9:

1. The Pill and the IUD are relatively safe when compared with the risk of death from pregnancy and childbirth when no fertility control method is used.

2. The risk of death increases significantly after the age of forty when birth control pills are used.

3. The use of traditional contraception, such as the diaphragm and condom backed up by early induced abortion of all unwanted pregnancies that result from contraceptive failure, is the safest method of birth control.

3
IUDS

An intrauterine device, or IUD, is a device inserted into the endometrial cavity and left there for various periods of time for the purpose of contraception. According to one legend, the first IUDs ever used were stones inserted by Arab camel-drivers into the endometrial cavities of their camels in order to prevent pregnancy on long desert crossings. The first twentieth-century IUD to be inserted into a woman was made of silkworm and animal membrane in the shape of a ring; it was used in Germany in 1909.

Modern IUDs are made of polyethylene plastic. (Copper has been added to the outside of some of the newer models.) Barium coating is present in all devices, which makes it possible for the IUDs to be seen on X-ray. Most IUDs have a nylon "tail" which protrudes from the cervix into the vagina. Today approximately four million women (approximately 8 to 10 percent of those of reproductive age) in the United States use one of the various IUDs for contraception.

Figure 3–1 shows some of the most famous (and infamous) IUDS.

What is the purpose of the IUD tail?
When you touch the tail or strings, or view them with a speculum as they protrude through the cervical os, you are assured that the IUD is in place. The person inserting the IUD should note the length of the tail, because if the length

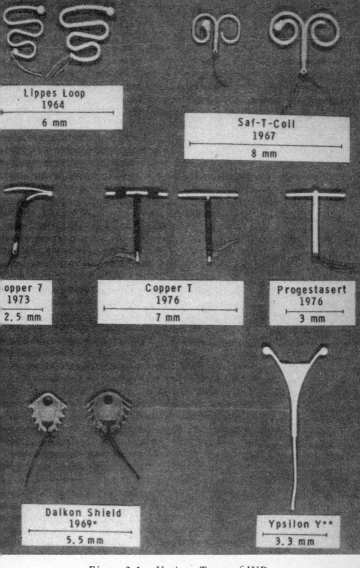

Lippes Loop
1964
6 mm

Saf-T-Coil
1967
8 mm

opper 7
1973
2.5 mm

Copper T
1976
7 mm

Progestasert
1976
3 mm

Dalkon Shield
1969*
5.5 mm

Ypsilon Y**
3.3 mm

Figure 3-1. Various Types of IUDs

suddenly increases or decreases on future examinations, it may mean that the IUD is not in its proper position. The strings also serve as a means by which the IUD can easily be removed.

Many women have not been told the type of IUD that has been inserted. However, the problem is solved if you have a speculum, since the tail of each device has a characteristic appearance. Descriptions of what the various IUD strings look like are listed in Table 3–1.

How is the IUD inserted?

All IUDs, with the exception of the Dalkon Shield, are elongated by pulling them into an inserter which has a small diameter. The inserter is then placed through the cervical os (Figure 3–2), and the IUD is pushed forward into the endometrial cavity, where it assumes its original shape (Figures 3–3 and 3–4). This is called regaining its "memory." The tail is then cut to a desired length, which usually is about two inches (Figure 3–5). When a T-shaped device is used, the two halves of the horizontal arm are folded downward against the vertical arm prior to insertion, and it is then inserted in this I-shape. When the inserter is withdrawn from the top of the endometrial cavity, the two arms open outward again and assume their original T-shape.

Should any special precautions be taken when an IUD is inserted?

An IUD should be inserted during the period or immediately after. At that time, the cervical os is slightly more open, and

TABLE 3-1 — IDENTIFICATION OF IUD STRINGS

TYPE OF IUD	COLOR OF IUD STRINGS		OTHER CHARACTERISTICS
Loop-A	Blue	2	Thin strings
Loop-B	Black	2	Thin strings
Loop-C	Yellow	2	Thin strings
Loop-D	White	2	Thin strings
Shields	Black	1	Knot on thick strings
Copper 7-200	Black	1	Thin strings
Copper T-200	Light Blue (variable)	2	Thin strings
Saf-T-Coil	Green	2	Thin strings
Majzlin Spring	White-Gray	2	Not as thin as most
Ypsilon Y	White	1	Thick Silastic tube
Progesterone-T	Black	2	Thin strings

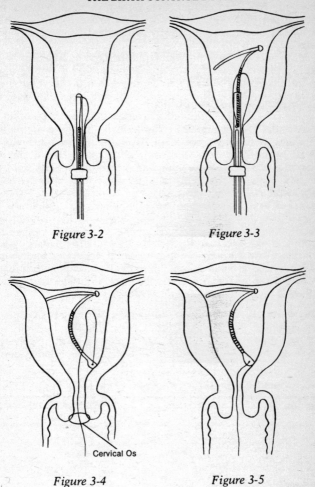

Figure 3-2

Figure 3-3

Figure 3-4

Cervical Os

Figure 3-5

you are assured that you don't have an undiagnosed pregnancy. In the absence of a period in a woman who menstruates only every few months, a pregnancy test should be done. If it is negative, she may take hormones to bring on the period before inserting the IUD.

It is vital that a pelvic exam be done immediately prior to inserting the IUD so that the position, size, and shape of the uterus may be determined (Figure 3–6). The IUD insertion should be gentle, and excessive pressure must never be applied. All equipment must be sterilized in order to minimize the risk of infection (Figure 3–6).

How painful is an IUD insertion?
A male gynecologist may tell a woman that insertion of an IUD is really easy and that the pain is "nothing at all." However, as most women with IUDs attest, this is usually

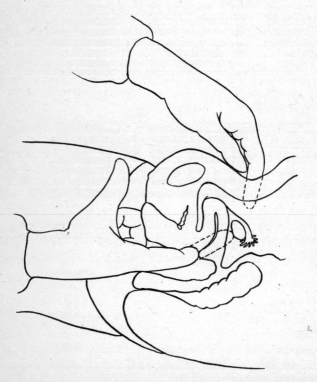

Figure 3-6.   Uterus in a Normal Forward Position

not true. <u>The degree of pain is variable.</u> There is usually little discomfort for women who have given birth several times, or for women who have IUDs inserted soon after delivery. For others, especially women who have never given birth, the cramping may be excruciating, necessitating instant removal of the device. Certain individuals who have never had previous dilation of the cervix may experience a *vasovagal stimulation* when the IUD inserter moves through the cervical canal. This reaction is characterized by a dangerously slow pulse, heartbeat irregularities, fainting, seizures, and even on very rare occasions a *cardiac arrest*, or stoppage of the heartbeat.

Use of a paracervical block is often helpful in relieving some, but certainly not all, of the pain associated with an IUD insertion. It is performed by injecting novocaine or a similar drug into the cervix before the device is inserted (see Chapter 7).

The diameter of the widest part of the inserter will determine to a great degree the amount of pain that an individual will experience. Table 3–2 lists the widest diameters of the various IUDs.

How do the IUDs prevent pregnancy?

This has been a subject of great controversy among physicians as well as religious leaders. Certain religious groups claim that the IUD works solely by preventing implantation of an already fertilized egg, thereby causing an early abortion. Although no conclusive medical evidence on the ques-

TABLE 3-2 — DIAMETER OF WIDEST PART OF INSERTER OF VARIOUS IUDs*

DIAMETER OF WIDEST PART OF INSERTER OF VARIOUS IUDs*	
	Millimeters
Copper 7	3.07
Saf-T-Coil (Nullip)	3.76
Saf-T-Coil (Standard)	4.50
Lippes Loop A	5.26
Lippes Loop D	5.33
Copper T	5.96
Dalkon Shield +	19.48

As measured by John Burson April 8, 1974
+ Measured with fins of shield crushed

tion has come to light thus far, the prevailing opinion is that the presence of the IUD in the endometrial cavity stimulates an inflammatory reaction. As a result, large microscopic cells called *macrophages* are released. These are believed to be capable of destroying sperm before they can get into the tube to fertilize the egg, and they probably are capable of destroying the fertilized egg as well. The addition of copper to an IUD appears to enhance this inflammatory reaction. Copper may also react with certain enzymes in the endometrium to diminish sperm movement.

Are there certain women who should not use an IUD?
The IUD should not be used by women with abnormalities, irregularities, or tumors of the uterus. Other contraindications are acute inflammation of the cervix, uterus, or Fallopian tubes; undiagnosed vaginal bleeding; extremely heavy periods; anemia; extremely painful periods; and cancer of the cervix or uterus.

Which IUD is best?
In evaluating the efficacy of an IUD, the most important factors are the pregnancy rate; the removal rate for medical problems such as bleeding, cramps, and infection; the expulsion rate; and the patient continuation rate.

You must take with a grain of salt all reports about a particular device, since the results are dependent on many factors and vary greatly from study to study. Factors that may prevent meaningful comparisons between two different IUD studies include differences in the motivation of the patient groups selected, the degree of experience among those individuals inserting the devices, and the attitude of medical personnel in encouraging or discouraging the use of a particular method of contraception. For these reasons it is extremely difficult for both the practicing physician and patient to obtain reliable data about a particular device. Table 3–3 is based upon the *most commonly quoted* results of using some of the more popular IUDs. The results are expressed as events per 100 women using the device over a specific period of time. For example, if 100 women used the small Saf-T-Coil for a period of two years, approximately 3.6 will become pregnant, and 57 out of 100 will continue to use it.

Skepticism of such statistics is only natural. For example, the most recent large-scale studies have indicated that the

Dalkon Shield was responsible for an unacceptably high pregnancy rate. In one astonishing report of 291 women, the pregnancy rate was 10 per 100 woman-years. When those rates are compared to the rates in Table 3–3, you can only surmise that someone's calculations were less than perfect.

Based on the numbers in Table 3–3, can I conclude that the copper-containing IUDs are best?

You should hesitate in drawing rapid conclusions until further studies are available. For example, it would appear from Table 3–3 that the expulsion rate of the copper devices is a very low 6 to 7 per 100 woman-years. This has been attributed to the special uterine muscle-relaxing property of copper. However, two more recent studies have demonstrated that the expulsion rate for copper devices, especially the Cu-7, may be much higher than originally quoted. In one twelve-month comparison study of the Cu-7 and TCu-200, involving 1,500 insertions of each device, tremendously high expulsion rates of 13.6 and 8.4 respectively were noted. A second comparative study, carried out by the Margaret Sanger Research Bureau, reported an expulsion rate of 17.1 for the Cu-7 and 9.1 for the TCu-200.

In 1974 the *British Medical Journal* reported the results of 1,156 Cu-7 insertions. After two years of use the pregnancy rate was 2.5 percent, the expulsion rate was 9.7 percent, and the continuation rate was 68.9 percent. Though these rates are probably better than with other IUDs, they are not as good as the initial reports indicated.

The three copper-covered devices are the Cu-7, TCu-200, and the Lippes Loop with added copper. The Cu-7 has been available to the public since 1973. The TCu-200 has been approved by the FDA and is scheduled for commercial distribution in 1978. The Lippes Loop with added copper has not been approved by the FDA.

Can any of the copper get absorbed into the bloodstream?

That supposedly was carefully examined by the FDA before it allowed distribution of the Cu-7. Apparently little copper is absorbed, and to date no harmful effects have been reported.

How often should the IUD be changed?

If you use an IUD that doesn't contain copper, there is little scientific evidence to guide you in making this decision.

TABLE 3-3 — SUMMARY OF IUD EFFECTIVENESS

DEVICE	SIZE	TYPE	MATERIAL	MANUFACTURER OR DISTRIBUTOR	PREGNANCY RATE PER 100 WOMAN-YEARS	EXPULSION RATE PER 100 WOMAN-YEARS	MEDICAL REMOVAL RATE PER 100 WOMAN-YEARS	CONTINU-ATION RATE PER 100 WOMAN-YEARS	REFERENCE
Lippes Loop	A(Small) B C D(Large)	Open with tail	Polyethylene Barium-Impregnated Nylon tail	Ortho	8.0* 5.8* 4.1* 3.6*	6.9* 6.5* 5.3* 3.6*	11.7* 21.1* 19.2* 19.5*	63.6* 59.2* 62.8* 65.6*	Tietze, C. "Evaluation of Intrauterine Devices: Ninth Progress Report." Cooperative Statistical Program, Studies in Family Planning No. 55 July 1970
Birm-berg Bow	Small Large	Closed with tail	Polyethylene Barium-Impregnated Nylon tail	I.C.D.	12.9* 6.1*	1.2* 0.8*	11.7* 18.4*	63.5* 69.3*	'' ''
Saf-T-Coil	Small Large	Open with tail	Polyethylene Barium-Impregnated Nylon tail	Julius Schmid	3.6*	7.8*	25.2*	57.0*	'' ''
TCu-200		Open with tail	Polyethylene Fine copper wire	Ortho And Population Council	2.2***	7.2***	5.6***	77***	Tatum, H. J. "The First Year of Clinical Experience with the Copper T Intrauterine Contraceptive System in the United States and Canada." Contraception 6(3) 179–189, Sept. 1972
7 Cu-200		Open with tail	Polyethylene Fine copper wire	Searle	Parous 0.97** Nulliparous 0.99**	4.77** 6.44**	7.37** 10.67**	83.5** 77.5**	Searle Laboratories, G.D. Searle & Co. January, 1974

80

TABLE 1-3 — SUMMARY OF IUD EFFECTIVENESS (CONTINUED)

DEVICE	SIZE	TYPE	MATERIAL	MANUFACTURER OR DISTRIBUTOR	PREGNANCY RATE PER 100 WOMAN-YEARS	EXPULSION RATE PER 100 WOMAN-YEARS	MEDICAL REMOVAL RATE PER 100 WOMAN-YEARS	CONTINU-ATION RATE PER 100 WOMAN-YEARS	REFERENCE
Ypsilon-Y		Open with silicone tail	Silicone surrounding stainless steel frame	Syntex	1.9***	2.1***	3.8***	88.2***	Fuchs, F., Cederqvist, L.L. and Lauersen, N.H.: The Antigon-F and Ypsilon Intrauterine Devices in "Proceedings from the Workshop on Advances on IUD Contraception for Lesser Developed Countries" at the Batteile Seattle Research Center, Oct. 18-20. 1973
Daikon Shield	Small Large	Open with tail	Polyethylene Barium-Impregnated Nylon tail	A. H. Robins	Parous (a) 1.5** Nulliparous (b) 1.2**	3.1** 3.5**	12.3** 9.7**	80.4*** 81.2**	(a) Ostergard, D.R., Broen, E.M. "The Insertion of Intrauterine Devices by Physicians and Paramedical Personnel," Obstet & Gyn. 41, No. 2 Feb. 1973; 257-258 (b) Ostergard, D.R., "Intrauterine Contraception in Nulliparas with the Dalkon Shield" Am. J. Ob. and Gyn. 116(8): 1088-91, 1973

*Data represents two years of use
**Data represents one year of use
***Data represents a minimum of six months' use

Parous: describes woman with previous pregnancy
Nulliparous describes woman without previous pregnancy

Some authorities suggest changing the IUD every three years because small amounts of calcification deposits may cover the surface of the device after that time. However, there is no evidence to suggest that it results in abnormal bleeding or higher pregnancy rates. On the contrary, most people have noted a normalization of menstrual pattern and a lower pregnancy rate the longer a device is left in. Changing an IUD often stirs up abnormal bleeding again, and therefore it has been my policy to leave the IUD in place as long as the patient is free of complications. I have not regretted this decision, nor have several patients who have had the same IUD for seven to ten years.

The IUDs which contain copper should be changed every three years, since much of the spermicidal and contraceptive action of the copper may be lost after this time. This is believed to be due to the loss of the ionized copper from the surface of the device.

Some research suggests that the loss of copper from the Cu-7 may take as long as four to eight years and that pregnancy rates may not increase during the second through fourth years of use. One recent study suggested that it isn't the loss of copper from the device, but rather the formation of a microscopic surface crust over the copper that prevents its release. When this occurs, the contraceptive effect is lost. Regardless of the mechanism, until more is known about the contraceptive action of copper, it would be wise to follow the manufacturer's recommendation that this IUD be changed every three years.

Changing or removing IUDs should always take place during or immediately after a period. Pregnancy may result at midcycle if intercourse has taken place within the preceding 72 hours before the IUD is removed.

What factors determine the expulsion rate of an IUD?
The expulsion rate is often determined by the skill of the person inserting the IUD. Many novices place the device too low in the endometrial cavity, and even into the cervical canal. It must be placed in the upper part of the uterine cavity in order to prevent pregnancy and expulsion.

The expulsion rate is higher for *nulliparous* women (those who have never had children), than for *multiparous* women (those who have had children), probably because the muscles of their smaller, more rigid, uteruses tend to contract and reject the device more readily. The highest expulsion rates occur with the smallest devices, and vice versa.

Time appears to be another important factor. Expulsion rates decrease with each month of IUD use, and the incidence of expulsion after the third year is extremely low. That is another major disadvantage of the Cu-7 and explains the reluctance of some doctors to frequently change IUDs which do not contain copper.

As you'd expect, the risk of expulsion is higher after a previous expulsion has taken place. Only two out of five women who have had a previous expulsion will be able to retain a second device for a full two years. It is for this reason that women should examine themselves after each period to determine the tail length as well as the absence of plastic or copper protruding from the cervix or vagina. For women with a previous history of expulsion, an additional self-examination prior to and after intercourse will enhance safety. It is known that the uterine muscle contracts vigorously during orgasm, and it has been suggested that this action may help to expel an IUD at this time. No studies have been performed which show a higher expulsion rate following orgasm.

What are some of the serious complications that a woman may experience while using an IUD?

Based on the federal study referred to at the end of Chapter 2, hospitalizations related to IUD use in the United States and Puerto Rico, during the first six months of 1973, are listed in Table 3–4.

TABLE 3-4 — HOSPITALIZATION OF WOMEN IN THE UNITED STATES AND PUERTO RICO FROM IUD COMPLICATIONS DURING THE FIRST SIX MONTHS OF 1973

COMPLICATION	NUMBER OF WOMEN
Pelvic infection	1,198
Other infection	72
Uterine perforation	795
Intestinal obstruction due to IUD	17
Hemorrhage	584
Pregnancy	999
Other	478
Unknown	29

Though bleeding problems such as heavy, prolonged periods are the most common complications among IUD users, actual hemorrhage requiring hospitalization is far less likely. Infection is certainly the most serious and deadly complication as well as the most common cause of hospitalization.

What type of infection may take place with an IUD?
When we speak of infection caused by an IUD, we are concerned with the growth of dangerous bacteria which somehow find their way into the uterus through the cervical os, and then spread through the muscle of the uterus and out into the lower pelvis, infecting the Fallopian tubes, ovaries, and other pelvic structures. Occasionally the tube and ovary may become matted together in a ball of pus called a *tubo-ovarian abscess*. The rupture of such an abscess has a very high mortality rate. The bacteria may also enter the bloodstream and attack distant organs, producing an overwhelming reaction and drop in blood pressure called *septic shock,* which may also be fatal. If a woman survives such an infection, she may be left permanently sterile and in chronic pain due to destruction of pelvic tissues.

The incidence of pelvic infection in women using the IUD is approximately 2 to 3 percent, though only a small fraction of those infected suffer the severe complications described above. Infection is more likely to occur in those individuals who have never been pregnant. This is believed to be due to the higher incidence of uterine contractions and cramping which follows IUD insertions in nulliparous women. It is theorized that these muscular contractions are responsible for allowing bacteria to enter the uterine cavity from the cervix and vagina. Similar uterine contractions are also present during coitus, becoming more intense at the time of orgasm. For this reason, it is not surprising that researchers have noted a higher infection rate among women having greater coital frequency.

Symptoms that should alert one to the possibility of an early pelvic infection are vague lower abdominal pain, any temperature above 99°, a foul-smelling yellowish discharge, chills, and pain with intercourse. Unfortunately, sometimes these infections become far advanced before a woman experiences any symptoms at all. Vague symptoms such as fatigue and flu-like aches and pains should also be cause for alarm.

When in doubt about the cause of a woman's low-grade fever or pelvic pain, your doctor should assume that the IUD is the culprit and immediately remove it while vigorously treating the infection with appropriate antibiotics. Placing the IUD in a sterile container and bringing it to a hospital laboratory for bacterial analysis will help determine if infection is present, the type of bacteria causing the infection, and the sensitivity of the bacteria to the antibiotic that has been prescribed. The habit of some doctors of leaving the IUD in the uterus while treating the infection with antibiotics is to be deplored.

If a tubo-ovarian abscess has formed (a very rare occurrence) and it does not respond to antibiotic treatment, surgical removal of the infected tube and ovary is necessary. When both ovaries are infected, removal of all structures involved in the infection, as well as hysterectomy, is necessary for cure. In 1975 two different reports were presented in the medical literature, one of sixteen women and the other of four women, in whom unilateral, or one-sided, tubo-ovarian abscess was present following IUD use. Removal of the infected tissue cured the disease. That one-sided involvement appears to be characteristic of IUD infection, whereas most infections produced by veneral disease such as gonorrhea affect both tubes and ovaries. If your doctor, on pelvic examination, feels a slight enlargement on one side, the prudent move would be to have him or her remove the IUD.

Is the new Progestasert IUD better than all other IUDs?

The progesterone T, or Progestasert, is a T-shaped IUD that contains progesterone in its vertical arm. The progesterone is slowly released into the uterine cavity over a period of one year, which produces hormonal changes in the endometrium that prevent implantation of the egg. In addition, it is believed that the progesterone alters the cervical mucus so that sperm are unable to penetrate it. It has been demonstrated that the small amount of progesterone released does not prevent ovulation. Several researchers have noted that the Progestasert may be more effective than other IUDs in relieving uterine cramps. In addition, excessive menstrual blood loss noted with other IUDs may actually be reduced with the Progestasert. Though pregnancy rates were originally reported to be less than one per hundred woman-years, Dr. Ridgely C. Bennett, Jr., of the FDA Bureau of Drugs has noted that following more extensive use of the Progestasert, the pregnancy rates originally quoted were greatly under-estimated. Based on over 46,000 woman-years of use, it has become obvious that the pregnancy rates are no better than those of currently used IUDs. The more recent statistics based on one year of Progestasert use are presented in Table 3-5.

The greatest concern about the Progestasert is the fact that wearers of this device may be at five times greater risk of ectopic pregnancy than users of other IUDs (see ectopic pregnancy, Page 90). In a study published in the April, 1977 issue of *Fertility and Sterility*, the percentage of ectopic pregnancies among pregnant Progestasert patients was 16 percent compared to 3 percent among women who inadvertently conceived while using a variety of other IUDs. It is for this reason that the FDA has requested that the Alza Corporation, manufacturer of this device, reanalyze their statistics and complication rates.

A distinct disadvantage of this IUD is the fact that it must be changed every twelve months, due to loss of the progesterone contraceptive effect beyond this period of time. It seems foolish to change an IUD so often, especially when one considers the three-to-four month adjustment phase of heavier periods immediately following an IUD insertion. Having an IUD removed and inserted so often is likely to cause both inconvenience and discomfort.

In addition, the cost of each Progestasert to a doctor is ten dollars more than the Cu-7. Finally, in the event of an accidental pregnancy no one knows what effects of progesterone in close proximity to a developing fetus may be (see Page 48).

Which IUD do you prefer in your private practice?
I prefer the Cu-7 to all other brands. My reasons are its extremely small diameter, allowing for ease of insertion (see Table 3-2) in both nulliparous and multiparous women, slightly lower pregnancy rates as noted in Table 3-3, and the very high continuation rates. Despite the pessimistic reports noted on page 79, I have personally experienced very low expulsion rates with the Cu-7. Its one drawback is that it must be changed every three years, which entails some discomfort and expense.

For the woman who is willing to sacrifice a slightly higher pregnancy risk in exchange for never having to change her

TABLE 3-5 — PROGESTASERT IUD STATISTICS

RATES PER 100 WOMAN-YEARS	PAROUS	NULLIPAROUS
Pregnancy	1.9	2.5
Expulsions	3.1	7.5
Continuation rate	79.1	70.9

IUD, I prefer to insert either the Saf-T-Coil or the B, C, or D size of Lippes Loop. These standard and reliable IUDs have been used with success for many years, and they are my first choice for many women in their midforties, who have somewhat reduced fertility, but who need reliable contraception until the age of fifty. Of the other IUDs listed in Table 3–3, the Birnberg Bow and the Dalkon Shield are best left in the gynecological hall of horrors, and the Ypsilon is still in its experimental testing stages, along with other promising IUDs (see Chapter 11). The TCu-200, or copper T, appears promising and should be available soon. Finally, the new Progestasert holds no advantages over the currently available IUDs, but has the added inconvenience of having to change it every year at a cost of $10 more than the Cu-7.

Why was the Dalkon Shield banned?
In early 1974 the A. H. Robins Company, maker of the Dalkon Shield, forwarded a letter to all doctors stating that the company had become aware of thirty-six cases of septic (infected) pregnancies in women who were using the Dalkon Shield. Most of these infections occurred after the first three months of pregnancy, and four of them resulted in death.

The controversial device was removed from the market in June of 1974. Two months later, the FDA reported that a total of 14 deaths and 219 cases of septic abortion had been attributed to the use of the Shield. In addition, they noted that the Lippes Loop was related to 5 deaths and 21 septic abortions, while the Saf-T-Coil was responsible for one death and 5 septic abortions. Other studies have subsequently confirmed that septic abortion and death, though more common with the Dalkon Shield, are possible with any IUD.

Dr. Howard Tatum sought to discover why the women using the Dalkon were more prone to infection when pregnancy occured. He studied the tails of all other IUDs under the microscope and noted that they consisted of a single or double segment of monofilament plastic thread. However, the Dalkon is made of a bundle of filaments encased in a thin plastic sheath (Figure 3–7).

When Dr. Tatum suspended the tails of various IUDs in a dye solution and in a solution containing bacteria, he noted that the many filaments in the Dalkon allowed both the dye and the bacteria to move rapidly up the tail by capillary action. This did not happen with the other IUDs.

During pregnancy with any IUD, the tail is often taken up into the endometrial cavity as the uterus enlarges. From the experimental model Tatum theorized that the infection with the Dalkon was carried into the uterus from the infected tail covered with bacteria from the vagina.

A modified Dalkon Shield with a monofilament tail was later approved by the FDA, but the manufacturer refrained from marketing the device.

Dalkon Tail   **Cu-7 Tail**

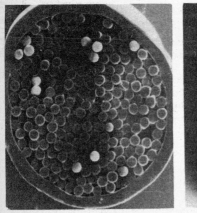 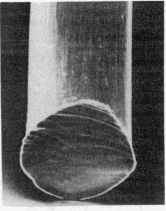

Figure 3-7.   Cross-Section of Dalkon Tail Compared with Cu-7 Tail

Should every woman wearing a Dalkon Shield have it removed?

Following the adverse news about the Dalkon Shield, Planned Parenthood encouraged all women under their care to have the device removed. Many gynecologists throughout the country have not followed this policy. At the present time it is estimated that 800,000 women in the United States are still wearing the Dalkon Shield. My personal policy has been to fully explain the Dalkon story to my patients. Following this, most elect to have it removed.

Those women who decide to keep using the device are cautioned to return immediately if pregnancy is suspected or at the first indication of infection symptoms such as abdominal discomfort, fever, or abnormal vaginal discharge. Under such conditions the Dalkon is always removed. Removal, however, is often an extremely difficult procedure for the doctor, and an extremely painful experience for his patient. This is due to its wide diameter (see Table 3–2) and to its tiny projections which tend to adhere to the endometrial cavity. While one is attempting to remove a Dalkon, it is not uncommon for the string to be pulled loose while the device remains within the uterus. If traction on the tail is too vigorous, laceration of the cervix and uterus is also possible. If removal of the Dalkon in the office is not easily accomplished, it is best to have the device removed in the hospital under anesthesia. The hysteroscope (Page 288) is often helpful in locating and grasping embedded Dalkon Shields.

If I become pregnant while using an IUD (other than the Dalkon Shield), what should I do?

Regardless of the type of IUD, if the strings are seen in your cervix and you decide to continue with the pregnancy, the device should be removed. By doing this, the risk of miscarriage will be approximately 25 percent, compared to 50 percent if the IUD is left in place. (The risk of miscarriage is normally around 10 percent.)

If the IUD strings cannot be seen, you can assume that it has been expelled without your knowledge, or it has been taken up into the uterus with the pregnancy, or it had previously perforated the uterus and is now either in the myometrium or in the abdominal cavity. Locating the IUD without radiation exposure to the fetus may be easily accomplished by use of ultrasound. However, most medical facilities do not have this sophisticated equipment available. Since even a single X-ray taken early in pregnancy to locate an IUD causes undue radiation exposure to the fetus, it is not recommended.

Women must understand the risk of infection while carrying a pregnancy with an IUD; early abortion may be considered. If you decide against it, maintain great vigilance and have the pregnancy terminated at the first evidence of sepsis, or infection. At the time of delivery the IUD will often be found attached to the placenta or in the endometrial cavity. If the IUD is not located at that time, an X-ray should be taken.

Women often express fears that an IUD may harm or cause deformity of the fetus by entangling a limb or other parts of the body. Fortunately, this does not happen since the IUD always lies outside the gestational or pregnancy sac of the baby. Of greater concern is our inability to predict the potential dangers of chemicals, such as copper and progesterone, in close proximity to the developing fetus. Certainly, from what is known about the relationship between hormones and the fetus (see Page 48), the risk of progesterone release from the Progestasert IUD could eventually prove to be dangerous. To date there have been no malformations reported of infants born following exposure to the Pogestasert in utero. However, the number of infants born under such circumstances is still quite small, and no conclusions can be drawn at the present time.

A recent report in the *British Medical Journal* describes two women who conceived while using IUDs containing copper. Both gave birth to newborns with similar limb defects in which there was an absence of some of the bones in the leg, arm, hand, and foot. Contrary to this is a 1976 study from the Population Council of New York. This extremely large project involved 157 women carrying a pregnancy to completion in the presence of a copper-containing IUD. Only one minor congenital anomaly was noted, and this was a benign growth of the vocal cord. There were no limb deformities in any of the offspring. Obviously, further information is needed.

Is tubal pregnancy more common in women using an IUD?
Women who become pregnant while using an IUD are more likely than other women to have an abnormal pregnancy in

the tube. This type of pregnancy, called an *ectopic* pregnancy, may cause the Fallopian tube to rupture, causing severe abdominal hemorrhage and even death. Among women not using the IUD, the incidence of tubal pregnancy is approximately 1 out of every 250 pregnancies. Among users of all IUDs except the Progestasert the incidence of ectopic pregnancy is between 2 and 3 per 100 accidental pregnancies, with progressively higher rates reported the longer the IUD is used. Furthermore, there is adequate evidence to suggest that the previous use of an IUD increases one's chances of suffering from an ectopic pregnancy. The increased incidence of ectopic pregnancy among IUD users is believed to be related to the greater likelihood of tubal infection among this group of women (see Page 84). Such infections hinder the fertilized egg from passing down the tube to its normal location in the uterus. As a result, it becomes trapped in the tube and grows in this abnormal location. Since the IUD prevents pregnancy in the uterus and not in the tube, even in the absence of infection a high percentage of women who conceive with the IUD will have a tubal pregnancy. One very disturbing report published in 1977 claimed that the Progestasert IUD was responsible for a five times greater number of ectopic pregnancies than any other device (see Page 85). The cause of this is obscure, but one of the authors of this paper, Dr. Howard Tatum, believes that it is due to the fact that the progesterone in the device may prevent the fertilized egg from moving down the tube as fast as it usually does. As a result, the pregnancy grows into the lining of the tube rather than into the endometrium of the uterus. At the present time, the FDA has requested that the manufacturers of this device reanalyze their statistics to determine the exact frequency of this very serious condition.)

Certainly, if you conceive while using the Progestasert or any other IUD, your doctor should strongly consider diagnosis of ectopic pregnancy. Symptoms of pregnancy accompanied by lower abdominal discomfort and a slight amount of dark vaginal bleeding can indicate a tubal pregnancy. Occasionally it is possible for your doctor to feel an enlargement in the tube which contains the ectopic pregnancy. Movement of the cervix either through intercourse or pelvic exam elicits extreme pain in the lower abdomen.

If only a minimal amount of tissue along with the IUD is removed during an abortion on an IUD user with a positive pregnancy test, ectopic pregnancy should be strongly suspected. Diagnosis of this condition prior to rupture is easily achieved via laparoscopy (see Chapter 9).

Can an IUD be inserted immediately after pregnancy or abortion?

The advantage of immediate contraception is in my opinion outweighed by the problems one may encounter. Heavy bleeding or infection several days following abortion or delivery adds confusion as to whether or not the IUD or some other factor is responsible. In addition, the threat of infection and expulsion appears to be greater at these times.

How does an IUD perforate a uterus?

It is the doctor who perforates the uterus, not the IUD. Perforation takes place at the time of insertion, and is the sole responsibility of the person inserting it. The one exception to that statement is the infamous Majzlin IUD. The FDA has removed that horrendous contraption from the market because of its tendency to penetrate deeply into the myometrium. The FDA has also banned the Birnberg Bow because of its high perforation rate.

Reports of so-called "silent" or asymptomatic perforations of the cervix and uterine wall associated mainly with the use of the copper T, and to a lesser extent with the Cu-7, have been a source of concern to many women. In one study of 62 women wearing the copper T, 30 demonstrated evidence of the device being partially imbedded in the uterine wall. This problem has been attributed to the three sharp points which made up the ends of the arms of the T, and the two sharp points at the ends of the Cu-7. In addition, the sharp point formed at the junction of the two arms of the Cu-7 was also believed responsible for the high perforation rates. Alterations in the design of the T and the 7 have apparently corrected this problem. The Cu-7 device which is now marketed, and the TCu-200 both have smooth, blunted edges rather than sharp ones. The two arms of the 7 now merge into a round ball or mushroom cap, thereby providing a smooth edge. Several reports studying these modified devices have confirmed extremely low perforation rates.

The incidence of perforation is listed as 1 in 2,500 insertions, but I am convinced that it is much higher, because many cases go unreported. Investigation has shown that when perforation rates are studied in terms of which doctor inserted the IUD, there is usually one culprit responsible for the vast majority of problems. If the person inserting the IUD is gentle, does not use excessive pressure, and performs a pelvic examination prior to insertion, perforation of the uterus should rarely happen (Figure 3–6).

Approximately 20 percent of all healthy women have a retroflexed uterus (one that tilts backward). If the person inserting the IUD omits the pelvic exam and assumes that the uterus is in an anterior position, as in Figure 3–6, the IUD inserter may perforate the cervix or the lower part of the corpus. The IUD then becomes embedded in the uterine muscle wall or passes beyond it into the abdominal cavity (Figure 3–8).

Before any IUD is inserted, a thin ruler called a *uterine sound* should be placed through the cervix and passed until the top of the corpus is reached. By doing this, the position and length of the cavity is easily determined. That allows the person inserting the IUD to know the limits beyond which the inserter should not be passed. That simple maneuver prevents perforation of the top of the corpus.

How can your doctor tell if an IUD has perforated?

Sadly, often the first clue is when a woman becomes pregnant within a few months following the IUD insertion. In the absence of a positive pregnancy test, perforation may be suspected when both you and your doctor are unable to see or feel the IUD tail. Since the tail may be taken up into the

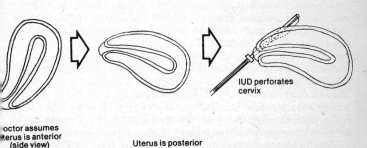

IUD perforates cervix

Doctor assumes uterus is anterior (side view)

Uterus is posterior

Figure 3-8.   Perforation While Inserting the IUD

endometrial cavity when the IUD is in its normal location, the mystery of the lost IUD may be solved by passing the uterine sound into the cavity and feeling for the IUD. If the IUD can be touched with the sound, you may be assured that all is well. If the IUD can't be touched, an X-ray taken with a probe in the uterus will confirm the presence of the IUD as well as its relationship to the endometrial cavity. An alternative method is to insert another IUD and take an X-ray. If both IUDs are in close contact, one may assume that they are in the right place, and the one with the visible string can be removed. A third technique is to fill the endometrial cavity with an X-ray dye solution and then take a picture called an *hysterogram*. If the IUD is seen outside the area of the dye, it means perforation has occurred.

A newer technique gaining popularity in this country is *hysteroscopy*. In that procedure, using local anesthesia to the cervix, a small viewing instrument is passed through the cervical os and into the endometrial cavity. If the IUD is present, it is easily located and may also be removed with a special forceps attachment (see Chapter 10).

When it has been determined that an IUD is located in the abdominal cavity, it may be removed through the laparoscope (see Chapter 9).

The IUD must not be left in the abdominal cavity, because it may be responsible for an inflammatory reaction of the surrounding intestine, or a blockage of a loop of intestine which may adhere to it. IUDs containing copper are the most difficult to remove, because they cause the greatest inflammatory reaction. The Dalkon Shield also produces a marked inflammatory reaction in the abdomen, due to the little-known fact, first revealed in the August, 1974, FDA investigations, that each Dalkon Shield actually contained 2 milligrams of copper.

Do women using the IUD have a higher incidence of vaginal discharge?

The characteristic discharge caused by use of the IUD is watery, mucus-like, clear, and odorless. It does not cause itching or irritation of the vulva, and is believed to be caused by stimulation of the glands of the inner cervix by the presence of the IUD tail in that location. Cutting the tail completely off will help to relieve the discharge somewhat, but it is not advised, since locating and removing the IUD will become more difficult.

Can the tail of my IUD cause discomfort for my partner during intercourse?

Discomfort with intercourse is a rather common complaint heard from men in the days immediately following a woman's IUD insertion. This is due to the firmness of the strings of the tail, which soften after they have been bathed in the vaginal secretions for a few weeks. If your partner continues to complain of penile irritation, your doctor can cut the strings so that they barely protrude through the cervical os.

Is fertility enhanced or diminished after the IUD is removed?

Assuming that there is no serious pelvic infection, as mentioned previously, the subsequent chances for pregnancy should be unchanged. However, one large study reported in 1977 has demonstrated that subsequent fertility may be diminished even in the absence of obvious pelvic infection. Dr. Anrudh Jain, of the Population Council, reported in 1977 on the fertility of 5,000 Taiwanese women following removal of the Lippes Loop. Over the course of six to nine years, these women were noted to have a very significant decrease in fertility. This problem was most prevalent among women who had used the IUD for at least three years and those who were at least thirty years of age at the time that the IUD was removed.

Ironically, IUDs have actually been used to enhance the possibilities of pregnancy in the rare case of women with scar tissue or adhesions of the endometrial cavity. That scar tissue usually forms following a D & C in the presence of an infected abortion. If your doctor performs a repeat D & C and immediately inserts a large IUD (Lippes D or large Saf-T-Coil), the cavity may be kept free of these adhesions. If the IUD is removed several months later, pregnancy is possible.

Can heavy and prolonged periods, often a major problem with the IUD, be prevented?

Many remedies have been tried, but all have failed, including Vitamins C and K, cortisone, and medication to contract the uterus.

Hormonal treatment in the form of birth control pills does control the bleeding, but most women have chosen the IUD specifically to avoid the hazards and discomfort of the Pill.

Heavy and prolonged periods, as well as bleeding between periods, can occur at any time after the IUD is inserted. However, the problem is most severe during the first three months. The birth control pill is often useful in controlling bleeding during this initial time period. Women who experience heavy periods while using the IUD should take supplemental iron preparations so that their hemoglobin remains at normal levels.

If I suddenly experience abnormal bleeding after several years with the IUD, should the IUD be removed and another inserted?

The presence of bleeding in a woman using the IUD does not necessarily mean that the IUD is responsible for the bleeding. In this particular case, inserting another IUD will only delay diagnosing the true cause of the abnormal bleeding. The more logical treatment in such situations is to remove the IUD and observe the menstrual pattern while another form of contraception is used. If the menstrual pattern reverts to normal, another IUD may be tried. If it doesn't, a diagnostic D & C should be performed.

Is there any relationship between the IUD and venereal disease?

Laboratory studies have definitely shown that the growth of the bacteria which cause gonorrhea is stopped in the area around the copper portion of the IUD. (The plastic affords no protection at all.) However, the copper is not effective in preventing all bacteria from passing out of the uterine cavity, and IUDs should not be thought of as providing protection against VD.

What is a reasonable fee for inserting an IUD?

Fees vary. They may range from ten dollars in a family planning clinic to more than $100 on fabulous Park Avenue. The cost of an IUD to a doctor ranges from three dollars to twenty dollars, with the Progestasert device being the most expensive.

What is the relationship between IUD use and cancer of the cervix or endometrium?

I have often heard this question from my patients. There is

no evidence thus far to indicate any relationship exists between use of the IUD and cancer of any type.

What safeguards should be made available to women before an IUD is inserted?

The FDA is asking that physicians obtain either oral or written consent from women before inserting the IUD. Women should have adequate time, well in advance of the time scheduled for actual insertion, to read the labeling and to study the list of all potential complications. Possibly, with more time to reflect upon the potential hazards of this form of contraception, safer alternatives may be chosen. In the following chapter I will discuss some of the safer, though admittedly less effective, methods of contraception.

4

DIAPHRAGMS, SPERMICIDES, AND CONDOMS

DIAPHRAGMS

A diaphragm is a flexible metal ring covered with a rubber in the shape of a shallow dome (Figure 4–1). It is placed in the vagina so as to completely encircle the cervix, thereby preventing sperm from entering the uterus (Figure 4–2). When used with a spermicidal or sperm-killing jelly or cream applied to the side of the dome facing the cervix, it can be a very effective contraceptive (Figure 4–3).

Though today's diaphragms resemble those first used at the end of the nineteenth century, it was Casanova who envisioned the first contraceptive diaphragm around 1750. It consisted of half a lemon rind placed against the cervix as a mechanical barrier against sperm. In addition, the citric acid of the juice proved a strong spermicidal agent. For centuries prior to that discovery, less effective mechanical barriers were used for contraception, such as leaves, wool soaked in oil, honey, fig pulp, sponges, and even animal dung.

With the popularity of birth control pills and IUDs, the diaphragm until recently had been looked upon as an old-fashioned and unpopular method of contraception. As more has been learned about the potential hazards of the Pill and IUD, there has been a sudden and well-deserved renewed interest in the diaphragm. Its one beautiful advantage is that

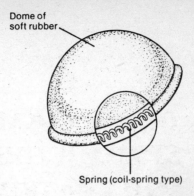

Dome of
soft rubber

Spring (coil-spring type)

Figure 4-1. Coil-Spring Diaphragm

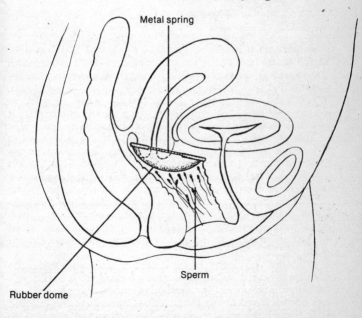

Metal spring

Rubber dome

Sperm

Figure 4-2. Correctly Placed Diaphragm

99

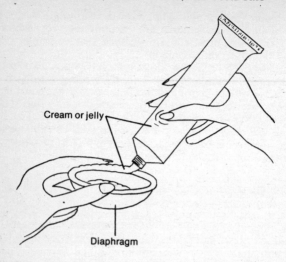

Cream or jelly

Diaphragm

Figure 4-3.   Spermicidal Jelly Applied to Diaphragm

it has never been responsible for a single hospitalization or death, and that's a lot to be said in its favor. It can safely be predicted that as public awareness of contraceptive alternatives grows, and newer complications of the Pill and IUD are revealed, the diaphragm will once again come into vogue. At the present time it is estimated that the diaphragm is used by 6 percent of all women who use contraceptives.

Where do I get a diaphragm, and how do I learn to use it properly?

You must be measured or fitted for the correct diaphragm size. That may be done in a doctor's office or in a family planning clinic. The prescriptions for the specific size, and the spermicidal cream or jelly, are then filled by a pharmacist. The actual measuring of the diaphragm takes only a few minutes, but once the size is determined, it is the obligation of your doctor to take the time to explain the simple anatomy involved as well as the proper insertion technique. You should take the time to practice inserting the diaphragm without assistance, and the doctor should then check its proper position by doing a vaginal examination. Regardless of how many failures are encountered, you shouldn't leave the office until you are satisfied that you fully understand the insertion technique.

Occasionally, when a woman has become discouraged after several unsuccessful insertion attempts, I will tell her to practice in the privacy of her home and then return to the office on another day wearing the diaphragm so that we can be sure that is now inserted correctly. (Obviously, I instruct her to use other contraception during this learning period.) Once the insertion technique is learned, it becomes extremely simple and is never forgotten.

What determines the diaphragm size?

The diaphragm size is dependent on the size and shape of the vagina, which in turn is determined by body size, body build, bone structure, previous intercourse, and previous childbearing. With childbearing, the vaginal walls and supporting muscles often undergo stretch and become weaker. When that happens the size required usually increases. Diaphragm sizes are measured in millimeters, the smallest being 50 and the largest 105.

What is the proper way to insert a diaphragm?

For greatest effectiveness the diaphragm should be inserted within the two hours prior to coitus, since the spermicidal creams and jellies lose their potency after this time. Inserting the diaphragm several hours earlier and then injecting cream into the vagina immediately before intercourse isn't enough, since these substances must first be applied to the side of the dome facing the cervix. When applying the cream or jelly to the diaphragm, put a very thin film on the rim to prevent the sperm from passing between the rim and vaginal wall (Figure 4–3). However, if you apply too much to the rim, it will be more likely to slip during intercourse. A teaspoonful of cream or jelly in the cup is usually adequate.

The diaphragm can be inserted while you are in any position you find comfortable; probably the most commonly used position is standing with one foot resting on a stool or toilet seat. After bending the diaphragm in half by pressing the rim between the thumb and middle finger, insert it (Figure 4–4). The diaphragm may be inserted by using the

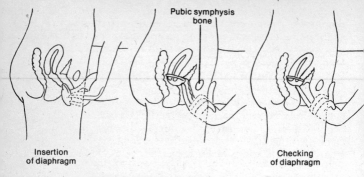

Figure 4-4.   Proper Insertion of Diaphragm

fingers or a small plastic or metal inserter can be used. The inserters may be purchased wherever diaphragms are sold.

Insertion is easier if you push the rim against the back wall of the vagina as far as possible. That insures that the back of the rim has passed behind the cervix. The diaphragm is then released from its bent position. Feel the dome with your finger to be sure that the cervix is in its center and that the rim completely encircles it (Figure 4–4). The front rim of the diaphragm should fit snugly under the pubic symphysis bone.

What different types of diaphragms are there?
There are four basic diaphragm types. The *coil-spring* type is made of a cadmium-plated coil spring encased in latex (Figure 4–1). The two most popular brands of this type are the Ortho Diaphragm and the Koromex Coil Spring. Sizes for both range from 50 millimeters to 105 millimeters at gradations of 5 millimeters.

The *flat-spring* diaphragm is also covered with latex, but it contains a flat watch-type spring which allows it to be compressed in one plane only, rather than in any point of the rim, as are the coil-spring types. That feature often allows for easier, less slippery insertions. The Ortho-White Diaphragm, which comes in Sizes 55 millimeters to 90 millimeters, is an example of a flat-spring.

If you can't place the back of the diaphragm behind your cervix, an *arcing-spring* diaphragm is probably best. This diaphragm, when compressed, assumes a half-moon or arc shape which makes it easier to pass it along the vaginal floor and beyond the cervix. Women with mild *cystocele* and *rectocele* (see Pages 229–230) may benefit the most from this type of diaphragm. Examples of arcing diaphragms are the Ortho All-Flex and the Koro-Flex Arcing Spring Diaphragm. The former is supplied in Sizes 50 millimeters to 105 millimeters, while the latter ranges from 60 millimeters to 90 millimeters.

The fourth type of diaphragm, called a Matrisalus, is rarely used. Its rim is in the shape of a special pessary named Smith-Hodge. Pessaries are devices made of plastic or rubber that come in a variety of sizes and shapes. When inserted into the vagina they are helpful in supporting sagging vaginal tissues found with cystocele, rectocele, and *uterine prolapse* (see Chapter 10). This type of diaphragm may be used both for contraception and for support of these tissues.

How is a diaphragm inserter used?

Diaphragm inserters or introducers are intended for use only with the coil and flat spring diaphragms. (Inserters cannot be used with an arcing spring diaphragm because the arcing spring is too flexible and becomes dislodged soon after it is placed on the inserter.) By far the most popular inserter is the Ortho Universal Introducer. This plastic device is designed for use with any coil or flat spring diaphragm brand from size 60 mm through size 90 mm.

One end of the Ortho Introducer has a smooth, round hook which may be used to remove the diaphragm simply by grasping it under the front rim. To insert the diaphragm, one end of the rim is placed in the notch at the end of the inserter not having the hook. Each of the little notches located in the middle of the inserter has a number which corresponds to each diaphragm size. The diaphragm is placed on the inserter by squeezing it and slipping one end of the rim in the end notch and the other end of the rim into the notch corresponding to your diaphragm size. It is best to apply spermicidal jelly or cream after the diaphragm is on the inserter. Otherwise, stretching the slippery, lubricated diaphragm onto the inserter may prove difficult and messy.

After you have inserted the diaphragm as far as possible, release it by giving the inserter a slight twist. After the inserter is removed, use your index finger to push the front securely under the pubic symphysis bone (Figure 4–5).

How successfully does the diaphragm prevent pregnancy?

Until recently, most studies have demonstrated pregnancy rates to be significantly higher with the diaphragm than with the IUD or birth control pills. Even in highly motivated women, the lowest pregnancy rates achieved were usually no better than six per hundred woman-years.

In 1974, a study in Oxford, England, involving 4,052 diaphragm users demonstrated a remarkably low pregnancy rate of only 2.4 per 100 woman-years. Furthermore, those rates fell sharply as the woman's age increased and the number of months that the diaphragm was used increased. It was also of interest to note that the pregnancy rate was lower for women who already had as many children as they wanted than for those women who desired more children or who were uncertain about their intentions in this respect. These findings demonstrate the importance of motivation in the success of this method of contraception.

In 1976, the Margaret Sanger Research Bureau published the results of the largest contemporary diaphragm study ever conducted in the United States. Of 2,168 using this method of contraception, accidental pregnancies in the first twelve months of use ranged from a low of 1.9 per 100 women less than eighteen years of age to a high of 3 per 100 women among thirty- to thirty-four-year-olds. At the end of one year, approximately 84 women out of every 100 elected to continue using the diaphragm. The Margaret Sanger research team attributed their success to patient motivation as well as the patience, motivation, and skill of the instructors teaching the proper use of the diaphragm. They also noted that once a patient chose the diaphragm method, it was used successfully regardless of the woman's age, ethnic background, marital status, or number of children.

It is interesting that the pregnancy rates cited in these reports are so much better than those quoted in several other large studies conducted in the United States. Rates have varied from six to fourteen per one hundred woman-years, and in one study, the pregnancy rate was an astonishing twenty-nine per one hundred woman-years. It is obvious from those discrepancies that the success of the diaphragm depends to a great degree on skillful instruction given by an

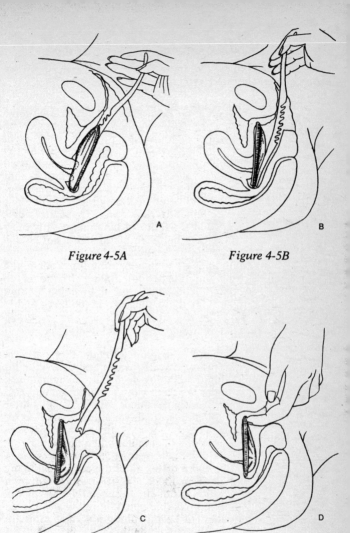

Figure 4-5A

Figure 4-5B

Figure 4-5C

Figure 4-5D

enthusiastic instructor to a motivated woman. With that combination, the pregnancy rate for diaphragm users should approach that of women using the IUD.

How can the pregnancy rate be reduced in diaphragm users?
Improper placement, because of either poor instruction by the doctor or excessive haste by the patient, is the main cause of pregnancy. In addition, the diaphragm must be left in for at least eight hours after intercourse to insure that all sperm in the vagina are dead. If you remove it before that time, living sperm can enter the cervix. A second intercourse within eight hours should be preceded by insertion of more spermicidal cream or jelly into the vagina. That offers additional protection against the influx of new sperm. It is most important that great care be taken at this time not to disturb the diaphragm from its secure position.

If the diaphragm appears to move during intercourse, the size should be rechecked. It is better to have a size that is too large than one that is too small, but if bleeding follows coitus, it may mean that the diaphragm is too large and is irritating the vaginal walls. Sizes should also be rechecked following pregnancy or if there is a weight gain or loss greater than ten pounds.

The diaphragm should be examined frequently for defects or holes by running water over the dome and observing for leaks. When removing the diaphragm from the vagina, hook your index finger under the front rim as it is pulled out, taking care to avoid puncturing the dome with your nails. After removal, wash the diaphragm with soap and water, dry it, and dust it with cornstarch but not talcum. A diaphragm lasts longer if it is kept in its container when not in use.

Perhaps the greatest obstacle against reducing pregnancy rates is the maturity and motivation of the couple using the diaphragm. Although all methods of contraception require a certain degree of motivation, it is especially true of the diaphragm. Too often a "diaphragm failure" really means that it was never used. The best diaphragm success rates are in those women who insert the diaphragm every night before going to bed, and remove it the following morning. When intercourse is spontaneous at other times during the day, a considerate, mature man patiently waits while his partner inserts the diaphragm. A woman is not the only one who can insert the diaphragm, and active participation by a man in this act can represent both a sensual and a mature expression of his feelings.

If all these precautions are followed, why does the pregnancy rate remain so high?

Unfortunately, other factors prevail. The vagina expands naturally during sexual excitation and intercourse, which can cause even the properly fitted diaphragm to become loose. Frequent penile thrusts and woman-above coital positions can also loosen the diaphragm and increase the pregnancy rate.

Which women can benefit most from using the diaphragm?

The diaphragm is an ideal contraceptive for women for whom accidental pregnancy would not be a physically, emotionally, or religiously devastating experience.

Women in their late forties, approaching the menopause, are well advised to use the diaphragm, since the chances of conception are lower at that age, while the dangers and side effects of the Pill and IUD are greater. The diaphragm is also an ideal contraceptive for a woman having infrequent intercourse. Taking birth control pills every day in anticipation of only an occasional sexual encounter appears to impose too high a risk on a woman. If you abstain from intercourse during the menstrual period because it is too messy, inserting the diaphragm over the cervix at that time solves the problem. Since the risk of pregnancy is minimal during the menstrual period, the diaphragm may be removed at your leisure over the next few hours following coitus.

Are there women who should not use the diaphragm?

Occasionally, anatomical factors, such as a severely anteflexed or retroflexed uterus, prevent proper diaphragm encirclement of the cervix (Figure 1–6). Complete uterine prolapse and severe cystocele and rectocele may also deter you from using the diaphragm (Chapter 7). Also, women who have not been accustomed to having intercourse may find a diaphragm uncomfortable, at least for the first few months.

If you feel uneasy about touching your genitals, chances are you will not be comfortable using a diaphragm. Some women find inserting the diaphragm and jelly to be repugnant and messy. (To avoid getting excessive amounts of jelly or cream on your hands, you can use an inserter rather than your fingers.) Still other women feel that the spontaneity of precoital lovemaking is lost when time is taken to insert the diaphragm. And finally, as previously mentioned, the diaphragm is extremely poor contraception for women needing 100 percent protection.

Can the diaphragm, jelly, or cream cause harmful side effects?

Occasionally a man or a woman may experience burning or irritation in the genital area from either the rubber of the diaphragm or the ingredients of the spermicide. Depending on the cause, one should either purchase a plastic diaphragm or switch brands of spermicide.

A few of the contraceptive jellies or creams, such as Certane Jelly and Contra Cream, contain phenylmercuric acetate, which is an organic mercury compound. Although it can't usually get absorbed through the vaginal wall and into the bloodstream, in the presence of a laceration within the vagina the chance of potential absorption does exist. Because of this, contraceptive jellies and creams without organic mercury are recommended. Examples are Kormex II and Ortho-Gynol Contraceptive Jelly.

Cream or jelly left at the vaginal opening during a hasty diaphragm insertion may be a source of displeasure for men during oral genital sex. Though most of these substances are safe and nontoxic, they do have a terrible taste, and if a man has a small laceration of the mouth or tongue, it is theoretically possible to absorb organic mercury from a cream or jelly which contains it.

The majority of women using a diaphragm prefer the contraceptive jelly to the cream because it provides better lubrication during coitus. The brand of contraceptive agent used does not have to be the same as that of the diaphragm, and you should sample a variety of brands to determine which you prefer. Table 4-1 lists the most commonly used vaginal spermicidal (sperm-killing) agents. Aerosols or foam should not be used with a diaphragm, because they are unable to adhere to the latex rubber and will not form a seal between the cervix and the diaphragm membrane. However, if intercourse is repeated within eight hours of the initial coitus, with the diaphragm already in place with cream or jelly, an applicator full of foam may be inserted into the vagina. Some women mistakenly use petroleum jelly with a

TABLE 4-1 — COMMONLY USED VAGINAL SPERMICIDAL AGENTS

COMPANY	BRAND	SPERMICIDAL AGENT	%SPERMICIDAL AGENT BY WEIGHT	COMMENTS
Ortho	Conceptrol Birth Control Cream	Nonoxynol-9	5	Contraceptive cream used alone, one single premeasured dose in applicator — very convenient
Ortho	Delfen Contraceptive Cream	Nonoxynol-9	5	Same as above, but 2.46-ounce tube for approximately ten refills
Ortho	Delfen Contraceptive Foam	Nonoxynol-9	12.5	Twenty applications per can — used alone
Ortho	Ortho-Gynol Contraceptive Jelly	p-diisobutylphenoxy-polyethoxyethanol	1	Used only with diaphragm
Ortho	Preceptin Contraceptive Gel	p-diisobutylphenoxy-polyethoxyethanol	2	Used only without diaphragm
Emko	Because™ Birth Control Foam	Nonylphenoxy-poly-ethylene-ethanol	8	Used alone. Same as Emko Contraceptive Vaginal Foam but contains six uses of contraceptive foam — very convenient ten-gram container
Emko	Emko Vaginal Foam Contraceptive	Nonylphenoxy-poly-ethylene-ethanol	8	45-gram and 90-gram aerosol
Emko	Emko Pre-Fil Contraceptive Vaginal Foam	Nonylphenoxy-poly-ethylene-ethanol	8	Applicator can be filled from aerosol any time up to one week before intercourse and kept in convenient location until needed — less delay in inserting before coitus
Holland Rantos	Koromex II Contraceptive Cream	Octoxynol	3	With diaphragm only, 75-gram tube
Holland Rantos	Koromex II Contraceptive Jelly	Octoxynol	1	With diaphragm only, 81 and 135 grams
Holland Rantos	Koromex II A Contraceptive Jelly	Nonoxynol-9	2	Used alone 135 gram tube
A.H. Robins	Dalkon Foam	Nonylphenoxy-poly-ethylene-ethanol	8	Used alone
National American Corporation	Semicid Contraceptive Suppositories	Nonoxynol 9	5	Used alone

diaphragm. This substance not only has little, if any, spermicidal effect, but can also cause deterioration of the latex
rubber.

Though the manufacturers of the various creams and jellies always specify whether a product is to be used alone or
only with a diaphragm, my conversations with representatives of Ortho and Holland Rantos have convinced me that
all of the creams and jellies listed in Table 4–1 may be used
with the diaphragm. However, the reverse is not necessarily
true, since not all creams and jellies designed for use with a
diaphragm are safe enough to be used alone. The pregnancy
rate achieved under such circumstances may range from a
not-so-low eleven to a high thirty-eight per one hundred
woman-years.

It is not clear why the stronger preparations are not pro-
moted for use both alone and with the diaphragm. Company
representatives have given me several answers, including
fear of deterioration of the rubber with prolonged use, and
fewer packaging problems by enclosing one jelly or cream
with each diaphragm rather than four or five possible
choices. The most logical reason given to me was that the
contraceptive action of the less concentrated spermicides
was more than adequate when they were used with a properly fitting diaphragm. Pregnancies that result from diaphragm use are rarely due to the concentration of the
spermicide.

Does a diaphragm help prevent VD?
Since the diaphragm forms a seal with the cervical os, it
may help to prevent the ascent of gonorrhea bacteria into
the uterus and tubes. This protection is quite limited, since
the bacteria may still enter the cervical os after the diaphragm is removed.

Cancer of the cervix is now believed to be a veneral disease. Evidence shows that it is most prevalent in women
who engage in intercourse both at an early age and with
numerous sexual partners. It is practically unheard of in
nuns, and in religious sects in which intercourse is forbidden
prior to adulthood. There is now considerable evidence to
suggest that the Type 2 herpes simplex virus (HSV–2) may
be the cause of cervical cancer. The virus is known to be
transmitted through sexual intercourse and has been iso-

lated from cervical cancer cells. A number of epidemiologic studies have demonstrated that women with cancer of the cervix more frequently have antibodies against HSV–2 than do other women. It has been suggested that the diaphragm offers a mechanical barrier against the herpes virus or any other agent which may be responsible for causing cervical cancer. The one study supporting that idea was presented in the *British Medical Journal* in 1969 and involved women attending Planned Parenthood Centers in New York. Comparison of Pill and diaphragm users was made, and after each year of contraceptive use it was found that the rates for cervical cancer were significantly greater in the former group. It should be pointed out that that study had many deficiencies, the main one being that the incidence of cancer in the Pill-user group was also higher before either form of contraception was started. Certainly other factors such as the personality, sexual habits, and lifestyle of a woman choosing one form of contraception over the other would have to be more intensely studied before definite conclusions could be drawn.

How much does a diaphragm cost?
The cost of a diaphragm at a retail pharmacy ranges between $7.50 and $8.50. Arcing-spring diaphragms, such as the Ortho All-Flex, are more expensive because of their unique construction. Discount pharmacies which I sampled sold their diaphragms for $6.90 to $7.50. If you take good care of a diaphragm it should last for at least two years. However, after that it may crack and lose its shape, and it is best to get a new one. Contraceptive jelly costs about $4.80 at a retail pharmacy and $4.50 at a discount pharmacy and one tube of jelly or cream contains enough for approximately ten applications.

What is a cervical cap?
A cervical cap looks like a small diaphragm, but fits securely over the cervix rather than against the vaginal walls. It is much more difficult to use than a diaphragm, and much more likely to result in contraceptive failure due to slippage during intercourse. While it was once very popular, it is rarely used today.

VAGINAL SPERMICIDES

Vaginal spermicides, or sperm-killing preparations, are available without prescription at all drugstores. They come in the form of creams, jellies, aerosol foam, tablets, and suppositories (Figure 4-6).

All spermicidal preparations consist of two components: an inert base which holds the spermicidal agent in the vagina against the cervix, and a spermicidal agent, such as nonoxynol 9 and octoxynol. All those agents must be inserted far up into the vagina, as close to the cervix as possible, if they are to be effective (Figure 4-7).

Insert them within the hour before intercourse, by filling the plastic applicator with the spermicidal agent. A large can of foam should be vigorously shaken prior to filling the applicator so that the spermicidal chemical is evenly dispersed. Some products are prefilled in the applicator and do

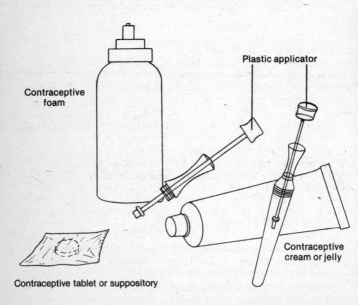

Figure 4-6. Vaginal Spermicides

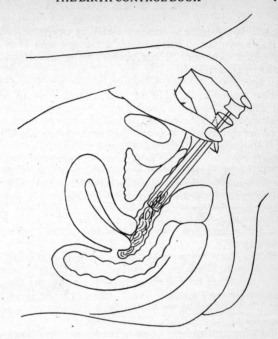

Figure 4-7. Insertion of Vaginal Foam and·Jelly

not require vigorous shaking prior to use (Table 4–1). The applicator may be used repeatedly and may be purchased with the initial starter pack of foam, cream, or jelly. Refill packs are slightly less expensive because they do not contain plastic inserters. The proper use of the applicator and its plunger is demonstrated in Figure 4–7.

Which of those agents is the best in preventing pregnancy?
Contraceptive aerosol foam is probably the most effective vaginal spermicide. The skepticism which exists about foam is based on studies which demonstrated pregnancy rates as high as twenty-nine per hundred woman-years. However, other investigators have claimed pregnancy rates equal to, or even lower than, those of the diaphragm. The crucial fac-

tor in the success or failure of contraceptive foams seems to be whether you are motivated to use the method correctly.

Are there other advantages to foam contraception?

Theoretically, foam should offer faster protection than other agents because it is more rapidly distributed throughout the vagina   quickly forms a barrier over the cervix. This advantage applies to contraceptive creams as well. Because of it, intercourse and ejaculation can immediately follow insertion of foam and cream. When using suppositories and tablets, it is best to wait at least fifteen minutes for them to completely liquefy. Since intravaginal distribution of jelly, tablets, and suppositories is partially dependent on penile thrusting, a greater chance of pregnancy will exist if the male ejaculates quickly after penetration.

Foam is also not nearly as messy as the other vaginal spermicides. It is less likely to drain out of the vagina after use, and is also less likely to leak out of the vagina during intercourse.

Delfen foam is considered to have the best spermicidal effect, though Emko would appear to be equally potent. To date, no studies have compared these two agents. Since they contain different spermicides, burning or irritation with one may be remedied by switching to the other brand.

What precautions help achieve the lowest pregnancy rates possible with the foam?

Shake the can or prefilled applicator twenty times before using. That insures that the foam will have the consistency of shaving cream, and that the spermicide will be mixed into the base. Since the bubbles start going flat after a half hour, it is best to insert it just before lovemaking.

A new applicator of foam must be inserted before each act of intercourse. Don't douche until at least eight hours later. To prevent foam from running out when getting out of bed and going to work or school, a tampon can be inserted after intercourse.

It is a good idea to always keep an extra container of foam on hand. With the large cans, there is often no way of telling when the supply is about to run out. Therefore use of a single, premeasured applicator, such as Conceptrol, is helpful.

What is Encare Oval?
Encare Oval is a suppository which, like many other vaginal contraceptives, uses nonoxynol-9 as its spermicide. Though the manufacturer of this product would have us believe it was the greatest invention since chicken soup, it is really no better, and possibly slightly worse, than Delfen foam which also contains nonoxynol-9. Because it is a suppository, Encare Oval has the disadvantage of taking ten minutes to dissolve completely before ejaculation is safe. I have noted that several of my patients have complained of intense vaginal burning soon after inserting it. Finally, the cost is not inexpensive. A box of twelve sells for $3.90, and about $3.15 at a discount pharmacy. One suppository has a sperm-killing effect of only two hours. To date, the only studies of Encare Oval's effectiveness were conducted in Europe, and though the pregnancy rates were reported as only 1 percent, I would reserve my optimism until reports from large studies in the United States are available.

What are the disadvantages of using vaginal spermicides?
The disadvantages mentioned for the diaphragm also apply to the use of vaginal spermicides. In addition, all of these preparations, including foam, are a little messy to use, tend to drip out, and have a rather unpleasant taste. The spontaneity of lovemaking is often interfered with. Finally, vaginal and penile irritation are not uncommon, especially with the stronger spermicidal preparations.

Do spermicidal agents protect against VD?
When the products currently used are studied in laboratory tests, all show some ability to retard the growth of bacteria which cause gonorrhea and syphilis. However, there are no data confirming the effectiveness of these agents in preventing the spread of venereal disease in people. Certainly they are less effective than either the condom or diaphragm in that respect.

What is the cost of these preparations?
A can of foam which contains twenty applications costs approximately $4.50 at a discount pharmacy and almost $6.00 at a regular pharmacy. The individual premeasured applicator of Conceptrol costs between $.50 and $.60 and is

sold in packets of six for $3.00 to $3.50. The brand Because is not premeasured, and has to be drawn up into the applicator. Because of that, it is less expensive at 6 for $2.25 at a discount pharmacy and $3.00 at a regular pharmacy. Contraceptive creams and jellies are about equally priced at $4.50 and $4.80 for a four and one-half ounce tube at discount and regular pharmacies respectively.

CONDOMS

The *condom* is a thin sheath of latex rubber or lamb membrane which fits over the penis and prevents sperm from entering the vagina. Other names for condoms are *prophylactics*, *safes*, *rubbers*, *sheaths*, *skins*, and *Trojans*. The latter is actually the name of one of the more popular brands (Figure 4-8).

The condom is an excellent method of birth control and probably the oldest, having first been described by Fallopius in 1564. Though the linen bag which he fashioned for the prevention of syphilis was not an instant success, he did achieve immortality by eventually having the Fallopian tubes named after him.

It was not until the eighteenth century that penile sheaths were given the name *condoms*, to be used for "protection from venereal disease and numerous bastard offspring." Once again, it was Casanova who was one of the first to popularize the condom. Today, it is the second most popular method of birth control, and is used by approximately 8-11 percent of all contraceptive users.

After all the problems that women have experienced with birth control pills, IUDs, unwanted pregnancies, and abortion, it is a pathetic commentary that this four hundred-year-old device is still the primary male contraceptive.

How "safe" is the condom?

In the three largest surveys, pregnancy rates for the condom were reported to be 11, 14, and 14.9 per 100 woman-years. Pregnancy rates in some other less extensive studies have varied from a low of 3 to a high of 36 per 100 woman-years. As with other methods of contraception that are used at the time of coitus, the effectiveness of the condom is dependent largely upon users' motivation and care in usage.

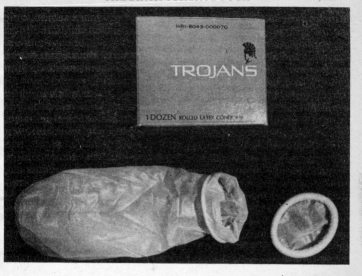

Figure 4-8.   Condoms

The risk of pregnancy from a defective device is extremely small and probably no greater than .3 percent. The chance of rupture or tearing of the high quality latex produced in the United States is less than 1 in 150 to 300 instances of use. The standard advice of testing a condom for leaks by filling it with water or blowing it up with air like a balloon is best ignored. These maneuvers only increase the risk of creating a defect in the latex.

When and how does a man put on a condom?
The man unrolls the condom onto the erect penis. Many condoms have a rubber receptacle at the end to catch the sperm; others do not. For the man using a condom without a receptacle, a little space should be left between the end of the condom and the penis for catching the sperm (Figure 4–9). It is a common misconception that by doing this the rapid ejaculation is prevented from bursting the rubber. The actual reason for the space at the end of the condom is that the receptacle's presence prevents sperm from being forced

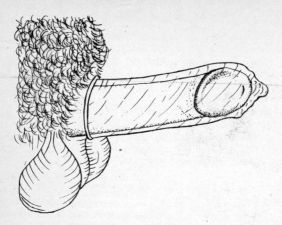

Figure 4-9.   Properly Placed Condom

down the penile shaft and out the lower part of the condom. Air should be squeezed out of that space, or the receptacle tip, with the fingers prior to intercourse. The condom should be unrolled the full length of the erect penis, and uncircumcised males should retract (pull back) the foreskin overlying the end of the penis.

Though men should be cautioned to put on the condom before intercourse rather than ejaculation, the usual reason given is incorrect. It is often stated that the first few drops of a man's discharge, which are present during erection and before ejaculation, contain enough sperm for pregnancy to occur. Most knowledgeable urologists dispute this, stating that pregnancy is nearly impossible from this small amount of preejaculatory discharge. The correct explanation for putting on the condom before inserting the penis is that a man may forget the condom once the penis is inserted.

What are the advantages of using a condom?
A man who uses a condom protects the woman he cares for from the risks involved in using the IUD and birth control pills. The condom is easy to use, may be purchased without prescription, is relatively inexpensive, and is small enough to be carried secretly in one's pocket or wallet without being detected by inquisitive parents or friends.

The condom is the only contraceptive which can prevent the spread of venereal disease when these infections are on or in the man's penis or the woman's vulva, vagina, or cervix. Provided the condom doesn't slip or tear, a woman or a man will have 100 percent protection against transmission of gonorrhea from an infected partner. The protection against syphilis and herpes virus is less, since these organisms are capable of entering through the exposed skin of the unprotected labia or scrotum. The spread of other sexually transmitted vaginal infections, such as trichomoniasis, may also be prevented by use of a condom. This condition is caused by a microscopic organism called a *protozoon*. Men usually have no symptoms, but women will almost always experience a heavy, yellowish-green, foul-smelling, and irritating discharge. Trichomoniasis is harmless but annoying, and treatment consists of taking tablets of Flagyl (metronidazole) by mouth for a period of seven to ten days. To prevent reoccurrence, asymptomatic men must also be treated at the same time, and both men and women must be reexamined by their physicians before resuming intercourse.

When VD, such as gonorrhea, is present, reinfection and transmission is still possible even though treatment has been started. Therefore condoms should be worn until all bacterial cultures are negative in both the woman and her partner.

How can pregnancy rates with the condom be reduced?
Many boys obtain a condom at the onset of puberty and hide it in their wallet while waiting for their first opportunity to use it. Sometimes the waiting period lasts a couple of years, and when the moment finally arrives the condom may disintegrate like old paper. For this reason it is important that a condom be no older than two years.

A nonlubricated condom should never be lubricated with petroleum jelly, since it causes rubber to deteriorate. If lubrication is necessary, K-Y Jelly is best. (This may be purchased at any pharmacy without prescription.) Adequate lubrication will also help prevent tearing of the condom.

Though the condom holds firmly to the erect penis, after ejaculation it may easily slip the flaccid penis. Because of this, the penis is best withdrawn soon after intercourse before it is completely soft. In addition, the base of the condom must be held firmly so that when it is removed it does not slip off. Penile thrusting may also loosen a condom, especially when it is lubricated on the inside and on the outside, as are XXXX Skins.

The use of foam in addition to the condom will add tremendously to its effectiveness. When foam and condoms are used together by a conscientious couple, the pregnancy rates approach that of the IUD. Even if foam is not always used, it is good to have it nearby in the event that a condom slips off or tears following ejaculation. If this happens, immediate injection of foam deep into the vagina may help thwart a potential pregnancy.

For maximum efficacy, each condom should be used only once.

Finally, one must not forget the ten most important letters in successful condom contraception: M-O-T-I-V-A-T-I-O-N!

Is it true that the condom is actually used by couples who are trying to conceive?
Some couples are infertile because a woman makes antibodies against the sperm of her partner. When the antibody level is high, sperm deposited in the vagina may be destroyed by these antibodies. In such situations, if a man wears a condom during coitus for periods of six months or more, the antibody level of the woman will diminish. When this occurs, attempting conception without a condom exactly at the time of ovulation often proves successful.

Why don't more people use the condom?
As with the diaphragm and vaginal spermicides, many couples complain that the spontaneity of sex is lost by stopping to put on a condom immediately before intercourse. For some couples it is a tolerable delay when the woman is the one placing the condom on the erect penis.

Men often complain that a condom diminishes the enjoyable sensation experienced when the penis is in direct contact with the vaginal walls. However, the newer lubricated condoms may actually enhance a man's penile sensitivity and enjoyment of coitus.

Allergic "rubber condom" dermatitis is a rare skin condition characterized by itching and swelling at the end of the penis due to an allergic reaction to a rubber condom. A rash may begin at the end of the penis and spread down the entire shaft to involve the scrotum, as well as other areas of the body. The same reaction in a rubber-sensitive woman is usually milder, producing a rash on the vulva and inner thighs. Individuals with rubber sensitivity will experience no further difficulty if they switch to a condom made of lamb membrane, such as XXXX Skins.

How are condoms packaged?

Unlike women, who must be measured for a diaphragm, men need not be "fitted" for a condom by their urologist. Condoms come in one standard size and are sold in drug stores in packages of three or twelve.

Which is the best condom?

XXXX Skins are made of a thin, though very strong, lamb membrane, and are thoroughly lubricated. Many men find that these condoms actually improve and enhance penile sensitivity. The two major disadvantages of this condom are its tendency to slip because of the degree of lubrication, and its high cost. Trojan-Brand Naturalamb is another lubricated condom made from lamb membrane. Ramses, Sheik, and Trojan produce condoms of excellent quality latex rubber that may be purchased with or without lubricant or a receptacle at the end. Regardless of the brand selected, the lubricated condoms are always more expensive than the nonlubricated variety. The lubricant most commonly used consists of a nonirritating surgical jelly, though the newest development in lubricated condoms is the special silicone lubricant which many couples now prefer. This so-called "dry" lubricant is not as messy, and is found in the golden colored Trojans Plus condoms. The newest condom is named Nuform. These condoms have a flared shape at the end, and come in a variety of colors. A disadvantage of Nuforms is that they are not lubricated. No one comdom is best for everyone, and couples are advised to experiment with a variety of types and brands to find one that is mutually satisfying. Recently, certain magazines have advertized condoms having very thin horizontal notches termed "ribbing." This is supposedly a stimulant to a woman during intercourse. If you believe this, you're being ribbed. Based on the objective evaluation of these condoms by several of my patients, I can assure the reader that the enhanced sexual benefits of this condom are strictly in the imagination of its manufacturer.

All rubber condoms produced in the United States undergo very precise quality control testing of their tensile

TABLE 4-2—CONDOMS AND COSTS

BRAND	BOX OF 3		BOX OF 12	
	DISCOUNT	REGULAR	DISCOUNT	REGULAR
Sheik	$0.75	$0.90	$2.25	2.50
Sheik with lubricant and reservoir end	1.00	1.10	3.00	3.25
Ramses	1.40	1.50	3.20	5.00
Ramses lubricated	1.50	1.75	5.00	5.25
Trojans	0.70	0.80	2.00	2.60
Trojans-Enz lubricated and reservoir end	0.80	0.90	2.20	2.70
Nuforms (not lubricated)	1.40	1.60	4.30	4.75
XXXX Skins	3.00	3.50	10.00	13.00

strength by the various manufacturers. In addition, the FDA has established standards for testing a condom's minimal thickness and pressures below which it should not burst or tear. Foreign brand condoms are not uniformly subjected to the testing given American condoms and are more likely to be defective. Condoms made of lamb membrane are also subjected to testing by the FDA and manufacturers in this country. However, because these condoms are made of an animal membrane rather than a uniformly manufactured substance such as rubber, the tests given them tend to be less specific and less standardized.

What do condoms cost?
Table 4–2 lists the prices per dozen of the brands mentioned. (Prices will vary in different locales.) When buying condoms in a box of three, the cost is slightly more.

The diaphragm, spermicidal agents, and the condom all provide contraception without risk of injury or death to the person using them. In the following chapter we will discuss methods of contraception which are equally safe in regard to your health, but unfortunately are far less reliable in preventing conception. These methods include rhythm, coitus interruptus, douching, and nursing.

5

COITUS INTERRUPTUS AND RHYTHM

COITUS INTERRUPTUS

What is coitus interruptus?

Coitus interruptus is intercourse in which the male partner withdraws his penis from the vagina before ejaculation. Emission of sperm then takes place completely away from the vagina and external genitalia of the woman. It is an ancient technique referred to in the Bible as "spilling the seed," and was first used by Onan. Other more modern synonyms are withdrawal, "pulling out," and the "French method". Worldwide (and among teenagers in this country), it is probably the most common form of contraception. Coitus interruptus has a failure rate somewhere between fifteen and twenty-five pregnancies per one hundred woman-years of use.

Why is withdrawal such an unreliable method?

As previously mentioned (see Page 118), it is doubtful that the first few drops of a man's discharge, which are present during erection but before ejaculation, are responsible for pregnancy. However, it is known that the first few drops of the true ejaculate released at the time of orgasm contain the greatest concentration of sperm. Depositing even a small amount of this fluid in the outer part of the vagina, or even the labia, may result in sperm migration to and through the cervical os. For this reason, withdrawal should never be used by men with poor ejaculatory control or those who suffer from premature ejaculation. Even when the method is practiced faithfully by a man with good control, the split-second timing required makes it inherently too dangerous.

Coitus interruptus can be objected to from the woman's point of view, because it places her at the mercy of her mate, giving him total control of both coitus and contraception. In addition, it is difficult to relax completely and achieve full sexual response when you must worry if he will or will not "make it out" in time. Your orgasm may not be achieved or may be blunted when withdrawal tends to be too early for your needs. Too often coitus is terminated abruptly and without any warning. Finally, for some women the postorgasmic warmth and closeness that they want is often spoiled by the messiness created by the external ejaculate.

Is there any way to improve coitus interruptus?
It would be unfair not to mention that many highly motivated couples have used withdrawal successfully for prolonged periods of time. When excellent communication and mutual respect exist between a couple, coitus interruptus is more likely to be successful. Frank discussion of coital techniques may be helpful in determining which position is most likely to give the greatest degree of ejaculatory control. The "spoon position," in which the couple curl side by side in the semifetal position, is often very satisfactory both physically and emotionally. In this position the male partner is unable to thrust very deeply, because he is behind the woman and has little leverage (Figure 5–1).

In the spoon position a woman's legs are together, which helps to close the labia so that if ejaculation does take place on the labia, there is less chance for sperm migration. This position also allows the woman to enjoy breast and clitoral stimulation during intercourse.

Another valuable aid for withdrawal users is the "squeeze technique." This method, first introduced by Semans and later popularized by Masters and Johnson, is also used as treatment of premature ejaculation. When the woman is in the superior position and not quite ready to achieve orgasm, she withdraws the penis from the vagina and places her thumb on the undersurface of the penile glans at the frenulum, while the first and second fingers are placed on the superior surface of the penis in a position immediately adjacent to one another on either side of the coronal ridge (Figure 5–2). Strong pressure is then applied by squeezing the

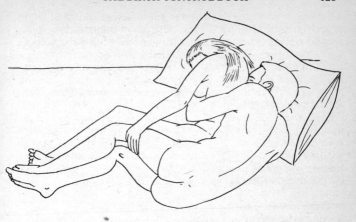

Figure 5-1.   Spoon Position

thumb and first two fingers together for approximately three to four seconds. When this technique is used on an uncircumcised male, the coronal ridge may be felt through the skin covering and the frenulum position estimated, since it can't be seen or felt in these individuals.

The effect of this maneuver is that a man will immediately lose his urge to ejaculate, though his erection will maintain 70 to 90 percent of its fullness. The penis is then reinserted and pelvic movements resumed 15 to 30 seconds after the squeeze. Following this technique there is little fear of imminent ejaculation for variable periods of time, and occasionally for as long as twenty minutes. The squeeze technique may be repeated throughout coitus whenever the man conveys to his partner that he is aroused and that orgasm may be imminent. It must be remembered that this technique will not work successfully if used at the very last second before ejaculation.

RHYTHM METHOD

What is the rhythm method?

The rhythm method is a birth control technique based on limiting intercourse only to those times of the month

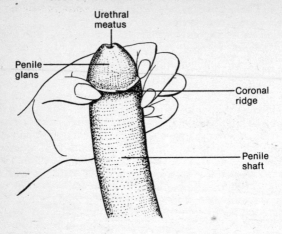

Figure 5-2. Demonstration of "Squeeze Technique"

thought to be free from the threat of pregnancy. It is the only contraceptive technique sanctioned by the Catholic Church. Many proponents of this method consider the name "rhythm" to be obsolete, and believe that the term "natural family planning" best describes the various techniques encompassed by this form of contraception. Because rhythm has and will continue to have such widespread use (despite a study released in 1977 which showed that in 1965 31.8 percent of white Catholics in the U.S. practiced rhythm but by 1970 that figure had declined to 17.8 and to 5.9 by 1975 while use of rhythm among non-Catholics went from 4.2 percent to 3.6 to 1.7 in the same years) the importance of achieving maximum success with it is readily apparent.

The rhythm method may be divided into three categories. One is the calculation of the "safe period," or calendar technique, based on the length of previous menstrual cycles. Another is the charting of the daily basal body temperature, and the third involves daily self-examination of the cervical mucus in order to avoid coitus at the time of ovulation. Knowledge and use of all three techniques will, I hope, lower the unacceptably high failure rates, sometimes quoted to be as many as thirty pregnancies per one hundred woman-years.

How do I calculate the safe period based on the length of previous menstrual cycles?

The success of the calendar technique in determining the safe time for intercourse is based on three biological phenomena. The first is that ovulation will occur fourteen days, plus or minus two days, prior to the onset of menses regardless of the length of the cycle. A woman with a thirty-seven-day cycle, measured from the first day before the next period, usually ovulates between Days 21 and 25. It is a misconception that ovulation occurs on the fourteenth day of the cycle, unless of course one has the twenty-eight day cycle described in textbooks, and only 8 percent of all women of childbearing age do. The second and third phenomena useful in the success of this technique are that the unfertilized egg survives no longer than twenty-four hours, and that most sperm remain viable no longer than forty-eight hours.

Chart the length of your cycle for a period of at least six months, then calculate your fertile days by subtracting eighteen from the number of days of the shortest cycle over those few months. That number represents the first fertile, or unsafe, day. Subtract eleven from the number of days of the longest cycle in order to determine the last fertile day, or the day on which the unsafe time ends. Table 5–1 demonstrates the method of calculating the unsafe days.

For example, if you note that your shortest cycle is twenty-five days and your longest, twenty-eight days, your first fertile or unsafe day will be Day 7, and your last dangerous day will be Day 17. You must therefore avoid unprotected intercourse from Day 7 through Day 17 of future menstrual cycles.

Obviously, if you are a sexually active woman with irregular menses, the restrictions placed on your sexual enjoyment will be totally unsatisfactory. Furthermore, when the calendar technique of rhythm is used as the sole form of contraception, the best pregnancy rate achieved is an unsatisfactory fourteen per one hundred woman-years.

How is the daily temperature used in determining the unsafe days?

Following ovulation, progesterone is produced by the corpus luteum and is responsible for an elevation of a woman's temperature for approximately fourteen days until the onset of menstruation. The basal body temperature (the temperature taken immediately upon rising in the morning before

TABLE 5-1 — CALCULATING THE UNSAFE DAYS OF THE MENSTRUAL CYCLE

LENGTH OF SHORTEST CYCLE IN DAYS	FIRST UNSAFE DAY AFTER START OF PERIOD	LENGTH OF LONGEST CYCLE IN DAYS	LAST UNSAFE DAY AFTER START OF PERIOD
21	3	21	10
22	4	22	11
23	5	23	12
24	6	24	13
25	7	25	14
26	8	26	15
27	9	27	16
28	10	28	17
29	11	29	18
30	12	30	19
31	13	31	20
32	14	32	21
33	15	33	22
34	16	34	23
35	17	35	24

getting out of bed), will rise between .4° and .8° F. during those fourteen days. By charting an accurate daily record of your temperature, you may determine your safe and unsafe times of the month (Figure 5–3). Some women, but not all, show a definite dip in temperature at the time of ovulation. This dip is illustrated in Figure 5–3.

The temperature rise usually takes place within twenty-four hours after ovulation. However, in actual practice, not all temperature charts are as easily interpreted as that demonstrated in Figure 5–3. Occasionally the temperature may rise gradually each day by less than .4°, and at other times it may have a step-like appearance, with a .2° rise every two or three days. That may lead to inaccuracies in interpreting the safe days.

The daily reading of the basal temperature is easier if you use a special thermometer with large, easy-to-read numbers and a temperature range of 96° to 100°. These thermometers may be purchased at any pharmacy under the trade name of Ovulindex and cost $5.60 at a regular pharmacy or $5.25 at a discount pharmacy (Figure 5–4).

For greatest accuracy, rectal or vaginal temperatures are preferred to the oral, but whatever method is used, it should not be changed from one day to the next.

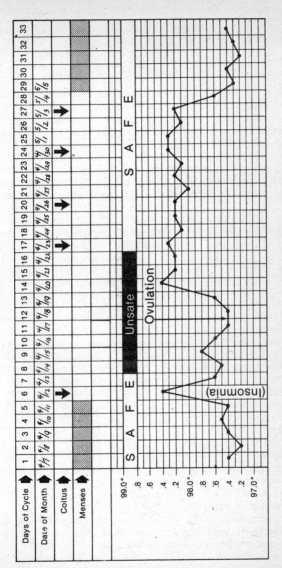

Figure 5-3. Temperature Method of Rhythm Contraception

Figure 5-4.   Basal Body Thermometer

Since the egg is usually incapable of being fertilized twenty-four hours or more following ovulation, a temperature rise for three or more days on the chart should provide safety from pregnancy at and after this time. For the woman with predicatable menstrual cycles, intercourse prior to ovulation should be safe until seven days before the earliest recorded day of temperature rise based on the cycles over the preceding six-month period. Though sperm have been known to live longer than forty-eight to seventy-two hours, it isn't usual.

Figure 5–5 shows one woman's earliest recorded day of temperature rise to be on Day 15. By deducting 6 days from this, it tells her that coitus should be safe for the first 8 days of the cycle. In addition, the third day of temperature elevation on Day 17 marks the first day that coitus can be resumed without fear of pregnancy. When the temperature chart is used in this manner to determine safe coital days

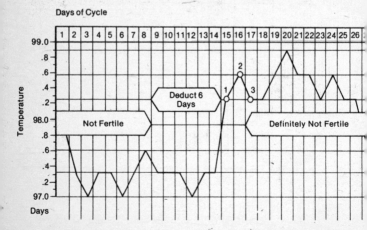

Figure 5-5.   Combined Form of the Temperature Method

both before and after ovulation it is referrred to as the "combined form" of the temperature method.

What are the chances of conception with the temperature method?

Three early studies demonstrated pregnancy rates between 14 and 24 per 100 woman-years. The only recent report was conducted in 1968 by John Marshall of London, who studied 502 women taking daily basal body temperatures. One group was instructed to start coitus at that time of the month when the basal body temperature was elevated for at least three consecutive days, and continue until the last day of the cycle. The resultant pregnancy rate was a low 6.6 per 100 woman-years (Figure 5–6). When coitus is limited to this short period of time, it is referred to as the "strict form" of the temperature method.

A second group in the study was allowed intercourse prior to ovulation as well, with the number of coital days determined by subtracting nineteen from the length of days in the shortest menstrual cycle that the woman experienced over the previous six cycles. This gave the day on which abstinence before ovulation should begin. The group experienced a pregnancy rate of 19.3 pregnancies per 100 woman-years.

Most investigators believe that the temperature method produces lower pregnancy rates than the calendar method.

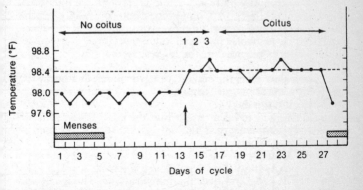

Figure 5-6. *Limiting Coitus to the Post Ovulation Phase (Strict Form of the Temperature Method)*

By using both methods together, the effectiveness of rhythm should be improved significantly.

Where can the temperature method go wrong?

Unfortunately one only knows in retrospect when ovulation has taken place. A surprisingly early ovulation is a real threat, even in a woman with previously predictable cycles. Statistically, only 8 percent of women of childbearing age have perfectly regular cycles each month. As mentioned, not all women experience the classic temperature dip at the time of ovulation, and if it does occur, it may not be seen in the early morning when the temperature is being taken. The burden of charting temperatures in the early moring when you are only half-awake may lead to inaccuracies both in taking the temperature and in recording it. A source of confusion may be a temperature elevation in the presence of an unrecognized infection or of tension, or following a sleepless night (Figure 5–3). Smoking a cigarette prior to taking the basal temperature may also falsely elevate it, while drinking large amounts of alcohol can falsely lower it.

The temperature change from low to high does not always follow the classic pattern depicted in Figures 5–3 and 5–5. Occasionally the temperature may rise gradually each day by approximately .2°, or even in a step-like fashion, such as .2° each two or three days. Other deviations from the classic pattern include the "zigzag," "double shifted," and "double shifted with 2 day plateau." These variations are illustrated below (Figure 5–7). (A woman does not necessarily exhibit the same pattern of variation every month.) In all instances, abstinence is necessary until there are three consecutive temperatures recorded at the highest level.

If I am a slow morning starter, or in too much of a hurry to take an accurate basal temperature, can I take it at another time during the day?

Most doctors have been taught that the basal (upon awakening) body temperature is the only accurate method used in determining ovulation.

In 1974 Zuspan and Zuspan studied the menstrual cycles of nineteen ovulatory women. These women recorded their basal, 5:00 P.M., and bedtime temperatures. Though it was found that the basal was the lowest, the 5:00 P.M. the highest, and the evening temperature somewhere in between, ac-

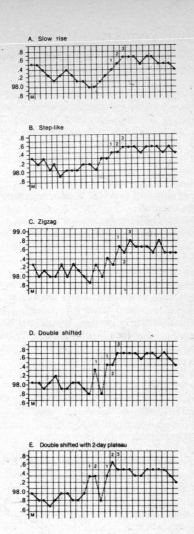

Figure 5-7. Variations in the Temperature Pattern at the Time of Ovulation

curacy in interpreting the results was easy regardless of when the temperature was taken. They calculated that if you forget to take your basal temperature, you can take it at 5:00 P.M. instead, then subtract .7° and record it on the basal body temperature chart for that day. When temperatures are taken at bedtime of the same day, subtract .3°. For many women it is much easier to take either 5:00 P.M. or bedtime temperatures on a regular basis and simply chart them as they are. Figure 5–8 demonstrates the similarity of all three temperature curves.

How does studying my cervical mucus improve the efficacy of the rhythm method?

As ovulation approaches, the glands of the cervix under the influence of estrogen secrete a progressively more abundant amount of thin, watery, lubricative, and stretchable mucus. Spinnbarkeit is the name given to the ability of the mucus to stretch, while "peak symptom" describes the raw-egg consistency and appearance of the mucus. That lasts for one or two days. Typically, ovulation occurs then or within a day or two before or after the "peak symptom" and maximum spinnbarkeit. Following ovulation, the mucus becomes thick, tacky, and opaque, and lacks spinnbarkeit. This is due to the

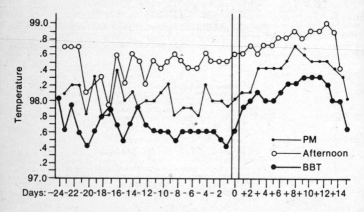

Figure 5-8.   Similarities Between Body Temperatures at Different Times of Day

effect of progesterone produced by the corpus luteum. To avoid conception, abstinence is necessary from the time the thin mucus is first noted until four days after the "peak symptom." This method of rhythm, based on analyzing changes in the cervical mucus, is also know as the the *Billings method*, named after E. L. Billings and J. J. Billings, two of its most ardent proponents.

If you use a speculum (Figure 1–6), you can easily learn to recognize your own pattern of cervical mucus secretion, thereby avoiding conception regardless of the length or regularity of each individual cycle. By gently touching the cervical os with a cotton applicator or long Q-tip, and then slowly withdrawing it, you can easily determine the distance that the mucus stretches between the cervix and the applicator. The amount of mucus and the degree of spinnbarkeit can actually be graded objectively (Table 5–2). A score of 3 in each category means that ovulation has just occurred or is imminent. Finally, as ovulation approaches, some women note a progressive opening of the cervical os (Table 5–2).

It has been reported that feeling the cervix daily may be helpful in detecting the approximate day of ovulation by changes in its position and consistency. For some women, the cervix is higher in the pelvis on the day prior to ovula-

TABLE 5-2 — MEASURING THE AMOUNT AND QUALITY OF CERVICAL MUCUS AND THE OPENING OF THE CERVIX AT THE TIME OF OVULATION

Score	0	1	2	3
Amount of mucus	None	Scant	Dribble	Cascade
		A small amount of mucus can be drawn from the cervical os	A glistening drop of mucus seen in the external os, mucus easily drawn from the cervical canal	Abundant mucus pouring out of the cervical os
Spinnbarkeit	None	Slight	Moderate	Pronounced
		Uninterrupted mucous thread may be drawn approximately one-quarter of the distance between the external os and vulva, or approximately one inch	Uninterrupted mucous thread may be drawn one-half of the distance between the external os and the vulva, at least two inches	Uninterrupted mucous thread may be drawn for the whole distance between the external os and the vulva, at least four inches.
Cervical os	Closed		Partially open	Gaping

tion, so that it is difficult to reach it with the examining finger. Following ovulation it assumes a lower, easier-to-reach position in the vagina, and remains in that position through menstruation and until a few days before the next ovulation.

The consistency of the cervix at the time of ovulation has been described as feeling like a lip—"rubbery" or "soft" to touch. Within a day or two after ovulation, the consistency of the cervix changes abruptly, becoming firm, like the tip of the nose.

Unfortunately, not all women experience the changes described, and when they do occur they are often too subtle to accurately predict the day of ovulation.

Is there any other way in which the cervical mucus may be used to enhance the accuracy of the rhythm method?
The cervical mucus also contains an abundant amount of glucose (sugar) at the time of ovulation. The concentration of sugar can be determined with fertility test kits which cost about $8.50 at a regular pharmacy and $7.50 at a discount pharmacy, or a roll of Tes-Tape, which costs $3.20 at a regular pharmacy and $2.34 at a discount pharmacy. Both can be purchased at a pharmacy without a prescription.

When you insert your index finger and touch it to the cervix, a small sample of mucus will usually remain on the fingertip when it is removed. Greater accuracy will be achieved if a woman is familiar with visualizing the cervix with a speculum (Figure 1–6). By touching the fingertip to a one-inch piece of yellow Tes-Tape, the yellow will usually turn to a dark blue color at the time of ovulation. Prior to ovulation, lesser shades of blue and green, representing lower sugar concentrations, are found. Though some doctors have recommended touching the cervix directly with the Tes-Tape secured on the index finger, this technique is not recommended at the present time. Tes-Tape paper contains certain chemicals which have not been adequately tested for its effects on the sensitive tissues of the cervix and vagina. Until such time when these chemicals are proven to be safe, the FDA suggests that they should not be used internally to determine the fertile period.

Finally, the woman who has access to an ordinary low-powered microscope, but preferably a high-powered one, can easily perform the fern test of the cervical mucus on the days prior to ovulation. Place a small amount of mucus from the cervical os on an applicator stick and rub it onto a glass slide. When the glass slide is viewed under the microscope at the time of ovulation, a beautiful, thick, branching pattern of the mucus, resembling a fern, may be seen throughout the whole slide (Figure 5-9).

A scant amount of ferning without branching means ovulation is still not imminent. Following ovulation, under the influence of progesterone, in practically all women, there is almost complete disappearance of ferning within two or three days (Figure 5-10).

The fern test may be totally inadequate in the presence of a slight amount of blood in the mucus, which some women experience at the time of ovulation. Inflammation of the cervix *(cervicitis)* may also be responsible for an absence of ferning at the time of ovulation. Since cervicitis is often without symptoms, a woman should be evaluated and treated for the condition by her gynecologist before relying on the ferning method.

The efficiency of the various cervical mucus methods has yet to be determined. Certainly when used conscientiously on a regular basis, they can only enhance the sensitivity of the calendar and temperature methods.

Use of a speculum, Tes-Tape, and a microscope for the purpose of avoiding conception may be considered absurd by some. Those skeptics never appreciate the turmoil created by the constant fear of pregnancy among women whose religious beliefs dictate against safer forms of contraception. All available variations of the rhythm method must be offered to those women if they are willing to use them. The price of a used microscope seems insignificant when compared to the emotional cost of an unwanted pregnancy.

What is Mittelschmerz and the "bounce test"?

Mittelschmerz is another name for painful ovulation. The small percentage of women who regularly experience it are at an advantage, because they can avoid intercourse from the time of the pain and for the next twenty-four hours, when the chances of fertilizing an egg are most likely. These women will also know in retrospect that there is a chance of pregnancy if coitus occurred two days or less before the painful ovulation.

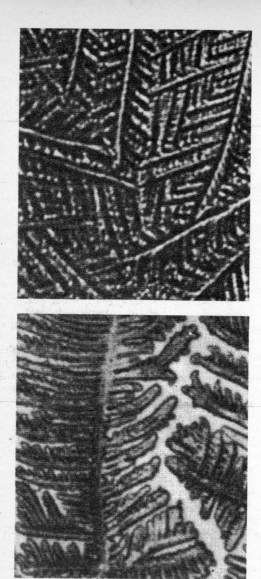

Figure 5-9. Fern Pattern at Ovulation

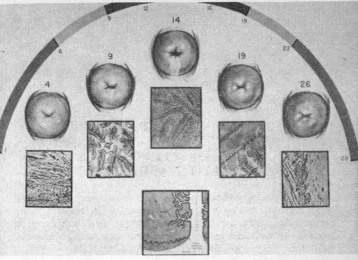

Figure 5-10.   Changes in Ferning and Cervix During Cycle

The bounce test may help one third of the women who do not experience Mittelschmerz to determine the day of their ovulation. Starting six days before the day that ovulation is expected, bounce on a hard surface such as a wooden chair by sitting down abruptly three to four times every morning and evening. Occasionally, by doing so, the pain of Mittelschmerz is reproduced when bouncing is performed on the day of ovulation.

Are there any dangers in using the rhythm method?

There is considerable evidence to suggest that a wide range of pregnancy problems, such as abortion and birth defects, may be related to the use of the rhythm method. It has been demonstrated that the optimum chance for normal pregnancy occurs when fertilization of the egg takes place just at the time of ovulation. Users of the rhythm method are more likely to abstain from intercourse at that time and for the few days before ovulation. Coitus twelve to twenty-four hours after ovulation is more likely to expose an overripe, unhealthy egg to fertilization.

Statistical data from three different studies conducted in New England have indicated a significantly higher rate of congenital fetal central nervous system defects in the Catholic population than in the Protestant population. Though other variables may certainly be responsible, it appears more likely that the rhythm method may be the significant factor.

CONTRACEPTIVE EFFECT OF NURSING AND RISK OF PREGNANCY FOLLOWING ABORTION AND FULL-TERM DELIVERY

Many women and their doctors hold misconceptions about when fertility is restored after abortion and following full-term pregnancy for both the nursing and non-nursing woman. In an excellent statistical review of this information, Dr. Helmuth Vorherr has helped to clarify some of these questions. The data presented below is based on his work.

How soon after abortion does fertility return?
Most women regain their fertility within a short time following an abortion. When the terminated pregnancy is between eight and fifteen weeks, the average return of ovulation takes two to three weeks. When the pregnancy is between sixteen and twenty weeks, ovulation usually returns four to six weeks later. The first period following an abortion is usually preceded by ovulation (Figure 5–11).

From those statistics I must conclude that contraception should be instituted immediately following abortion if repeat pregnancy is to be avoided. There is no such thing as a safe period following pregnancy termination.

What are the chances of conception after full-term childbirth?
Generallly, menstruation is not resumed before four to five weeks following childbirth, and the first periods are usually not preceded by ovulation. In both the nursing and non-nursing woman, ovulation rarely takes place before the fourth to fifth week following full-term delivery.

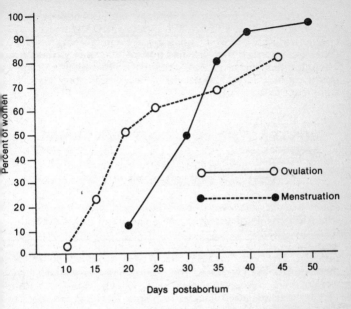

*Figure 5-11.   Return of Ovulation and Menstruation
Following Abortion*

Both ovulation and menstruation are more likely to occur earlier in one who does not nurse. These comparisons are listed in Table 5-3.

The most amazing statistic in Table 5-3 is that ovulation and the threat of pregnancy may be as high as 25 percent in nursing women at twelve weeks following delivery, and 65 percent of women at twenty-four weeks. These statistics should dispel the myth of reliability on nursing as the sole method of contraception after the sixth week postpartum.

DOUCHING—A NON-METHOD

Douching with various solutions is an ancient postcoital contraceptive technique that is totally worthless. Current re-

TABLE 5-3 — COMPARISON OF POSTPARTUM REPRODUCTIVE FUNCTION IN THE NURSING AND NON-NURSING WOMAN

WEEKS UNTIL RETURN OF OVULATION	PERCENT OF NURSING WOMEN	PERCENT OF NON-NURSING WOMEN
6	5	15
12	25	40
24	65	75
WEEKS UNTIL RETURN OF MENSTRUATION		
6	15	40
12	45	65
24	85	90

search has demonstrated that sperm may be found in the endocervix, beyond the reach of the douche solution, within ninety seconds after ejaculation. (This doesn't mean that the ejaculate is not capable of entering the endocervix in five seconds, but ninety seconds is the fastest that the researchers were able to collect and examine the postcoital specimens). In addition, recent studies have demonstrated sperm in the Fallopian tube ten to forty-five minutes following insemination. Even if a douche is used within ten seconds following ejaculation, it is highly improbable that it would kill all the sperm in the vagina or prevent the ascent of many through the cervical os.

For the woman in need of postcoital contraception, douching is valueless. In the next chapter I will discuss effective methods of postcoital contraception.

6
POSTCOITAL CONTRACEPTION

Estimates of your chances of conception following one act of unprotected intercourse at ovulation vary from a low of 2 to 4 percent, to a high of 20 percent. Until recently, women threatened with that anxiety-producing situation have had no alternative but to helplessly await the onset of menses.

Effective postcoital contraception is now available in the form of the "morning-after pill," the "morning-after IUD," and menstrual extraction. Those new and popular methods have given women the opportunity to safely terminate both the potential and the diagnosed pregnancy following unprotected coitus.

"MORNING-AFTER PILL"

What is the "morning-after pill"?
Diethylstilbestrol, or DES, is the "morning-after pill," which—when taken within seventy-two hours after unprotected coitus at ovulation—is highly effective in preventing survival of the fertilized egg. The drug is classified as a non-steroidal synthetic estrogen, which is a fancy way of saying it is made in the laboratory and not in the body, and is of a chemical structure totally different from the steroidal shape of natural estrogens and those contained in birth control pills.

How does DES prevent continuation of pregnancy?

Dr. John Morris of Yale University defines the term *interception* as the process of preventing implantation of the egg after fertilization has occurred. It is theorized that DES may act as a pregnancy interceptor at several locations. One of its main effects appears to be on the corpus luteum, causing it to malfunction and produce inadequate amounts of progesterone which is essential for support of an early pregnancy. The decline of progesterone is occasionally reflected by a premature drop in the basal body temperature during the second half of the menstrual cycle.

A second, and also very likely, site of DES action is in the endometrium, where it causes a deficiency of an enzyme called *carbonic anhydrase*. Without that enzyme, the fertilized egg can't dispose of its carbon dioxide waste products and therefore dies. Other studies of the endometrium have noted microscopic retardation of growth, in addition to a lack of another enzyme, called *alkaline phosphatase*.

In the past it was theorized that DES was responsible for both slowing down and speeding up the passage of the fertilized egg down the Fallopian tube. The former "tube locking" effect was believed to be responsible for a higher incidence of ectopic (tubal) pregnancy in women who conceived despite DES treatment. However, as is the case with the IUD (see Page 90), DES prevents intrauterine pregnancy, not tubal pregnancy. Therefore, if a pregnancy does take place, the chances that it will be in the tube are greater, though the actual number of tubal pregnancies is no higher.

How effective is DES as a postcoital contraceptive?

In a review combining the results from several studies totaling 5,593 women, 26 pregnancies were reported. The authors estimated that without DES, 1,100 women, or 20 percent of those exposed, would have conceived. Other, more recent reports have sampled more than 1,000 women using DES without a single pregnancy. Opinion is unanimous that it is an excellent postcoital contraceptive.

What are the disadvantages of using DES?

To achieve effectiveness, five 5—milligram tablets must be taken twice a day for five days. The extremely high dose of estrogen frequently causes nausea as well as vomiting in approximately 16 to 25 percent of all women. For this reason, I

TABLE 6-1 — SIDE EFFECTS OF DES AMONG 1,217 PATIENTS

	NUMBER OF PATIENTS	PERCENT
None*	407	33.44
Nausea—slight, hardly noticeable	157	12.90
Nausea without vomiting	277	22.76
Nausea and vomiting, intermittent; one day	162	13.31
Nausea and vomiting, intermittent; more than one day	37	3.04
Headache	15	1.23
Vaginal spotting while taking DES or soon after finishing course	13	1.07
Dizziness	12	0.99
Diarrhea	10	0.82
Bloated or swollen condition	10	0.82
Miscellaneous (breast tenderness, increased vaginal secretions, mild lower abdominal cramps, etc.)	44	3.61
Unknown	117	9.61

Note: As some patients had more than one side effect, the total number of side effects was 1,261 in the 1,217 patients.
*Includes 43 patients with only tired feeling.

always prescribe five extra tablets, or a total of 55. If vomiting occurs within four hours after the pill is swallowed, another pill must be taken, since there is a chance that not all of the DES from the vomited pill is absorbed into the body prior to this time. Enteric-coated DES dissolves in the intestine rather than in the stomach and is less likely to cause vomiting. However, more often than not, that form of DES delays rather than prevents the onset of vomiting. It is a good idea for a doctor to prescribe medication to prevent nausea and vomiting to be taken one hour before each DES tablet.

Other side effects include extreme breast tenderness, headaches, dizziness, and menstrual irregularities. Table 6-1 lists 1,261 side reactions reported in a group of 1,217 women taking DES.

If you are medically unable to take the estrogen in birth control pills—due to hypertension, phlebitis, or breast cancer, for example—the enormous dose of estrogen in DES certainly contraindicates its use. Sudden onset of symptoms such as blurring of vision, severe leg cramps, chest pain, cough, shortness of breath, or severe headache, while using DES, necessitates stopping the drug immediately and seeking medical evaluation.

What type of menstrual irregularity should a woman expect after taking DES?

The character of the menses following a course of DES may be quite variable. Of one thousand women studied, only 40 percent noted that their next period came at the normal time and was normal in flow. Some 7.6 percent had a lighter flow that came on time, 6.2 percent had a late onset of flow from one to seven days beyond their expected date, and 5.9 percent had the onset of flow seven days or more beyond their expected date. Adding those three groups together, we find that approximately 20 percent of all women will have a menstrual irregularity suggestive of pregnancy following DES ingestion. This fact should be reassuring to women fearing that the DES they took did not successfully intercept their pregnancy. However, to be on the safe side, a pregnancy test or a menstrual extraction (see Page 156) should be performed on all women with light or delayed menses following a course of DES treatment.

Is there another estrogen, with fewer side effects than DES, that can be used as postcoital contraception?

Other estrogen preparations have been used with great success. Yussman treated 200 rape victims with 50 milligrams intravenous conjugated estrogens (Premarin) for two days without a pregnancy, while others have administred Premarin orally, 10 milligrams three times a day for five days, to 125 women without a pregnancy. The incidence of nausea appears to be less with this medication, especially when it is given intravenously.

Haspels and Adriesse administered ethinyl estradiol tablets to 524 women without one pregnancy, and Hans Lehfeldt in his review noted a lower incidence of headache, nausea, and vomiting with the same medication. Lehfeldt's technique is to give ethinyl estradiol 5 milligrams a day for five days. However, to reach the 5-milligram dose a woman is instructed to take a total of ten .5-milligram tablets in many divided doses throughout the entire day. By doing so, only 10 percent of his patients were nauseated and only 2 percent vomited. Table 6-2 lists the dosage of all estrogens which will successfully intercept pregnancy. To date, only DES has been approved for clinical use by the FDA. The approximate cost for a prescription of fifty-five 5—milligram tablets of DES varies tremendously from one pharmacist to another. The lowest price quoted to me was $3.50, the highest $4.60.

If DES fails to successfully intercept a pregnancy, its effects on the fetus at that early stage, though still unknown, may be similar to those of other hormones (see Page 48). Due to its nonsteroidal configuration, DES—when inadvertently taken after pregnancy is already a few weeks along —increases the risk of vaginal and cervical abnormalities and cancer in any daughter of that pregnancy. An advantage of using ethinyl estradiol, conjugated estrogens, estrone, and esterified estrogens is that they are all steroidal estrogens. As a result, they are not likely to initiate those potentially deadly effects. Ethinyl estradiol and mestranol, the two estrogens in birth control pills, are also steroidal estrogens.

TABLE 6-2 — POSTCOITAL ESTROGENS

DRUG	TRADE NAME	DOSAGE
Diethylstilbestrol (DES)	———	25 milligrams twice a day for five days
Ethinyl estradiol	Estinyl	2.5 milligrams twice a day for five days or Ten .5-milligram tablets a day for five days
Conjugated estrogens	Premarin	10 milligrams two or three times a day or Intravenous 50 milligrams a day for two days
Esterified estrogens	Evex, Menest	10 milligrams twice a day for five days
Estrone	Ogen	5 milligrams twice a day for five days

How was it determined that DES, given to a mother, was capable of causing vaginal cancer in her daughter?

Practically all medication given to a mother is capable of crossing the placenta and reaching the fetus. During the late 1940s, and until 1969, DES was widely used to prevent miscarriage, especially for women with a poor obstetrical history, diabetics, and others who experienced vaginal bleeding early in pregnancy. It has been estimated that between 500,000 and 2,000,000 pregnant women took DES or two other equally harmful nonsteroidal estrogens, Dienestrol and Hexestrol. In most instances, treatment with those substances began in the seventh week of pregnancy. Coincidentally, that is the time when vaginal and cervical development and demarcation becomes most active in the female fetus.

In 1972, three Boston physicians noted a sudden increase in the number of a previously rare cancer, *clear-cell adenocarcinoma*, of the vagina and cervix among young women. Upon further investigation they discovered that the majority of the mothers of these young women had taken nonsteroidal estrogens during their pregnancies. In addition, benign, though highly abnormal, changes in the cervix and vagina of many of the daughters exposed to DES, Dienestrol, and Hexestrol were also noted. The Registry of Clear-Cell Adenocarcinoma of the Genital Tract of Young Females was formed in 1972 with the purpose of reporting all such tumors in women born in the United States and abroad after 1940. To date, at least one hundred vaginal and seventy cervical adenocarcinomas have been reported. Of these, maternal use of a nonsteroidal estrogen has been confirmed in approximately 65 percent. So far more than forty women have died of adenocarcinoma, while several others have undergone radical and mutilating operations to prevent the spread of the disease.

What are the benign cervical and vaginal changes caused by DES?

Adenosis is a word used to describe the presence of strawberry-red, mucus-secreting glandular tissue on the outer part of the cervix and the vagina. These glands are normally located inside the cervix, and are usually not readily seen with a speculum.

Using sophisticated diagnostic techniques, skilled

gynecologists have noted adenosis in anywhere from 80 to 97 percent of daughters exposed to *in utero* DES. In addition to adenosis, the cervix in approximately 40 to 50 percent of these women often appears characteristically deformed, so that the diagnosis of maternal DES ingestion can be made simply by viewing its unusual shape during the speculum examination. One of these distorted shapes, called a vaginal *hood* or *collar*, is seen as a circular fold in the upper vagina into which the cervix containing adenosis appears to merge. Another is the classical *cock's comb*, a small, triangular protuberance seen at the upper pole of the cervix. Complete deformities can make identification of the cervix and its os a nearly impossible task.

In addition to abnormalities of the cervix and vagina, uterine anomalies have recently been described by doctors at Baylor College of Medicine. In a report published on May 1, 1977, in the *American Journal of Obstetrics and Gynecology*, the authors presented the results of hysterograms, or uterine X-rays, performed on sixty young women exposed in utero to DES. Unusual deformities were noted in forty of these women, and included underdevelopment of the uterus combined with a peculiar T-shaped configuration of the uterine cavity. In addition, constricting bands were noted in the uterine cavity along the horizontal arm of the T. The significance of these abnormalities as they relate to a woman's future fertility remains unknown at the present time.

How does a doctor diagnose small areas of adenosis when they are not visible to the naked eye?

The simplest method of diagnosing adenosis is by applying a special iodine solution over the cervix and vagina, and biopsing or taking a small piece of tissue from those suspicious areas that do not absorb the iodine stain.

A more accurate and sophisticated method of detecting adenosis or cancer is with an instrument called a *colposcope.* When used skillfully, the colposcopic magnification of abnormal areas allows for painless evaluation of adenosis in either a clinic or doctor's office (Figure 6–1).

Many doctors believe that they achieve maximum accuracy by combined use of the colposcope and iodine techniques.

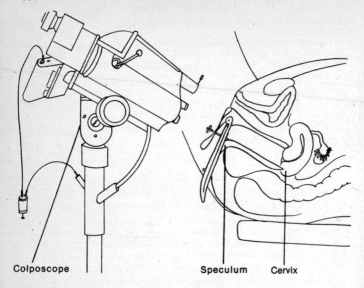

Colposcope Speculum Cervix

Figure 6-1.   Colposcope

Does the week of the pregnancy in which DES was first taken determine the likelihood of developing adenosis?
Table 6–3 demonstrates the likelihood of adenosis, based on when DES was first taken.

It appears unlikely that a fetus can develop adenosis when the first dose is taken after the eighteenth week of pregnancy. Surprisingly, the amount of DES ingested was less important than the pregnancy week in which it was begun. There are instances of adenosis resulting from use of very small amounts of DES for only a few days during the critical seventh week of pregnancy.

Should adenosis be treated?
This is a source of great controversy among gynecologists. The use of aggressive therapeutic approaches by some doctors is based on the assumption that benign adenosis has the potential to become clear-cell adenocarcinoma. Though it is true that adenosis has been found in almost all patients with

TABLE 6-3 — PERCENT OF WOMEN WITH ADENOSIS BASED ON WEEK THAT DES WAS STARTED

WEEK OF PREGNANCY DES STARTED	PERCENT
7 - 8	100
9 - 10	89
11 - 12	70
13 - 14	20
15 - 16	Less than 15

clear-cell carcinoma, a direct transition from adenosis to cancer has never been observed under a microscope. For this reason, other physicians believe that adenosis is not precancerous but is present coincidentally along with cancer in only a very few unfortunate women. The same doctors argue that if adenosis is precancerous, there would be many more women afflicted with cancer than the very low .2 percent of the total number exposed to DES. Extensive studies, such as that from the University of Southern California, have included hundreds of women with adenosis, but not one instance of clear-cell adenocarcinoma has been diagnosed. Since the oldest patients exposed to DES are now only twenty-nine years old, it is impossible at the present time to give a prognosis as to the chances of adenosis becoming malignant.

Dr. Arthur Herbst, one of the men who originally reported the relationship between DES and cancer, warns, "Iatrogenic damage from overtreatment might well be worse" than the adenosis itself. He advises careful and frequent examination of a woman with adenosis rather than aggressive forms of therapy. Dr. Duane Townsend, another authority, speaks of the prevailing opinion in dealing with adenosis as one of "cautious optimism and careful observation."

How often should an adenosis patient see her doctor?
It is suggested that a woman with adenosis have a pelvic exam and Pap smear at least every six months. The frequency of the colposcopic exam should vary according to the amount and severity of the adenosis present, but should be no less often than once per year. The iodine staining tech-

nique may be performed at the same time as the colposcopy, though it is certainly not advised that that be the sole method of examination. If your gynecologist does not have a colposcope or is inexperienced at using it, seek out a skilled colposcopist who performs several such examinations each week. The fee for colposcopic examination may vary from twenty-five to one hundred dollars, and most insurance policies pay for the procedure as long as it is noted on the insurance form that, "Mother took DES during pregnancy. Possible precancerous cervical and vaginal changes noted requiring colposcopy and further follow up." Also, if a biopsy is made at the time of the colposcopy, insurance policies must pay since it is a surgical procedure. Many large teaching hospitals have special colposcopy clinics, where the fee is often lower than that of the private practitioner. If biopsies are taken, the pathologist who studies them will usually charge an additional twenty-five dollars or less. That is also usually paid for by most insurance plans.

The minority group of doctors who believe in more aggressive management of adenosis have claimed success with various methods including cauterization (burning), cyrosurgery (freezing), carbon dioxide laser beam, and the use of progesterone suppositories. More radical techniques have included excision (cutting out) of the adenosis, or even partial vaginectomy or removal of part of the vaginal wall. It is to that group of enthusiastic physicians that Dr. Herbst has directed his remarks about "iatrogenic overtreatment."

At what age should a young girl exposed to DES undergo her first pelvic examination and colposcopy?
Of the first 170 patients with adenocarcinoma in the registry, only 16, or 9 percent, were girls aged twelve years or younger. Because of the difficulties involved in examining young girls, most authorities suggest that the examination be delayed until after the first period, or the age of fourteen if menstruation still has not begun. Immediate examination before that time is indicated if any abnormal bleeding or discharge is noted. If that happens, the examination is best performed with the patient under anesthesia in a hospital operating room. It is fortunate that practically all of the sixteen patients under the age of twelve experienced bleeding as an early warning sign and were treated successfully. Others, in the older age groups, were not nearly as fortunate

and died despite surgical removal of the pelvic organs involved with the disease.

Though the youngest patient reported with adenocarcinoma has been seven years old, and the oldest twenty-nine, the peak incidence appears to be at nineteen years of age. The figure has not changed significantly, despite the fact that more women have been diagnosed with this disease each year. It is encouraging to note that the incidence of adenocarcinoma drops precipitously after the age of nineteen, and is most unusual after the age of twenty-four.

How can I find out if I was given DES during my pregnancy?

All women in doubt should attempt to contact the obstetrician who treated them during their pregnancy. Many obstetricians have sent notices to patients who were given stilbestrol in order to alert them. If the doctor is deceased or retired, another doctor often has access to the original doctor's old records. Women who were hospitalized during their pregnancy in question may be able to obtain transcripts of their old records, which are occasionally kept on microfilm in hospital record rooms. Nevertheless, most women will be unable to know for sure if they did or did not receive DES. If there is a reasonable suspicion that it was given, examination is essential.

Can a daughter who is exposed to DES in utero use birth control pills?

Whether or not abnormal changes in the vagina and cervix may be precipitated by the hormones in birth control pills is still not known. Some doctors believe that alternative contraception should be prescribed for DES offspring. Other authorities, such as the famous Dr. Adolf Stafl, see no indication for denying birth control pills to these women.

If a woman uses DES as a morning-after pill, is it possible that she may increase her chances of malignancy at a later date?

It does not appear that a woman taking DES over a short period of time will experience any harmful effects at a later date. Though no extensive studies have been conducted on women who took DES throughout several months of pregnancy, the incidence of vaginal and uterine cancer in the

group has not been significantly higher. At the University of Chicago a study begun in 1951, and not yet completed, has compared the incidence of breast malignancy among 693 former DES users with a group of women who never used the drug. Based on the statistics available to date, Dr. Arthur L. Herbst has noted no statistical difference in breast cancer rates between the two groups. Representatives of governmental agencies have prematurely interpreted Dr. Herbst's findings and have concluded that DES users are at a greater risk of developing breast cancer at a later date. It is obvious that this very important controversy will not be settled until more data is available.

Are there any harmful effects to men whose mothers received DES during pregnancy?

Research conducted at the University of Chicago on 134 DES-exposed men has revealed abnormalities of the genital tract in 36, or 27 percent. Of these, 19 had cysts of the epididymis (Figure 1–14), 11 had abnormally small testes, 3 had undersized penises of 4 centimeters or less, and 5 had *induration*, or thickening of the capsule, of the testicle. The sperm count, as well as the sperm motility, was also found to be significantly lower in 43 percent of 28 DES-exposed men when compared to a control group. It is too early to determine whether lesions comparable to vaginal and cervical adenocarcinoma will develop in these males, though it appears unlikely. The suggestion of the investigators is that all DES-exposed men undergo a complete urological examination.

One interesting animal study conducted on male mice exposed to DES *in utero* revealed that six of nineteen were sterile, and eighteen of twenty-four had some abnormality of the reproductive system, including ten with the same type of epididymis cysts reported in humans.

A psychosexual study conducted at Stanford University on boys exposed to *in utero* DES concluded that they were significantly "less masculine" than a comparative group not exposed to this drug. Psychiatrists rated six-year-olds and twenty-year-olds according to masculinity factors such as athletic coordination, behavioral movements, heterosexual experience, masculine interests, and aggression-assertion attitudes. The control group was significantly "more masculine" than those whose mothers took diethylstilbestrol.

While the potential inaccuracies of such a study are readily apparent, it does suggest that those hormones may be capable of influencing some aspects of postnatal psychosexual development in boys.

Isn't DES the same medication used to fatten cattle?

Cattle are given DES in their feed so that they will require less grain to supplement their diet and will produce more lean meat at a faster rate.

To prevent the dangers of DES ingestion by a pregnant woman or a woman with an estrogen-dependent disease, such as breast and uterine cancer, cattle are killed after they have been given no DES for forty-eight hours. It was formerly believed that that was the time needed to reach a zero level of DES in the cattle prior to slaughter. However, newer, more accurate radioactive methods of detecting DES have clearly demonstrated residues in these animals beyond forty-eight hours.

Can these minute amounts of DES cause problems for those women at risk?

Several experts have calculated that the risk is infinitessimal, but Dr. Sidney Wolfe of the Ralph Nader-sponsored Health Research Group in Washington, D.C., disagrees and has called for an immediate ban on DES use in animal feed. In addition, the FDA in January, 1976, renewed its efforts to ban DES.

On January 25, 1977, a team of agricultural scientists and physicians announced that they had been unable to find any evidence of a cancer risk to humans resulting from the use of DES in cattle. However, they also commented that "It is beyond the capability of science to prove that anything is completely safe and without hazard."

POSTCOITAL IUD

What is the "morning-after IUD"?

For those women who are unwilling or medically unable to tolerate DES, insertion of an IUD after unprotected intercourse will effectively prevent pregnancy. Since fertilization takes place in the tube followed by a three-day journey of the egg to the endometrium, the IUD usually sets up an inflammatory reaction in the endometrium capable of destroying the egg as it reaches its destination. When used in that way the IUD probably causes early abortion.

In one study, ninety-seven women had a Cu-7 inserted following unprotected intercourse. Of those, seventeen women had it inserted within 24 hours, thirty-one within 48 hours, seventeen within 72 hours, seventeen within 96 hours, fourteen within 120 hours, and two within 144 hours. There were no pregnancies. The advantage of the procedure over DES or the morning-after pill, is that it causes none of the nausea, vomiting, and potentially dangerous side effects found with DES. In addition, it may be left in the uterus for contraception during future cycles.

MENSTRUAL EXTRACTION

What is menstrual extraction?

Menstrual extraction is a highly successful method of fertility control in which tissue is removed from the endometrial cavity through a small, flexible, plastic Karman cannula attached to a source of suction. The suction source may be either a machine (see Chapter 7) or a specially designed syringe (Figure 6–2).

Menstrual extraction is usually performed on a woman whose period is late, and who is fearful of pregnancy but prefers not to wait the two weeks beyond the missed period for the standard pregnancy test to become positive.

It should be noted that the criterion for calling a procedure a menstrual extraction, rather than an abortion, is not whether the pregnancy test is positive or negative. If your uterus is of normal size or only slightly enlarged, and if you are three weeks or less beyond your missed period, the criteria for a menstrual extraction are satisfied regardless of the pregnancy test results. In some areas of the country, a positive pregnancy test is required before a doctor will perform a menstrual extraction. Dr. William J. Cameron addresses himself to this attitude when he says, "To insist that pregnancy be known before the procedure can be carried out smacks of the attitude we physicians, mostly male, held in the past, the attitude that led to the designation of the number of children a woman must have before she can be offered tubal ligation." If your psychological and religious

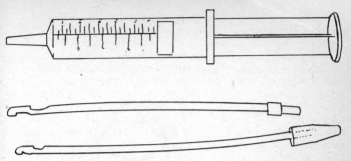

Figure 6-2.   Small Karman Cannula and Aspiration Syringe

well-being is best served by menstrual extraction without a pregnancy test, then your doctor is obligated to abide by your wishes.

Names synonymous with menstrual extraction are *menstrual induction, menstrual planning, menstrual regulation, instant period, mini abortion,* and *minisuction.* The crude term *lunch-hour abortion* has also been used to describe this procedure.

Where and how is menstrual extraction performed?

Menstrual extraction may be safely accomplished in a doctor's office or in a clinic which also performs abortions.

The doctor inserts a speculum and then washes the cervix with an antiseptic solution. The cervix is then held in position by means of an instrument called a *tenaculum.* Application of the tenaculum may cause a slight "pinching" sensation (Figure 6–3).

Novocaine, or a novocaine-like medication, is then injected into the area around the cervix. This *paracervical* (around the cervix) *block* is actually painless when administered correctly, and it significantly reduces the discomfort of menstrual extraction.

After allowing the anesthetic to take effect for three minutes, a 4-, 5-, or 6-millimeter plastic Karman cannula, well lubricated with K-Y Jelly, is then inserted through the cervix and into the uterine cavity. With menstrual extraction, dilatation of the cervix is usually not necessary, but if it is, it is best performed with *Pratt* dilators. The largest Pratt di-

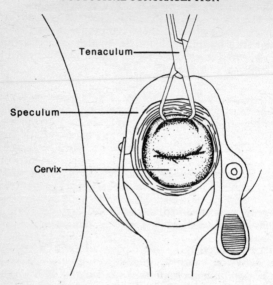

Figure 6-3.   Tenaculum

lator that should ever be used for menstrual extraction is numbered 17–19. This is equivalent to a diameter of approximately 6 millimeters.

The cannula is then attached to suction, and moved around the endometrial cavity with an in-and-out motion until all the tissue is removed. When the cavity is emptied, the cannula moving against the walls of the endometrium creates a characteristic "grating" sound and a feeling of resistance is noted by the person performing the extraction. That phase of the menstrual extraction may be totally painless, but more often than not, a woman will experience menstrual-like cramps. For some women, especially those who have never borne children, the pain may be quite intense, even following an adequate paracervical block.

The total operating time is usually no longer than ten minutes, and you can leave the office unaided within thirty minutes. If you want contraception, birth control pills may be started on the same day. However, insertion of an IUD at the time of menstrual extraction is not advised, because if bleeding or fever is noted postoperatively, it will be difficult to determine if the cause of these symptoms is the IUD or retained tissue fragments from the menstrual extraction. In any case, avoid intercourse for at least a week, or until there is no evidence of bleeding.

What determines the cannula size that a doctor will use?
Because of its larger diameter, the 6-millimeter cannula is more likely to cause pain when introduced through the cervix than the 4-millimeter cannula. However, if there is abundant tissue, or if the uterus is slightly enlarged, the larger cannula will more rapidly and more efficently empty the uterine contents. Incomplete evacuation of the uterus is the most common complication of menstrual extraction, and occurs from 2 to 12 percent of the time. Retention of pieces of pregnancy tissue will often cause secondary infection and bleeding, necessitating antibiotics, repeat extraction, D & C (see Page 53), and sometimes even hospitalization. That complication is far more likely to occur with a 4-millimeter cannula than with one of 6 millimeters. In one large study of menstrual extraction performed on women with a positive pregnancy test, the pregnancy remained completely intact and uninterrupted in 5 percent of those on whom the 4-millimeter cannula was used. With a 6-millimeter cannula, the continuing pregnancy rate was a very low .7 percent. Regardless of the cannula size used, both a pregnancy test and reexamination should be performed two weeks following all menstrual extractions in order to be certain that the pregnancy has been successfully terminated.

Should I take any other precautions following menstrual extraction?
All Rh-negative women should receive an intramuscular injection of immune globulin (Rho GAM) within seventy-two hours after the procedure, to prevent the formation of antibodies against Rh-positive fetuses during future pregnancies. The one exception to this would be if the father is known to be Rh-negative, in which case you don't have to take the medication.

Taking your temperature twice a day for one week will enable early detection of a fever over 100.4°. Approximately 3 percent of all women undergoing menstrual extraction note such an elevation. It often indicates retained tissue fragments, or an inflammation of the endometrium, called *endometritis*. A foul-smelling vaginal discharge accompanied by lower abdominal cramps may also signify inflammation. All of these symptoms necessitate immediate reexamination and treatment by a physician.

Medications which contain aspirin should not be taken either before or after menstrual extraction and abortion. Aspirin significantly prolongs the bleeding time and decreases platelet activity, thereby increasing the blood loss. Aspirin also lowers body temperature and as a result masks a fever caused by retained tissue and endometritis. Aspirin is also an antagonist of prostaglandin, a substance used to induce second-trimester abortions.

The flow following a menstrual extraction should be no heavier than a normal menstrual period. Heavy bleeding, defined as soaking one sanitary pad or more every hour, is abnormal and must be evaluated by a doctor.

Is it true that many women undergo menstrual extraction unnecessarily, since they are not pregnant?
It has been determined that when menstrual extraction is performed prior to the seventh day after the missed period, only 50 percent of these women are actually pregnant. Between the seventh and fourteenth day about 85 percent are pregnant, while after that time the number increases to 95 percent. In one study of 500 menstrual extractions, 177 women were noted not to be pregnant when the removed tissue was studied under a microscope.

The accuracy of the standard pregnancy urine test leaves a lot to be desired. Among a group of pregnant women the test is positive in only 40 percent when it is done six days after the missed period, and in 95 percent at fourteen days or more beyond the missed period. The discovery of a new pregnancy test by Dr. Brij B. Saxena, professor of endocrinology and biochemistry at Cornell University Medical College, may soon prevent practically all unnecessary menstrual extractions. The blood test, called the *radioreceptor assay*, appears to be 100 percent accurate in detecting pregnancy six to eight days after conception, or on the first day after a missed period. Though the test, when universally available, will be of great help in preventing most unnecessary menstrual extractions, there will still be a significant number of women who, for religious or other personal reasons, prefer the risk of an unnecessary procedure to the knowledge that they are terminating an actual pregnancy.

Can I perform menstrual extraction on myself or a friend if I have the proper equipment?

A small minority of radical feminists have advocated monthly menstrual extraction both as a form of contraception and as a method of shortening the number of days of the menstrual flow. Fortunately this notion has been soundly discredited by other feminists. The risks of endometritis, hemorrhage, and even perforation of the uterus are just too great when this procedure is performed on a monthly basis, especially by a novice.

What is the cost of menstrual extraction?

The fee for a menstrual extraction is less than that for an abortion, and may range from a low of fifty dollars to a high of one hundred dollars. For the 15 percent of women who are Rh-negative, the expensive Rho GAM injection will increase the total cost by forty to fifty dollars. The cost of this procedure in terms of your future reproductive capacity is still in question. However, weakening of the cervix during subsequent pregnancies (see Page 169) would appear unlikely, since the cervix is not significantly dilated. In those rare cases when endometritis appears, infertility can be prevented if the infection is treated immediately and vigorously with antibiotics.

When pregnancy is terminated beyond the mini abortion or menstrual extraction stage, it is then classified as an early abortion. Chapter 7 deals with the methods and complications of early and late pregnancy termination.

7
ABORTION

What procedures should be carried out prior to a first-trimester abortion?

Some women neglect to have a pregnancy test performed because they are certain that they are pregnant. I have personally examined several nonpregnant women referred to my office for an abortion solely on the basis of missed periods. I have also examined women with false-positive pregnancy tests inaccurately performed in a doctor's office rather than in a certified laboratory, where such errors are less likely. There have been instances in which women consumer advocates have purposely submitted a man's urine specimen to an abortion facility and been told the test was positive for pregnancy. For this reason, it is always best to have the pregnancy test performed by a qualified laboratory, and not at the abortion facility on the day of the proposed procedure. When you submit urine for a pregnancy test, it is vital that it be the first morning specimen (and therefore undiluted by day's intake of liquids) in order to insure accuracy. Of course, more and more laboratories are using the newer, more accurate blood test for detecting early pregnancy.

First trimester abortion (abortion performed during the first three months of pregnancy) may be done in clinics, doctors' offices, or hospitals. Choosing the right facility and the most qualified doctor to perform the abortion requires some investigation (see Page 176). A complete list of Planned Parenthood Centers for each state is provided in the Appendix of this book. They offer confidential abortion and contraceptive counseling, and can refer you to the nearest sympathetic doctor, clinic, or hospital.

Regardless of where the abortion is performed, be sure the procedure is thoroughly explained to you beforehand, all possible complications discussed, and all questions answered to your satisfaction. Counseling should include a discussion of the possible options, such as continuing with the pregnancy and keeping the child, or continuing with the pregnancy and giving up the child for adoption. It is significant that 5 to 6 percent of women who apply for abortion rethink their preliminary decision and elect to continue with the pregnancy. It is for this reason that some authorities suggest that the counseling session not take place on the day that the abortion is scheduled. For some women, two or three days of reflection prove invaluable in convincing them that the decision made is a correct one. If the final decision is to proceed with the abortion, most facilities require that a letter of informed consent be signed, indicating that the method of abortion and its potential complications have been fully explained. Most abortion clinics discuss contraceptive techniques before, as well as after, the procedure is completed.

It is imperative that all women relate a complete medical history and receive a physical examination before the abortion. Essential laboratory tests include a hemoglobin and hematocrit test to check for anemia, urinalysis, a test of the blood type and Rh factor and a Pap smear for cancer detection. Some clinics also perform a routine chest X-ray and cervical cultures for detecting gonorrhea.

Regardless of the type of anesthesia used (see Page 173), make sure you don't eat or drink for at least eight hours prior to abortion. If an emergency dictates the use of general anesthesia, the potentially dangerous risk of food regurgitation from the stomach into the windpipe, or trachea, will be avoided if that precaution is taken. If general anesthesia is requested, a preoperative dose of atropine is given. This medication helps to dry up excessive secretions in the mouth which may cause breathing difficulties under general anesthesia. If local anesthesia is used, many facilities give a preoperative intramuscular or intravenous injection of a tranquilizer. Most abortion clinics do not use general anesthesia. Therefore, check beforehand, if that is the method you prefer.

Some clinics continue to employ the archaic pubic "prep," or shaving of some of the hair surrounding the vaginal opening. There has never been a study to prove that this annoying and uncomfortable custom is more likely to prevent infection, but old customs die hard. Some clinics and hospitals require a preoperative enema, which also is a waste of time. A very small number of clinics insert *laminaria* (see Pages 185–186) twelve to twenty-four hours prior to the abortion. Patients who have laminaria inserted should report to their doctors any temperature elevation, severe cramps, or bleeding.

Finally, a woman should be sure to determine the policy of fee collection at the facility she chooses. Practically all abortion clinics and doctors' offices require most, if not all, of the fee before they perform the abortion. Some clinics include the Rho GAM injection for Rh-negative women in the fee, but others do not. All laboratory tests are usually included in the fee. There is usually an additional fee if general anesthesia is requested. The fee for an abortion may vary significantly from one clinic to another, and it is a good idea to do some comparison shopping before selecting a particular clinic. Some clinics base their fee on the number of weeks of pregnancy, as determined by the size of the uterus, and the larger the size, the more expensive the procedure. I know of no abortion clinic that accepts personal checks.

How is abortion performed during the first trimester of pregnancy?

Of the almost one million elective abortions performed in the United States in 1975, three fourths were terminated during the first trimester.

In the first eight weeks of pregnancy, as measured from the first day of the last menstrual period, an abortion may be easily accomplished with a 6-millimeter plastic cannula in a manner identical to that described for menstrual extraction. Because a greater amount of suction is needed, the cannula should be attached to a suction machine rather than to a syringe (Figures 7–1, 7–2).

If the pregnancy is further advanced than eight weeks, dilatation of the cervix with Pratt dilators is almost always

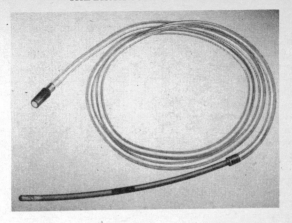

Figure 7-1. 6-Millimeter Cannula Attached to Hose

necessary in order to allow insertion of larger suction cannulas or curettes, called *vacurettes*. Those instruments may be curved or straight; the largest size is 12 millimeters. Metal suction cannulas have also been used, but they lack the flexibility of the softer disposable types. Theoretically, this characteristic would appear to increase the risk of uterine perforation. However, in the one study which compared these two cannulas, no differences were noted in the incidence of complications.

The uterine cavity is completely evacuated within five minutes when the curette is gently moved in, out, and around the uterine cavity. The same "grating" sound and the tightening of the uterine muscle noted after menstrual extraction is also observed following abortion (Figure 7-3). Rapid tightening or contraction of those muscles is essential in preventing excessive bleeding. The process may be improved by intramuscular or intravenous injection of *oxytocin*, muscle-contracting drug.

The contractions of the uterine muscles may cause moderate to severe cramps during the first few minutes following the abortion. They usually subside within twenty minutes, and pain medication given intramuscularly or by mouth should relieve the discomfort. Medications such as Darvon

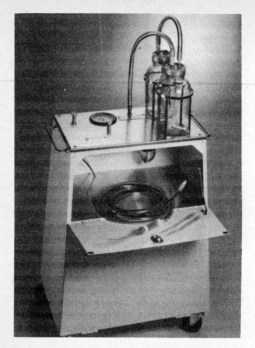

Figure 7-2.   Suction Machine

Compound, Percodan, Fiorinal, and Darvocet-N 100 are best avoided since they all contain aspirin, which may interfere with the coagulating ability of the blood. Most abortion facilities have a well-equipped recovery room, staffed by nurses, where postabortal patients are observed for a period of two hours or more. Most women are able to get dressed and are ready to leave within a half hour if local anesthesia is used. Following general anesthesia or a substantial dose of preoperative tranquilizer, a woman who is sensitive to the effects of medications may feel drowsy for even longer than the two hours.

Most abortion facilities dispense a total of six ergotrate tablets with the instructions that one be taken every four hours for the first twenty-four hours. That helps to keep the

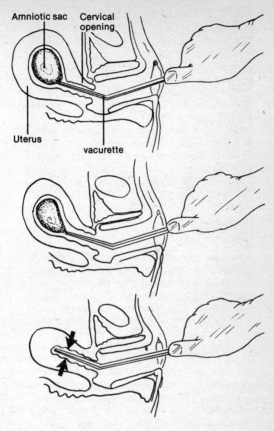

Figure 7-3. Evacuation of Early Pregnancy with 8-Millimeter Curette

uterus contracted and diminishes the amount of bleeding. Uterine cramping after you take each tablet is to be expected. Ergotrate tends to elevate the blood pressure, and because of that it should not be prescribed to hypertensive women.

Most women will experience a menstrual-like flow following an abortion. That bleeding should be no heavier than the

heaviest menstruation, is occasionally dark in color, and
may be accompanied by passage of an occasional clot. It is
not uncommon for the bleeding to stop completely and then
return a few days later. The use of four or five pads per day
for the first ten postabortal days may be considered normal.
However, passage of several clots over a short period of
time, or the soaking of two pads with bright red blood
within the period of one hour, is cause for concern and must
be reported to a doctor.

Rest is advisable on the day of the abortion, but most
women are able to resume normal activities, including work,
on the following day. Douching and intercourse should be
avoided during the first two weeks, and sanitary napkins
rather than tampons are preferred during the first postabortal week. Showers and baths are both permissible. Contrary
to popular belief, you can't introduce infection into the vagina by taking a bath, but for esthetic purposes baths are best
avoided during the first few days, when the bleeding is
heaviest.

In addition to reporting heavier-than-normal bleeding,
other symptoms requiring medical advice are severe cramps
which begin later than a day after the abortion; a temperature over 100.4° orally; a greenish, foul-smelling vaginal discharge; and burning and frequency of urination.

Fertility rapidly returns following a first-trimester abortion, with 60 percent of all women ovulating within the first
twenty-five postabortal days. Normal menses return between four and eight weeks, with 80 percent menstruating
prior to the fifth postabortal week. These statistics demonstrate the urgency of starting adequate contraception immediately. If the Pill is the contraceptive of choice, it may be
started on the day of the abortion. Some clinics insert IUDs
at the time of the abortion, but many don't (see Page 83). All
women undergoing abortion should have a pelvic examination two weeks later, and if you want an IUD, it can be inserted at that time. Postabortal exams are usually included
in the abortion fee, though the insertion of the IUD or the
fitting of a diaphragm during the visit usually involves an
additional fee.

After Week 8 of pregnancy, it is customary to use a vacurette with an outside diameter in millimeters equal to, or
two millimeters less than, the duration of the pregnancy in
weeks, counting from the first day of the last period. The

curette size should never be greater in diameter than the uterine size in weeks. It is not unreasonable to ask your doctor the curette size that he or she intends to use. If the reply is a 9-millimeter cannula for a pregnancy of six weeks, seek abortion at another facility.

There have been a few reports on the use of vacurettes with diameters greater than 12 millimeters. Supposedly they are capable of evacuating the uterus even when the pregnancy has advanced beyond the first twelve weeks. Most gynecologists with abortion expertise agree that that procedure is extremely dangerous and ill-advised since the risk of hemorrhage, uterine perforation, cervical laceration, and *incompetent cervix* can only be increased.

What is an incompetent cervix?

An *incompetent cervix* is one that is weakened, and unable to carry the weight of a growing pregnancy. It usually results in a spontaneous and premature dilatation or opening of the cervix, followed by miscarriage after the twelfth week of pregnancy.

Though the cause of cervical incompetence is usually unknown, trauma in the form of forceful dilatation may be responsible for the problem in some women. Reports from Hungary, England, and Japan, where abortion has been legalized for several years, indicate that the incidence of spontaneous midtrimester pregnancy loss may be significantly higher among women who have experienced previously induced abortions. Other reports, from Japan and Yugoslavia, have failed to demonstrate such a relationship.

In 1975, a fascinating experimental study was reported in the *British Journal of Obstetrics and Gynecology*. Dilators were passed through the cervix of surgically removed uteri in an attempt to detect the stage of dilatation at which microscopic tissue rupture could first be detected. In almost 50 percent of the specimens tested, evidence of tissue damage was apparent at a dilatation of 9 to 11 millimeters. The investigators concluded that use of a dilator of 8 millimeters or less caused a harmless dilatation of the cervix, while those above that critical size were more likely to cause damage. Though it is possible to question the applicability of that experimental data, the lesson to be learned is obvious: only the smallest possible dilator should be used while performing a suction curettage if the potential problem of an incompetent cervix is to be avoided.

What are some of the more common complications of first-trimester abortion?

Hemorrhage is the most common immediate complication, and may occur in as few as two, and as many as ten women of every one thousand undergoing abortion. Only a very small percentage of those women bleed to the point of needing a blood transfusion.

Hemorrhage usually occurs when the endometrial cavity is not completely emptied of all its pregnancy tissue, or when, for some unknown reason, the uterine muscle becomes flaccid and fails to contract immediately following the abortion. The latter condition, *uterine atony*, usually responds to intravenous oxytocin. It is more likely to occur in a uterus of twelve weeks' size than in one of six or eight weeks' size. Statistically, the average blood loss resulting from an abortion at five weeks is about three tablespoons, while at twelve weeks it is equal to sixteen tablespoons.

Perforation of the uterus may occur when the end of a sound (see Page 84), a dilator, or a vacurette actually passes through the uterine wall and into the abdominal cavity. This complication, estimated to occur from .1 to 2.7 percent of the time, is extremely dangerous. The amount of hemorrhage caused by perforation may be severe, and the presence of a suction curette in the abdominal cavity can easily cause damage to the intestine.

Perforation rates are inversely related to the skill and care taken by the doctor, and directly related to the size of the uterine cavity. As the pregnancy advances, the enlarging uterine muscle becomes softer and thinner, making it much easier to perforate. In addition, the 10- or 12-millimeter vacurette is a much more dangerous instrument than the small flexible 6-millimeter Karman cannula.

When perforation is suspected, the abortion should be stopped immediately, and the woman transferred to a hospital if the abortion is being conducted in an office or a clinic. Blood should be made available for transfusion, and exploratory surgery performed if bleeding appears to be heavy or if intraabdominal hemorrhage is suspected. At the time of surgery the site of perforation can usually be located and easily sutured. Occasionally surgery may be more complex and involve *ligation*, or tying, of the larger blood vessels near the area of the bleeding. On rare occasions, hysterectomy may be the only method of controlling the hemorrhage.

When the blood loss following perforation is not excessive, the suction curettage may be completed safely and successfully in the hospital by one doctor, while another views the perforated uterus through a laparoscope (see Chapter 9). Laparoscopic visualization helps to determine whether or not the perforation site is actively bleeding and if the vacurette is in danger of again perforating or injuring a piece of intestine. By such use of the laparoscope, major exploratory surgery may be avoided.

Laceration and hemorrhage from the cervix may be caused by a doctor who does not dilate the uterus in a slow, gradual manner. It is more likely to occur in a young woman with a small, rigid cervix who has never had a previous abortion or pregnancy. Cervical laceration may occur as often as 2 percent of the time and usually requires suturing to stop the bleeding.

When bleeding occurs several days following an abortion, it is often the result of retained fragments of pregnancy tissue. That complication has been quoted to occur from three to eleven times per one thousand abortions performed. It usually requires repeat suction curettage or a D & C to remove those fragments. As with menstrual extraction, when fever accompanies the bleeding, it means that the retained tissue is infected, and antibiotics must also be given.

When a D & C is performed for removal of infected abortal tissue, it is vital that the curettage or scraping of the endometrium be extremely gentle. If not, permanent scarring of the endometrium may be a late complication. This condition, called *Asherman's syndrome*, though rare, can lead to permanent sterility.

Fever, lower abdominal pain, and a yellowish vaginal discharge in the absence of bleeding may signify endometritis (inflammation of the endometrium). Endometritis complicates the abortions of as few as eight and as many as thirty-five women of every one thousand undergoing first-trimester pregnancy termination. Antibiotics without curettage usually cure endometritis. That condition is also more common as the size of the uterus increases.

The total complication rate of first-trimester abortion —including hemorrhage, perforation, retained pregnancy tissue, and endometritis—has been estimated at an average of 22 per 100,000 women aborted. It is clear that the number and severity of complications greatly increases with each week that you delay before undergoing abortion, as demonstrated in Table 7-1.

What is the chance of death following first-trimester abortion?

Deaths following early abortion are described by some as extremely rare, but they are not rare enough. In one study combining statistics from California and New York, there were 20 deaths following 759,647 abortions, for a fatality

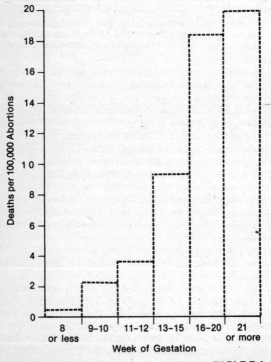

TABLE 7-1

rate of 2.6 per 100,000 women. Others have reported the rate
to be 1.7 per 100,000 women. In the combined California and
New York study, infection was a leading cause of death,
closely followed by hemorrhage and cardiac arrest, or unexplained stoppage of the heart while anesthesia was being
given. A large and more recent study in New York of 26,000
women showed no deaths.

The latest and most complete study on first-trimester
abortion deaths was published in April, 1977 by the Center
for Disease Control. In their evaluation of the 850,000 legal
abortions reported in this country in 1975, the death rate
was less than 1 per 100,000 when the procedure was performed within 8 weeks of the last menstrual period. In the 9
to 10 week interval the death rate was 1.2 per 100,000 abortions, while in the 11 to 12 week category the death rate
jumped to 4.7 per 100,000.

What is the safest type of anesthesia for first-trimester abortion?

Without doubt, paracervical block, occasionally sup-
plemented by small amounts of intravenous or intramuscular tranquilizer, is the safest form of anesthesia. Of the
26,000 successful abortions reported above, all patients received only paracervical block.

A few abortion clinics, and practically all ambulatory
abortion facilities in hospitals, offer you a choice of paracervical block or general anesthesia. The sensible choice should
practically always be paracervical block.

(However, it is important to realize that no anesthetic is
100 percent safe, and even local anesthetics used for
paracervical block can be potentially dangerous. Since
January 1, 1972, 5 women in the United States are reported
to have died from paracervical block used for first trimester
abortions. Three of these deaths were caused by improper
injection of the anesthetic; two may have been caused by
rare allergic reactions.)

With general anesthesia, a short-acting barbiturate is injected intravenously. That puts you to sleep. A mask is
placed over your face, and a light anesthetic gas, such as
nitrous oxide, is administered. Upon completion of the abortion, recovery is usually quite rapid. General anesthesia is
preferred if you are sensitive or allergic to local anesthetics,
or extremely apprehensive, to the degree that even a routine

examination may be difficult, if not impossible, for the doctor to perform.

Cardiac arrest under general anesthesia may occur, for totally unexplained reasons, as often as 1 in 2,500 operations performed on hospitalized patients. This statistic includes people of all ages and health conditions; and cardiac arrest does not occur as frequently among younger and healthier women who undergo early abortion. However, it still remains a threat in this group as well, as the nine anesthetic deaths reported in the New York–and–California study verify.

If general anesthesia is used, it is essential not to eat or drink anything for at least eight hours prior to the procedure. That assures adequate emptying of food from the stomach, and prevents the potentially fatal risk of food regurgitation into the windpipe while you are asleep under anesthesia.

Newer drugs, *neuroleptics*, produce a trance-like state of dissociation without sleep. They have been used successfully for abortion and are gaining in popularity. However, difficulties may occasionally be encountered because their anesthetic effects may vary considerably among different individuals.

Should first-trimester abortions be performed in a hospital rather than in a clinic or a doctor's office?

Several studies have actually demonstrated complication rates to be lower when abortions are performed in clinics rather than in hospitals. The 26,000 successful abortions mentioned above were all performed in an abortion clinic in New York. The explanation for the excellent results may be that in most clinics and offices, only paracervical anesthesia is used. In addition, doctors working in abortion clinics perform a large number of abortions daily and naturally become proficient at them.

Certain potentially dangerous bacteria live in a hospital environment and are resistant to many antibiotics used against them. The chance of infection with these resistant bacteria is much lower in a setting outside the hospital.

In all fairness, it should be noted that when a complication does occur outside the hospital, the patient is transferred to the hospital. If she dies there, the hospital and not the clinic is recorded as being responsible for the complication.

For this reason clinics may have overly deflated complication rates.

Are there any medical conditions which make a hospital preferable for a first-trimester abortion?

It is my preference not to perform an outpatient abortion if the uterus measures greater than eleven weeks' size, counting from the onset of the last menstrual period. I adhere strictly to this rule and have not regretted it. The increased risk of hemorrhage from a uterus of that size makes the hospital a better location in the event that a blood transfusion is needed immediately. I am aware of the fact that a skilled operator can practically always successfully terminate a pregnancy of twelve weeks, but even an expert will encounter an occasional severe hemorrhage in a uterus of that size. It seems foolish and terribly unfair to subject even the smallest percentage of women to such a potentially lethal complication. Occasionally, the uterus may be filled with fibroids (see Page 248), making it difficult to accurately determine the length of the pregnancy. Fibroids may also distort the endometrial cavity, making it difficult to insert the dilators or the curettes. Abortion under such conditions is best performed in a hospital. Some women are born with congenital abnormalities in the shape of the uterus. In such individuals there may actually be a septum, or wall, between the two halves of the uterus, or two separate uteruses with separate endometrial cavities. If the doctor is lucky enough to detect that prior to surgery, he would most likely perform the abortion in the hospital.

Women with serious medical problems should also be hospitalized for an abortion. They include diseases such as hypertension greater than 160/100 (see Page 42), diabetes requiring insulin, heart disease or a significant heart murmur as a result of previous heart disease, a history of deep vein phlebitis or pulmonary embolus (see Page 37), blood coagulation disorders, chronic debilitating diseases, and anemia. A normal hemoglobin level for women ranges between 11 and 15 percent grams per one hundred milliliters of blood, and any number below that signifies anemia. When the hemoglobin is less than 10 percent grams per one hundred milliliters of blood, abortion in the hospital is preferred and should be preceded by laboratory tests to determine the cause of the anemia. A significant number of women with severe psychiatric problems are also best managed in a hospital environment.

How do I choose the right clinic and doctor to perform my abortion?

In choosing a doctor's office or an abortion clinic, determine if the facility is within ten minutes' driving time to a hospital in which the doctor has operating privileges. Don't be timid. Ask to inspect the treatment and recovery area for intravenous equipment, a tray of emergency drugs, oxygen and mask for resuscitation, and adequate staffing with registered nurses supervising.

Planned Parenthood has listed the physical facilities which an abortion clinic must have if it is to be considered acceptable:

1. Adequate, private space specifically designated for interviewing, counseling, and pregnancy evaluation

2. Conventional gynecologic examining or operating accessories, drapes, and linen

3. Approved and electrically safe vacuum aspiration equipment, and conventional instruments for cervical dilatation and uterine curettage (in adequate supply to permit individual sterilization for each patient)

4. Adequate lighting and ventilation for surgical procedures

5. Facilities for sterilization of instruments and linen, and for surgical scrub for all personnel

6. Laboratory equipment and personnel (or immediate access to laboratory facilities) for preoperative and emergency determinations and for tissue diagnosis of uterine contents

7. Postoperative recovery room, properly supervised, staffed, and equipped

8. Adequate supplies of drugs, intravenous solutions, syringes, and needles, including four to six units of plasma volume-expander liquids for emergency use (until blood is available)

9. Dressing rooms for staff and patients, and appropriate lavatory facilities

10. Ancillary equipment and supplies, including stethoscopes, sphygmomanometers (for taking blood pressure), anesthesia equipment—including oxygen and equipment for artificial ventilation and administration of anesthetic gases—and resuscitation equipment and drugs

11. Ability to transfer a patient without delay to a conventional operating theater and a written letter of agreement from a full-service hospital regarding transfer of emergency patients

12. Special arrangements for patient emergency contact (on a twenty-four-hour basis) for evaluation and treatment of complications, for postoperative followup and examination, and for family planning services

Some doctors still perform first-trimester abortions with a sharp curette (see Page 53) rather than with a suction apparatus. With that technique, the blood loss is greater, the incidence of retained pregnancy tissue is almost tripled, and the pain is intolerable and prolonged. If there is no suction apparatus in the office, find another doctor. If there is a suction apparatus, then ask the doctor the size of the dilator and curette that he or she intends to use.

Though many doctors perform abortions, not all are board-certified obstetricians and gynecologists. Though certification by that specialty board is no absolute guarantee of a doctor's competence or manual dexterity, it does show that he or she has completed an approved residency program and has demonstrated the ambition and knowledge to study for and pass extensive qualifying examinations. I would certainly be more inclined to have a board-certified obstetrician-gynecologist treat a potential complication of an abortion than a family practitioner or general surgeon.

A telephone call to a local family planning clinic, such as Planned Parenthood, may be helpful in locating a competent physician. These centers receive followup evaluation from women who are referred for abortions. If treatment has been below par, it is unlikely that the doctor or clinic will remain on the referral list for long. Some Planned Parenthood affiliates perform first-trimester abortions. All personnel at these facilities must meet very high standards of care and undergo a thorough inspection before they are approved. Furthermore, those Planned Parenthood affiliates not performing abortions will not usually refer you to a physician's office or abortion clinic unless they have sent a representative to personally inspect it beforehand.

A call to an operating room nurse or an obstetrical resident at a local hospital will often be the most helpful in securing a qualified physician. A senior resident in an approved obstetrics and gynecology program is often the most critical and best judge of the relative talents of the attending staff physicians.

What is the cost of a suction curettage?

When an early abortion is performed in a clinic or a doctor's office, the fee should not exceed $200, though a more reasonable fee would be $100 to $150. Some clinics include Rho GAM (see Page 159) in the fee, but others do not. If you know you are Rh-negative, telephone beforehand to find out if Rho GAM is included in the fee. There is usually an additional fee if general anesthesia is given. Most abortion clinics request payment in full prior to the abortion, and some can be very blunt about collecting every last dollar. Included in the fee is a reexamination two weeks later, as well as contraceptive counseling both at the time of the abortion and at the two-week visit. If an IUD is to be inserted at or after the two-week visit, an additional fee is usually added.

The ambulatory facilities at most hospitals are more than adequate, but are usually twice as expensive as those of a clinic or doctor's office. However, many insurance companies provide full or at least partial payment for abortions performed in a hospital, as well as those in a clinic or office.

For the indigent woman who is unable to afford an abortion, local family planning centers will usually be able to make special financial arrangements through a clinic or private doctor. Because most hospitals in the United States are not meeting their obligations in caring for these women, more than one half of all abortions are now being performed in private clinics and offices.

When a pregnancy has advanced beyond twelve weeks, how is it terminated?

Beyond the twelfth week, a pregnancy may be terminated by injecting either *hypertonic saline* (see Page 180) or *prostaglandins* (a group of lipid, or fat-like, substances that produce intense uterine contractions) into the amniotic fluid which surrounds the fetus. This fluid is contained in the amniotic sac, or bag of waters, and increases in quantity as pregnancy advances. An adequate quantity of amniotic fluid must be present before either of these solutions can be safely injected. This is usually not achieved until at least the sixteenth week of pregnancy, when the uterus is enlarged to a height slightly more than half the distance between the pubic symphysis (see Chapter 1) and the umbilicus. As previously mentioned, some medical centers have advocated use of suction curettage and other instruments to terminate pregnancies beyond the twelfth week and as late as the seventeenth week following the last menstrual period. However, this method has not gained favor among most gynecologists in the United States.

For the woman who is slightly more than twelve weeks pregnant, the four-week delay in terminating the pregnancy is often unnerving. However, if the procedure is performed too early, the chances of failure and subsequent physical and psychological trauma may be far greater than the anxiety produced by waiting the full four weeks.

What is that abortion procedure like?

You must urinate immediately before receiving the injection in order to be certain that the needle does not perforate a distended urinary bladder lying in front of the uterus (Figure 1–5).

The skin overlying the enlarged uterus is then cleansed with antiseptic solution, and a local anesthetic such as novocaine or xylocaine is injected into the skin.

A long needle is then inserted through the anesthetized skin and the uterine muscle, and into the amniotic sac. That may cause a moderate amount of pain below the skin, but it can be greatly relieved if the needle is inserted rapidly. Correct placement of the needle is confirmed by a free flow of clear amniotic fluid through the tip of the needle.

At this point, some doctors prefer to thread a plastic catheter through the needle and into the amniotic sac, and then remove the needle, leaving the catheter in place. Withdrawal of amniotic fluid and injection of either hypertonic saline or prostaglandin is accomplished by attaching a syringe to the catheter. Other doctors prefer to inject the solution from the syringe attached to the needle.

The advantage of a plastic catheter is that it can be left in place, taped to the abdomen, so that if the initial injection is unsuccessful in producing abortion within twenty-four to forty-eight hours, reinjection is simplified. However, the disadvantage of leaving a plastic catheter in place is that it may increase the risk of infection both on the skin and along the path of the catheter. If a plastic catheter is not used, the discomfort of reinjection with the longer needle must be repeated.

Within a variable interval of several hours following the injection, contractions usually begin, followed by labor and eventual expulsion of the fetus and the placenta. The labor is often described by insensitive gynecologists as a "minilabor," slightly more painful than severe menstrual cramps. Nothing could be further from the truth. Despite the small size of the fetus, the labor is often prolonged and very painful, usually requiring liberal amounts of pain medication.

What is hypertonic saline and how dangerous is it?

Hypertonic saline is a highly concentrated 20 percent salt solution which, until recently, has been the most popular method of terminating second-trimester pregnancies in the United States. It was first introduced in Japan but is no longer used there because it was found to be associated with some very serious complications. These complications have been observed in this country as well. Though many doctors have performed hundreds of saline abortions and have claimed only minimal side effects, the fact remains that midtrimester abortion with saline is a far more dangerous procedure than first-trimester suction curettage. The total complication rate for saline abortion in various studies has been estimated at 20 to 26 per 100 women aborted. The death rate has varied between 12 and 18 per 100,000 abortions, which means it is at least four times as likely as suction curettage to cause death.

What are the most common complications of saline abortion?

The first potentially serious complication experienced with hypertonic saline may occur while it is being injected. If the doctor accidentally injects the solution into a uterine blood vessel, rather than the amniotic fluid, the *hypernatremia*, or increased levels of salt solution in the blood, can cause instant death. This complication has been estimated to occur in less than .4 percent of all women undergoing saline abortions, and may be avoided by very slow injection of the saline with frequent withdrawal of the syringe handle. This insures that clear fluid, and not blood, returns into the catheter. If there is even a trace of blood returned in the catheter or the syringe, no more saline should be injected until the fluid becomes perfectly clear again. The amount of saline required to produce abortion is approximately 200 cubic centimeters, or the volume equivalent of a drinking glass. When such a large amount is being used, the chances of accidental intravenous injection are greater. Because of that, your doctor must constantly observe you for early signs of hypernatremia while the solution is being injected. Those signs include headache, restlessness, numbness of the fingers, a sensation of increased body warmth, and excessive thirst. The procedure must be stopped immediately when any of those warning signs are noted. It is obvious that the patient must be fully awake and alert, and never sedated before or during the saline injection.

If the needle is accidentally placed in the muscle of the uterus, and saline is then injected, *necrosis*, or death of the muscle, may occur. That complication, though very rare, may require hysterectomy, but it should not happen if the doctor strictly adheres to the precautions outlined above. Rarer still is the placement of the needle into the abdominal cavity rather than into the amniotic sac. Injection of saline into the abdominal cavity usually causes immediate and severe pain. No harm results if the injection is stopped immediately.

Following accurate placement of the saline into the amniotic sac, some of it is absorbed into the bloodstream over a period of several hours. If you have such medical problems as heart disease, the increased salt load and expansion of the blood volume may be quite dangerous.

A temperature greater than 100.4° may occur in as many as 16 percent and as few as 2 percent of women undergoing saline abortion. Those temperature elevations are usually due to either necrosis or death of tissue, but may also be a result of infection. When infection is the cause of the fever, it can become a potentially lethal complication, and as I previously mentioned, it is the leading cause of saline abortion death.

The incidence of hemorrhage has been calculated at 2.6

percent, while 1 to 2 percent of all women aborted with saline hemorrhage to the point of requiring a blood transfusion. An unexplained but very serious complication of saline abortion is a decrease of several blood coagulation (clotting) factors. Without those factors, uncontrolled hemorrhage may occur in 1 of every 1,200 women receiving saline.

Finally, 10 to 16 percent of women who abort the fetus retain the placenta, and do not pass it within one to two hours. That necessitates its removal, either by hand or with a sharp curette and other instruments, under anesthesia. All these complications, while rarely mentioned to patients by their doctors, are potentially very serious and serve to emphasize the dangers that may occur with hypertonic saline abortions.

Is there any way to reduce the incidence of complications with hypertonic saline?

If difficulty is encountered while the doctor is trying to insert the needle into the amniotic sac, it may be overcome by direct visualization with an ultrasound machine. Unfortunately, most hospitals are not equipped with this sophisticated and expensive device.

By shortening the time interval between injection of the saline and passage of the aborted fetus, the incidence of some complications may be reduced. In one study, in their extensive review of the literature, Drs. Lonnie S. Burnett, Ian Colston Wentz and Theodore M. King noted that when oxytocin was given in an intravenous solution following saline injection, some 48 percent of these women aborted within twenty-four hours, compared with only 22 percent when saline was used alone. After forty-eight hours, 93 percent of the saline-plus-oxytocin group aborted, compared to 85 percent in the saline-only group. In addition, the incidence of fever and infection was reduced by one-third, while there was a significant drop in the number of women with retained placentas from 16 to 2 percent. On the negative side, the incidence of hemorrhage was actually tripled, and the risk of hemorrhage from diminished coagulation factors was increased to 1 in 300 women, from 1 in 1,200 women.

What are prostaglandins and how do they compare with saline?

Prostaglandins are lipid, or fat-like, chemicals found in their natural state in the bodies of all men and women. These potent substances may be synthesized in the laboratory as well. Originally, prostaglandins were thought to be present only in the prostrate gland of men, and that is how the name was derived. There are many different types of natural and synthetic prostaglandins, each classified according to their individual chemical structure. Two such prostaglandins, named PGF$_2\alpha$ and PGE$_2$, have been used successfully to induce abortion, since both are capable of stimulating intense uterine contractions resulting in expulsion of the fetus and placenta. At the present time, only PGF$_2\alpha$ has been approved by the FDA for intraamniotic injection while PGE$_2$ received FDA approval as a suppository in 1978.

Several studies have confirmed that there are five definite advantages of using PGF$_2\alpha$ over hypertonic saline:

1. Only 8 cubic centimeters (40 milligrams) has to be injected into the amniotic fluid in order to induce abortion. When compared with the 200 cubic centimeters saline, the chances of that small amount entering the bloodstream are much less.

2. Prostaglandins have a much more rapid injection-to-abortion interval. In one (the Burnett et. al.) study previously referred to, 69 percent of patients given prostaglandins aborted within twenty-four hours, and 93 percent within forty-eight hours, compared to 22 percent and 85 percent with saline. Practically speaking, you spend less time in the hospital, and therefore incur less expense, when prostaglandins are used. (The injection–abortion interval may be lengthened if pain medication containing aspirin is given to relieve the discomfort of contractions, because aspirin is a prostaglandin antagonist. Therefore, never take such commonly used pain medications as Darvon Compound and Percodan when undergoing prostaglandin abortion.)

3. Prostaglandins do not cause significant changes in the blood volume or salt load, and can therefore be given with greater safety to women who have cardiac or other coexisting medical problems.

4. Prostaglandins do not alter the blood coagulation factors.

5. There is no risk of death from hypernatremia or necrosis

of the uterine muscle when prostaglandins are given incorrectly.

Are there any adverse reactions when prostaglandins are used for an abortion?

The most frequent side effect is vomiting, which has been reported to occur in at least 50 percent, and as many as 75 percent, of all women. There is a 25 percent incidence of extreme nausea without vomiting. These symptoms do not usually occur until several hours following the initial injection, and use of a rectal suppository to alleviate these symptoms before they occur is sometimes helpful. Diarrhea has been a problem in 16 percent of those women.

A transient temperature elevation, without apparent fever, has been noted 6 percent of the time.

The most frightening side effect for both patient and doctor occurs as often as 1 to 3 percent of the time: the immediate onset of an asthma-like shortness of breath, nausea, vomiting, restlessness, and even seizures, drop in blood pressure, slowing of the pulse, and irregularities of the heart beat. This is believed to occur because of inadvertent passage of the prostaglandins directly into the circulation. Fortunately, the prostaglandins are metabolized rapidly by the body, and all symptoms disappear within twenty minutes. However, because of this possibility, it is recommended that prostaglandins not be used in aborting asthmatic women.

The uterine muscle contractions caused by prostaglandins are often so strong that they can cause lacerations, or tears, of the lower cervix in approximately .5 percent of all patients. It is for this reason that the cervix must be carefully inspected following prostaglandin abortion, and all lacerations sutured immediately. The complication is more likely to occur in young women who have never experienced childbirth. It is the lack of control over the force of the contractions which prevents use of prostaglandins for safe induction of full-term pregnancies. An infant subjected to such potent contractions may become severely damaged.

In Anderson's study of 600 prostaglandin abortions, he noted that 30 percent of the women did not go into labor within twenty-four hours, and required reinjection of one half of the initial 40-milligram dose. In addition, 140 women experienced retained placenta following passage of the fetus. Some 10 of these placentas were successfully removed in bed, 117 required removal in a nearby treatment room, and only 13, or 2.2 percent, required removal in the operating room. A total of 25 of his patients were readmitted because of retained placental fragments and bleeding, while 5.3 percent of the 600 women experienced bleeding equal to or greater than one unit of blood (500 cubic centimeters).

A 1977 report published by the Center for Disease Control compared 1,200 prostaglandin abortions with 10,000 saline abortions. The authors of this study concluded that prostaglandins had the advantage of a more rapid injection-to-abortion interval, but the disadvantage of a higher rate of fever, uterine infection, retained placental fragments, and rehospitalization for complications following the procedure.

Can a prostaglandin abortion ever be successfully performed between the twelfth and sixteenth week of pregnancy?
In December, 1977, the FDA approved PGE2 use as a vaginal suppository for the termination of pregnancy from the twelfth gestational week through the second trimester. The drug is marketed by Upjohn under the name Prostiń E2. One 20 milligram suppository is inserted in the vagina at 3-to-5 hour intervals until fetal expulsion occurs. In one study of 102 patients, complete evacuation of the uterus occurred in 100 patients in a mean time of 9 hours, and at a mean total dose of slightly less than three suppositories. Only two patients experienced retained placental fragments requiring a D & C. The most frequent side effects were vomiting in two-thirds of the women, temperature elevation of more than 2° F in one-half, diarrhea in one-third, and nausea in one-tenth. One-tenth of the patients also experienced a transient though significant drop in blood pressure.

At the present time, most physicians in the United States are totally unfamiliar with this new suppository. However, if the experimental data prove to be accurate, the use of intraamniotic methods should become obsolete in the near future. Suppositories have the distinct advantage of safe and painless administration and require no special skill on the part of the person inducing the abortion.

Is there any way to decrease the risk of trauma to the cervix during both first- and second-trimester abortions?
Laminaria digitata is dried sea weed that has been used, both legally and illegally, as a cervical dilator for over one

hundred years. Due to its hydroscopic (water-absorbing) ability, a sterile piece of laminaria, when inserted into the cervix (Figure 7–4), absorbs the secretions and increases its diameter by three to five times over a period of six to eight hours. This slowly and painlessly dilates the cervix prior to suction curettage and prostaglandin abortion. Small, medium, and large laminaria sizes before and after hydration are demonstrated in Figure 7–5.

The insertion of laminaria into the cervical canal causes only minimal discomfort, and allows for suction curettage without dilatation several hours later. When inserted fourteen to nineteen hours prior to prostaglandin or saline abortion, the interval between injection and abortion has been noted to be shortened by as much as six hours.

Though the incidence of cervical injury may be greatly reduced with laminaria, the incidence of cervical and uterine infection may be slightly higher because the opening of the cervix prior to abortion may introduce potentially harmful bacteria. That is especially true when the laminaria is inserted more than twenty-four hours prior to the abortion.

Are prostaglandins harmful to women with sickle cell trait?

In 1973, a Stanford University study suggested that prostaglandins were more likely to increase the rate of sickling in blacks with sickle cell trait (see Page 44). Two subsequent reports by other researchers have refuted this claim. In one of these studies the blood from eighty patients with sickle cell trait was mixed with a prostaglandin substance, and in another, prostaglandins were actually given to eight patients

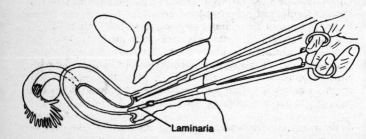

Laminaria

Figure 7-4.   Insertion of Laminaria into the Cervix

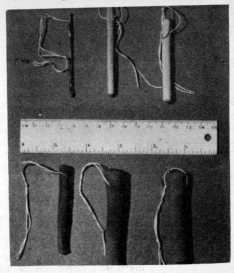

Figure 7-5.   Small, Medium, and Large Laminaria Before and After Hydration

with sickle cell trait. In both instances sickling was not in-creased. Since then, the Stanford group has modified their position, saying that prostaglandins may worsen sickling once it has begun. At the present time, the use of prostaglandins in terminating the pregnancy of a woman with sickle cell trait or sickle cell disease remains controversial. Until more is learned about this relationship, hypertonic saline may be considered a logical alternative.

What is hysterotomy?
Hysterotomy is termination of a pregnancy by removing it through a Cesarean section-like incision in the uterus.

The mortality rate from hysterotomy has been estimated to range from a low of 45, to an astronomical high of 271, per 100,000 women, with a total complication rate between 23 and 51 per 100 women aborted. The latest statistics reported for abortion via hysterotomy is 61 per 100,000 in 1975. In addition, future full-term pregnancies usually necessitate Cesarean section because of the weakening of the uterine muscle caused by the hysterotomy. Hysterotomy should rarely, if ever, be used today as a means of pregnancy termination.

How expensive is a second-trimester abortion?

Because midtrimester abortions are often associated with many serious complications, a doctor's fee will almost always be higher than for suction abortion. The minimum fee is usually $150, but it may run as high as $500. Hospitalization may be necessary for three or four days, and that will cost several hundred dollars. If a D & C is necessary to remove the placenta, anesthesia and operating room fees must be added to the already-high total. Some insurance policies will pay part or all of the hospitalization costs. There are smaller hospitals that specialize in performing midtrimester abortions, and actually offer a fixed fee for the entire hospitalization. At some hospitals the set fee for midtrimester abortion of less than twenty weeks may be less than $500.00.

In the past, attempts have been made to reduce the cost of these abortions by doing them in a clinic. Other attempts have been made to reduce the total hospital stay by injecting prostaglandins or saline in a clinic or office, and then admitting those women to the hospital only when labor is well established. However, that has proven to be a very dangerous and unacceptable practice. In 1974, a report from the Medical Society of New York demonstrated that the risk of death was three times as great for women undergoing second trimester abortion without remaining continously in the hospital from the time of induction of the abortion until its completion. Some 43 percent of statewide maternal deaths were due to hemorrhage, many of which could have been prevented if the patient was in a hospital with an adequate blood bank and transfusion facilities.

What is a "super coil"?

The "super coil" was introduced rather spectacularly in 1973 by Harvey Karman. This nonphysician, encouraged by his success with the very useful Karman cannula (Figure 6–3), claimed that the insertion of several of these plastic IUD-like devices into the uterus, with removal the next day, could safely terminate second-trimester pregnancies. Amid great television and radio coverage, super coils were inserted under his direction in an abortion facility in Philadelphia. Naturally the results were catastrophic, with 60 percent of these unfortunate women experiencing major complications. Needless to say, further exhibitions of that type are not likely to happen. I hope Karman will give up the practice of medicine while he is still at the break-even point of success.

Are women who undergo abortion likely to experience emotional problems and guilt feelings later on?

In one study at Johns Hopkins University Hospital, a total of 373 women were evaluated. One group was aborted with suction curettage, another was aborted with saline, and the third group carried their pregnancies to term. In comparing the three groups, there was no significant variation in "sense of alienation from society" or in "self-esteem." Furthermore, subsequent sexual enjoyment and marital happiness appeared unchanged when comparing the three groups.

A second psychological study of 380 women undergoing abortion in New York revealed that almost 79 percent were happy with the decision, while only 7 percent experienced some self-anger, and 1.5 percent were very angry with themselves and negative about their decision. Among Catholics, it was noted that guilt and difficulty with the decision to abort occurred somewhat more frequently than among non-Catholics, but even among that group, negative feelings were minimal.

Robert Athanasiou in his review noted that religion did not seem to play an important part in the general population's use of abortion facilites. He referred to several studies showing that Catholics tend to be slightly overrepresented in abortion patient groups relative to their population percentage in the states of Maryland, Colorado, New York, Connecticut, and Hawaii. He noted that Catholic women were less likely to prevent pregnancy or define it as unwanted when it occurred. However, when the pregnancy was defined as unwanted, they sought abortion as readily as non-Catholic women. In conclusion, he stated that there was a definite, though small, percentage of women who do experience mild, transient depression following first- and second-trimester abortion. However, there are no data to support the claim that serious psychological problems will develop in a previously normal woman.

Can my husband legally prevent me from having an abortion?

The Supreme Court decision liberated women in early pregnancy from any form of state control. Since the state has no direct authority to prevent a woman from having an early abortion, neither does it have indirect authority to prevent abortion because a husband disapproves of his wife's decision. Since husbands have no enforceable right to deny abortion, their consent is not legally required prior to abortion during the first trimester.

When a second-trimester abortion is performed in a hospital, the situation may be different, because each hospital sets its own guidelines for abortion consent. A hospital is within its legal rights to request a husband's consent prior to performing abortion or any other surgical procedure. In addition, the state may also exert influence over the hospital, since it has the authority to regulate second-trimester abortions.

Can a doctor perform an abortion on a minor without parental consent?

Many doctors believe that it is their moral obligation to inform parents that their daughter is pregnant if she is below the age of eighteen. However, betrayal of her confidence is unjust and contrary to the principles of the Hippocratic oath. Certainly, a physician should encourage a young woman to have her parents share in the decision on abortion, but if she is unwilling to do this, the doctor has no right to act against her wishes.

The report of the Committee on Education in Family Life of the American College of Obstetricians and Gynecologists entitled The Management of Sexual Crises in the Minor Female in 1974 stated it clearly in their report: "However, when she (a minor) is unwilling to tell her parents that she is sexually involved, or that she is pregnant, the physician may not be free to do what he believes is in the best interest of the patient, because the law is either restrictive or unclear. In such situations, the physician has three choices: he may refuse to help the girl unless she agrees to inform her parents; he may himself inform them, thus betraying her confidence; or he may agree to give her advice and help without the parents' knowledge. The third choice probably represents a less serious violation of the physician's duty than either of the other two."

In situations where the physician judges that the minor who refuses to tell her parents is incapable of making a rational decision, the committee recommends that the doctor not act on his or her own judgment, but should carefully select a medical colleague or a member of another helping profession, such as a clergyman or psychologist, as a consultant, and share the decision and responsibility with that colleague and the young girl.

Does easy access to abortion make a woman less likely to use adequate contraception?
On the contrary, several studies, including those of Dr. Christopher Tietze, have shown that more women are using effective contraception than ever before. That, says Dr. Tietze, is reflected in the overall decrease of 7 percent in the total pregnancy rates between 1971 and 1973. He noted that the greatest decline in pregnancy rates was 12.4 percent in women in the twenty-to-twenty-four age group, most of whom were married. Unfortunately, teenage pregnancy showed the smallest decline of all age groups, though teenagers had the highest increase in abortion rates. To improve the statistics for that particular group, he suggests more widespread availability of free and confidential contraceptive counseling services and supplies for young people of both sexes.

The statistics from a New York City review from 1970 to 1974 demonstrate beyond a doubt that most women who undergo abortion will, in the future, use adequate contraceptive techniques. A study of white, Puerto Rican, and black women aborted in 1970 revealed that members of all three groups used adequate contraceptive techniques following their abortion and at the time they were reevaluated in 1974. Though black women were noted to have a slightly higher repeat pregnancy rate, it was not nearly as high as would have been if adequate contraception had not been used. The conclusion reached was that a "very consistent level of use of the most effective contraceptive measures" was practiced among all three groups.

8

VASECTOMY

All too often, vasectomy in this country is still looked upon with skepticism and fear, and misinformation about the operation is widespread. Many individuals mistakenly believe that vasectomy causes such ill-effects as the inability to ejaculate, loss of virility, inability to achieve orgasm, hair loss, premature aging, and a change in voice pitch. Vasectomy has even been accused of causing skin disease, kidney, lung and liver diseases, narcolepsy (inability to stay awake), and multiple sclerosis. Sadly, such misinformation has been responsible for many men's avoidance of this simple and relatively harmless procedure.

In 1974, more than 1.3 million voluntary sterilizations were performed in the United States. Of these, 51 percent were vasectomies. Though the figure sounds impressive, it is not high when you consider its relative ease and safety when compared with female surgical sterilization. Figure 8–1 shows the total male and female sterilizations in the United States between 1969 and 1974. The statistics for 1975, not charted in Figure 8–1, are quite disturbing. Despite the fact that the total number of sterilizations decreased slightly, female sterilizations increased by 22,000 from the previous year and accounted for 51 percent of all sterilizations. This is an exact reversal of the percentages reported for 1974, when 51 percent of the total sterilizations were vasectomies. The change, attributed to the increasing popularity of laparoscopic sterilization, is disappointing in view of the fact that vasectomy remains the safest method of surgical sterilization.

What is vasectomy?
Vasectomy means cutting of the vas deferens, the two tubes which carry sperm from each testicle (Figures 1–14, 8–2).

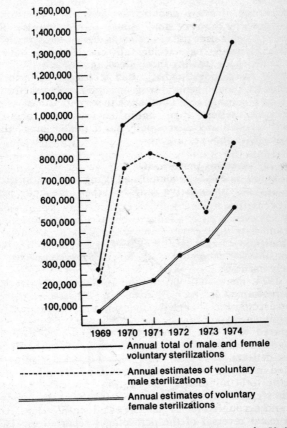

Figure 8-1. *Sterilizations of Men and Women in the United States Between 1969 and 1974*

Vasectomy is a minor surgical procedure also referred to as "clipping the cords." It is the simplest, surest, and safest surgical or medical method known to prevent unwanted pregnancy.

The first vasectomy was performed more than three hundred years ago, and it has been used routinely as a means of sterilization since 1925. It may be performed in hospitals, clinics, and doctors' offices with equal ease. The preference of some doctors for hospital vasectomy is influenced by the very small chance of encountering bleeding if the veins near the vas deferens, called the *pampiniform plexus* (Figure 8–2) are accidentally cut. Hospitals have better facilities for treating those bleeding problems.

Most vasectomies in the United States are performed by urologists, though general surgeons and family practitioners also do a considerable number of these operations. As with abortion, when rare complications do occur, a board-certified specialist usually has a greater knowledge in dealing with these problems.

How is vasectomy performed?

Vasectomy is easily accomplished using local anesthesia. A tranquilizer or sedative may be taken one hour before

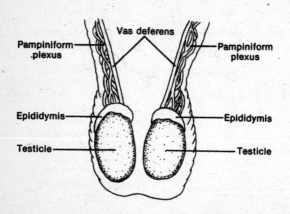

Figure 8-2.   Male Genitalia, Showing Epididymis and Vas Deferens

surgery, and then the area over the scrotal incision is shaved. Some doctors prefer one midline scrotal incision; others use two incisions, one over each vas deferens (Figure 8–3). The scrotal incision usually measures less than one inch in length and is made after adequate amounts of novocaine or xylocaine are injected into the skin.

The two vas deferens are then located, pulled out through the incision (Figure 8–4), and cut. The two loose ends of each vas may then be closed with a suture, cauterization (burning), or special metallic tantalum clips (Figure 8–4).

Most doctors remove a small portion of each vas deferens, to keep the loose ends apart. The skin is then closed with absorbable sutures which dissolve in seven to ten days. Upon completion of a successful operation, the sperm produced by the testes are blocked from passing beyond the point of surgery (Figure 8–5).

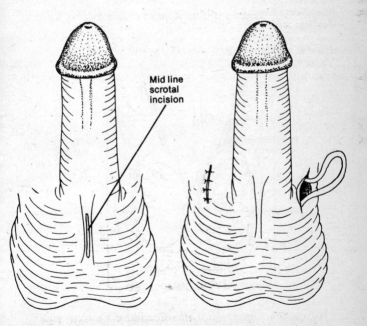

Mid line
scrotal
incision

Figure 8-3.   One- and Two- Incision Vasectomy Technique

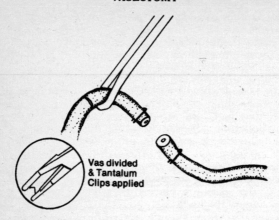

Figure 8-4. *Tantalum Clips Applied to Cut Ends of Vas Deferens*

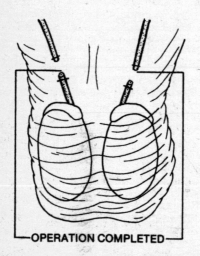

Figure 8-5. *Appearance after Completed Vasectomy*

What instructions should be given to a man following vasectomy?

Most men experience a moderate amount of pain on the day of surgery and the following day. It is best to spend the day of surgery in bed. Return to work is not advised until three days after surgery if he has a sedentary job, and seven days if he performs manual labor. Strenuous athletic activities should also be avoided for seven days. It is also a good idea to wear an athletic supporter for about one week. That provides scrotal support and help in preventing swelling and pain over the operative area.

Pain medication may be taken, but it is probably best to avoid those which contain aspirin, since they may have a detrimental effect on the coagulation factors in the blood. That in turn may increase bleeding at the operative site.

It is best to keep a small gauze bandage over the stitches for a few days in order to avoid irritating the skin. The dressing should be changed every two days and kept clean. Some swelling and oozing of a clear liquid from the incision is not unusual, but if the amount of swelling is greater than the diameter of a quarter, it may mean that there is an infection or a *hematoma*, a collection of blood in the area just under the skin. Slight discoloration of the skin, resembling an abrasion, is not unusual.

How soon after vasectomy can a man resume coitus?

Coitus with use of contraception may be resumed after seven days. However, before he can rely on vasectomy for permanent contraception, spermatozoa stored in the upper part of the vas deferens and the seminal vesicles (Figure 1–14) must first be emptied. To accomplish that, as many as fifteen ejaculates may be necessary, though the usual number is six to eight. Following the surgery, the doctor must examine sperm specimens until two ejaculates in succession contain no active sperm. When that occurs, additional contraception is no longer needed.

Following vasectomy, sperm production in the testes continues, but at a slower rate than before vasectomy. Fewer mature sperm are produced, and those that reach maturity disintegrate in the testes and the epididymis.

Many men fear vasectomy because they believe that it significantly diminishes the volume of their ejaculate. Actually, more than 90 percent of the fluid in the ejaculate comes from accessory glands, such as the seminal vesicles and prostate. These glands are unaffected by vasectomy, and so the 10 percent diminution in total semen volume is never even noticed.

What are some of the complications of vasectomy?

Several studies—including one with 1,500 and another with 2,700 men undergoing vasectomy—have demonstrated a death rate of 0. Complication rates have been consistently 5 percent or lower. In one study from Baylor College of Medicine, major complications were reported in 4.1 percent, and minor complications in 1.7 percent, of all men undergoing this procedure. *Epididymitis*, or inflammation of the epididymis, was responsible for 1 percent of all major complications. Adhesion of the vas deferens to the scrotal skin complicated surgery in another 1 percent. Abscess or infection caused by the stitches around the tied vas deferens occurred in slightly less than 1 percent of the men, but was absent when metallic clips were used instead of sutures.

The remaining 1.2 percent of complications included such entities as hematoma, or blood clot formation, at the surgical site; *orchitis*, or inflammation of the entire testicle; and recanalization, or reopening and recommunication of the two cut ends of the vas. The latter condition occurred in 10 of the 2,700 patients, for a failure rate of .37 percent. Even when surgery is performed by an expert, between .1 and .4 percent of the time the two cut ends amazingly find each other and reestablish communication, resulting in an unwanted pregnancy.

Rarely, a painful nodule or lump may be found at the site of surgery. This is called a *sperm granuloma* and appears to be caused when some of the products of the dead sperm actually leak through the walls of the ligated vas deferens and epididymis. The granuloma produced is actually a localized immune or allergic reaction, and it may take weeks or even months to heal. When the granuloma does not subside, it must be surgically removed.

Can other allergic reactions to sperm occur following vasectomy?

It was first noted in 1964 that some men developed antibodies against their own sperm following vasectomy. This is believed to happen when some of the products of the dead sperm, unable to pass through the closed vas, become absorbed into the bloodstream. The circulating sperm products then stimulate the body to produce the antibodies against them. More recent investigations have demonstrated as many as 50 to 60 percent of all men in the first year following vasectomy will have elevated antibody levels. After the first year, the antibody concentration will decrease to very low levels. It should be noted that some fertile men, who have never undergone vasectomy, for some unknown reason also have antibodies to their own sperm.

Can vasectomy be responsible for diminishing the sexual drive and potency in some men?

On the contrary, most men report that their sexual potency is the same as before the operation or greater. In a study of 189 men undergoing vasectomy at the Margaret Sanger Research Bureau, two thirds reported an increase in sexual desire attributed mainly to removing the anxiety of a possible pregnancy. Only 1 man in the entire study reported less sexual desire, and he was sixty years old. Some 98 percent of the patients stated that they would recommend the operation to others.

Testosterone, a hormone produced by the testes, is believed to be responsible for a man's normal sexual drive as well as for maintaining his male characteristics. Blockage of the vas deferens does not alter testosterone release, which takes place directly into the bloodstream from the testes. Several studies have measured blood testosterone levels before and after vasectomy without noting any change.

As I previously mentioned, some men incorrectly look upon vasectomy as the termination of their masculinity. It has been demonstrated that most men who experience sexual problems following vasectomy have had underlying psychological problems prior to the surgery. For this reason, it is the responsibility of their doctors to carefully evaluate each patient preoperatively. If doubt exists about an individual's mental status, psychiatric consultation should be obtained prior to surgery.

What type of man is most likely to request vasectomy?

It has been demonstrated that men with higher incomes and more schooling than that of the general population are most likely to want vasectomy. Minority groups, especially blacks, have been consistently underrepresented in choosing vasectomy as a form of contraception. Reasons cited have included the fear of loss of masculine gender role, fear of genocide, fear of surgery, and the predominant feeling among less-educated black men that the ability to father children is intimately related to their masculinity.

There also appears to be significant regional differences between men who choose vasectomy and those who do not. In one study conducted in 1970, the lowest rate of vasectomies was noted in the mid-Atlantic states, and the highest in the Pacific states. Among indigent couples, the West again demonstrated the highest vasectomy rates, while the South had the lowest incidence of vasectomy.

What is the cost of vasectomy?
When performed in a doctor's office, the fee may range from $150 to $350. Hospital costs are usually much higher and include use of the operating room, anesthesia, and the fee for the pathologist if a portion of the vas deferens is removed. Insurance policies usually cover all or most of this expense.

Aren't there special banks where men can store their semen prior to vasectomy?
For men who want "fertility insurance" prior to vasectomy, there are special sperm banks where ejaculates are frozen in liquid nitrogen at a temperature of $-196°$ for months or even years. If a man decides that he wants children at a later date, those specimens may be thawed, and artificially inseminated into his wife's vagina. The number of ejaculates stored in those cryobanks for each man is usually five to eight, and the fertilizing capacity of the frozen specimen is two thirds of that expected when fresh semen is used. The initial cost of sperm storage is approximately twenty-five dollars per specimen, with an annual storage fee of twenty to thirty dollars per year.

It does not appear that freezing causes harm to the sperm cell. The incidence of miscarriage and abnormal births is actually lower with frozen semen. Some investigators believe that the reason is that freezing helps to eliminate the unhealthy and fragile sperm.

To date, published reports have documented more than five hundred normal infants resulting from clinical use of frozen semen. The greatest success has been achieved with specimens stored for less than six months, though pregnancy has been reported following storage of sperm for ten years. Several investigators have questioned the condition of most frozen specimens stored beyond three years.

The first commercial semen bank was established in 1970. In 1973, there were twenty-three sperm banks in the United States, with optimistic plans for the building of many more profit-making commercial banks. However, the response of American men to the idea of "fertility insurance" has been disappointing, and several of those commercial sperm banks have gone bankrupt or have closed for lack of financial success.

Human sperm banks must still be considered experimental, and a man should not delude himself into believing that he can deposit his semen in one of these banks and return a few years later with the guarantee of having children with these stored specimens. To quote the National Medical Committee of Planned Parenthood—World Population, "The promise of fertility insurance to be achieved by storing semen may be misleading. Moreover, it may lead to the persuasion of immature or poorly motivated individuals to undergo vasectomy."

9
TUBAL
LIGATION

Voluntary sterilization for women has increased significantly during the 1970s. It was estimated that in 1974 approximately 550,000 women underwent tubal sterilization in the United States (Figure 8-1). Female sterilization has increased at a faster rate than male sterilization despite the fact that statistically, vasectomy is far safer than any surgical procedure performed on a woman. The upward trend has been attributed to the development of newer, more sophisticated instruments and techniques, as well as the removal of most legal barriers preventing permanent contraception. Until 1970, most hospitals used the so-called age-parity formula, or "rule of 120," for determining which women would be fortunate enough to be granted sterilization. By this ignominious method, sterilization was permitted only if the age of the woman multiplied by the number of her living children was equal to or greater than the number 120.

What is tubal ligation?

By definition, *tubal ligation* means *ligating*, or tying, the Fallopian tubes (Figure 9-1). The more general term of *tubal sterilization* refers to any procedure which prevents fertilization of the egg by the sperm within the tube. Traditional methods have often involved ligation combined with excision, or cutting out a piece of the tube. Newer techniques have utilized coagulation, or burning, as well as the place-

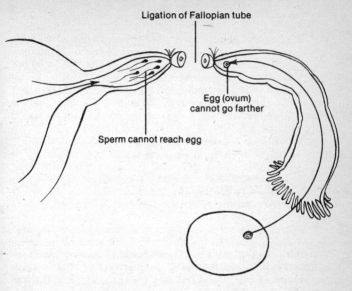

Figure 9-1. Tubal Ligation

ment of elastic bands and clips around a segment of the tube. Tubal sterilization immediately following childbirth is called *postpartum* or *puerperal* sterilization, while *interval* sterilization refers to the procedure when it is not associated with pregnancy. Tubal sterilization may also be performed in combination with an abortion (Figure 9-1).

What is the difference between abdominal and vaginal tubal ligation?

Abdominal tubal ligation, performed by means of an abdominal incision, is still the most commonly used method of tubal sterilization in this country. It is by far the most popular method employed in the immediate postpartum period. Methods of *vaginal tubal ligation* (see the sections in this chapter on colpotomy and culdoscopy), in which the surgery is performed via the vagina, are also used, though never as postpartum procedures. The doctor's fee alone for either of these procedures can range from $300 to $700.

What procedures are followed before tubal ligation is performed?

Prior to surgery the area over the proposed operative site is shaved and scrubbed with an antiseptic solution. If the incision is to be made just above the pubic hair line, most, if not all, of the pubic hair is removed.

All solid foods and liquids are restricted for eight hours prior to surgery, to be sure that the stomach is empty in the event of inadvertent retching under general anesthesia. If the stomach is full, food particles and liquids may be aspirated into the trachea, or windpipe, producing a potentially dangerous situation. Intramuscular premedication is given one hour before surgery and usually consists of a tranquilizer combined with atropine. The latter drug helps to dry up excessive secretions in the mouth and throat, which could cause breathing difficulties when general anesthesia is used.

Though abdominal tubal ligation is most commonly performed under general anesthesia induced with intravenous pentothal, patient preference and medical indications occasionally make other methods more attractive. Local anesthesia may be easily injected into the incision, though there is usually some discomfort when the tubes are grasped. Spinal and epidural anesthesia have also been used successfully. Both of those procedures involve injection of an anesthetic into the lower back, resulting in complete absence of pain at the operative site. Of the two, epidural is usually preferred, because it allows movement of the legs as opposed to the complete paralysis produced by the spinal. In addition, epidural anesthesia doesn't cause the sometimes excruciating postoperative headache which may follow a spinal anesthetic. The only disadvantage of epidural anesthesia is that it is more difficult to administer, and not all anesthesiologists have the experience and delicate touch needed to achieve consistent success with it.

Most doctors prefer to have the lower bowel emptied prior to surgery, so they order a preoperative enema. Catheterization of the urinary bladder immediately before surgery allows better visualization of the uterus, which lies behind it. However, the introduction of a catheter increases the risk of a postoperative urinary tract infection. Catheterization can usually be avoided if a woman completely empties her bladder immediately before entering the operating room.

ABDOMINAL TUBAL LIGATION

How is an abdominal tubal ligation performed?

When abdominal tubal ligation is performed within the first two days following childbirth, a one-inch skin incision is usually made just below or through the lower border of the umbilicus, or navel. This is the level at which the top of the enlarged uterus is located. The resulting scar is hardly noticeable.

For interval abdominal tubal ligation, the skin incision is usually longer and is located in lower position on the abdomen, just above the upper part of the pubic hair line. The incision may be up-and-down or side-to-side.

After the abdominal cavity is entered, many methods may be used to tie the tubes. As with the various types of IUDs, each method of tubal ligation is named after the man who devised it. The easiest and most popular is the Pomeroy technique, in which a knuckle of tube is elevated and a catgut suture is tied below the knuckle (Figure 9–2).

The knuckle of tube is then cut off, and by the time the catgut is absorbed several weeks later, the two stumps retract and leave a scarred gap in between (Figure 9–3). The subsequent pregnancy rate is .3 percent following the Pomeroy technique.

Variations used by other doctors have included excision or removal of the middle portion of the tube, use of different suture material (such as silk), and either excision or suture of the fimbria, which are necessary for picking up the egg as it passes from the ovary (Figure 1–8).

Several investigators have demonstrated higher subsequent pregnancy rates when tubal ligation is performed at the time of Cesarean section or immediately postpartum.

What are the disadvantages to abdominal tubal ligation?

The complication rate following abdominal tubal ligation is 2 to 4 percent. Most of these are problems such as superficial inflammation of the incision, and urinary tract infections caused by bladder catheterization, which precedes the surgery.

Fatal pulmonary embolus (see Pages 36–37) may occur following any abdominal operation, with a death rate reported at approximately one per one thousand hospital operations. Though this tragic complication is less likely in a young,

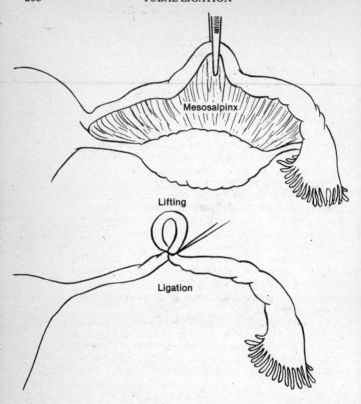

Figure 9-2. Pomeroy Technique of Elevating and Tying the Fallopian Tube

healthy woman undergoing tubal ligation, it still must be considered a real threat.

Abdominal tubal ligations are usually performed under general anesthesia, so an additional risk is incurred (see Page 173).

Hemorrhage from the blood vessels in the mesosalpinx, undetected at the time of surgery, is a rare cause of post-operative death.

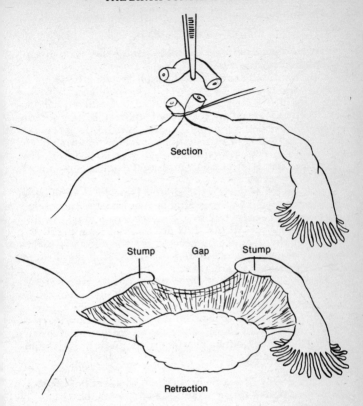

Section

Stump   Gap   Stump

Retraction

*Figure 9-3.   Pomeroy Technique for Cutting Tube and
Eventual Retraction of the Stumps*

Adding all these factors together, the total mortality rate
for women undergoing abdominal tubal ligation has been
estimated at between 10 and 25 per 100,000 operations performed.

On the practical side, other disadvantages are that the
hospital stay following interval abdominal sterilization averages five to six days, at a cost of more than one thousand

dollars, and the recovery time following surgery averages six weeks.

What are the advantages and disadvantages of postpartum abdominal sterilization?

Postpartum abdominal tubal ligation is not as costly as interval sterilization. The incision is smaller and is usually less painful. The surgery is easier than abdominal tubal ligation and may even be performed under local anesthesia, though most doctors prefer general anesthesia. When performed immediately after delivery or on the following day, a woman can return home three to five days later. This lengthens her total postpartum hospitalization time an average of only two days.

One disadvantage of immediate postpartum sterilization is that occasionally a congenital or acquired disease or infection is not recognized in the newborn during the first twenty-four hours of life. It is not unusual for a previously healthy baby to suddenly become ill. The effects of such a tragedy will only be compounded if irreversible sterilization has been performed prematurely.

Emotionally, a woman may believe that she wants sterilization following a difficult nine months of pregnancy. However, she may later regret the decision. In one study, a significant number of women who requested postpartum sterilization, but had surgery delayed for various reasons, declined to undergo the operation when given the opportunity at a later date.

If I later decide I want more children, what are the chances of reconstructive surgery following abdominal tubal ligation?

In the hands of the best surgeons the success rate will be no higher than 40 percent. Attaching the two ends of the tube is often difficult because each end has a different diameter. Often it is impossible to bring the two ends together, and in this situation the segment of tube farthest from the uterus is transplanted directly into the endometrial cavity. Successful pregnancy following this technique occurs in less than 20 percent of those women operated on. When pregnancy does occur following reconstructive surgery, the chances of tubal pregnancy may be as great as 10 to 15 percent of the total pregnancy rate. Tubal reconstruction should be performed only by a gynecologist who specializes in this type of surgery.

Dr. Robert M. L. Winston of London's Hammersmith Hospital has recently reported on the use of microsurgery in joining the two ends of the separated tube. In this operation, surgery is performed while viewing the operative area under a microscope. The method is quite similar to that used in reversing a previous vasectomy (see Chapter 11), and requires a great deal of surgical expertise and training. To date, of 30 women who have undergone this surgery, 23 have become pregnant.

What is a "minilap"?

A "minilap," or minilaparotomy, is a new method of interval abdominal tubal ligation. It is gaining great popularity in the United States, as well as in other countries throughout the world. In this procedure, an instrument is inserted through the cervix and into the uterine cavity in order to push the uterus up against the lower abdominal wall. A one-inch skin incision is then made directly over the top of the elevated uterus. The tubes are then brought up into the operative field and are either tied or cut (Figure 9–4).

A special retractor, resembling a small vaginal speculum, may be inserted through the incision to aid in visualizing both tubes (Figure 9–5).

Though sufficient data has not been accumulated on "minilaps," one great advantage is that they may be performed under local anesthesia as outpatient procedures, so you can go home four to six hours later. Because the minilap does not require elaborate surgical equipment, it has been used to great advantage in indigent countries such as India and Thailand, where it is routinely performed by trained technicians rather than doctors. Recently, Planned Parenthood and the Association for Voluntary Sterilization announced that they are jointly backing a $300,000 program to establish five minilap pilot programs in the United States. Surgery will be performed in outpatient clinics, such as Planned Parenthood centers, under local anesthesia.

Potential disadvantages are perforation of the uterus with the elevating instrument, difficulties encountered with obese women, and the possibility of intestinal or bladder injury if either of these organs happens to lie between the skin and the top of the uterus when the incision is made. Chronic pel-

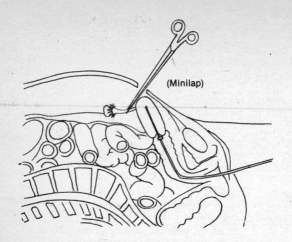

(Minilap)

Figure 9-4. *"Minilap" Technique*

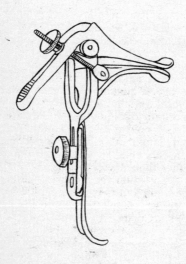

Figure 9-5. *Special Retractor for "Minilap"*

vic infection, endometriosis, and previous extensive intestinal or urinary bladder surgery appear to be contraindications to using a "minilap."

What is laparoscopy?
A *laparoscope* is an instrument with a diameter slightly larger than a pencil. It contains a powerful light source which, when inserted through the navel, allows visualization of the abdominal and pelvic contents.

The injection of two or more liters of carbon dioxide or nitrous oxide gas into the abdomen moves the intestine out of the lower pelvis and makes viewing of the pelvic organs easier. Specially designed instruments can then be passed through the laparoscope to accomplish such procedures as tubal sterilization; biopsy of the overy, liver, or intestinal wall; removal of misplaced IUDs; diagnosis of tubal pregnancy; and evaluation and treatment of infertility, pelvic pain, and endometriosis (see page 58).

When the laparoscopic procedure is completed, the carbon dioxide is removed from the abdomen, and the tiny incision in the navel is closed with one absorbable suture. The suture is then covered with a Band-aid—hence the name "Band-aid surgery." (Another synonym for laparoscopy is "belly-button surgery".)

Though newspaper and television coverage of laparoscopic surgery during the past six years has been spectacular, few people realize that the first laparoscopy was actually performed in 1806 by Philip Brozzini. His light source was a candle and his laparoscope was a urological cystoscope. Throughout the years others have attempted laparoscopy, but it was the recent refinement of the optical equipment and light source which allowed for its popularity today.

How does laparoscopy compare with other methods of tubal sterilization?
When compared with all other forms of tubal sterilization, the total complication rates of less than 3 per cent are unmatched. In addition, the pregnancy rate following laparoscopy is less than 1 per 1,000 women. Postoperative hospitalization is usually less than one day, and total recovery time ranges from zero to five days. Because of this, hospital costs are at least one-third less than for traditional abdominal tubal ligation.

What are the details of the laparoscopic sterilization procedure?

Often doctors simply fail to take the time to explain the details of laparoscopic procedures to their patients. Consequently, you may be uninformed about and unprepared for some of the events which take place before, during, and after surgery. This may be particularly upsetting for those women having laparoscopy performed under local anesthesia.

As with all abdominal surgical techniques, don't eat or drink for eight hours prior to laparoscopy. Intramuscular premedication is given one hour before surgery and usually consists of a tranquilizer combined with atropine. The latter drug is used to dry up excessive secretions in the mouth and throat which could cause breathing problems when general anesthesia is used. Atropine is also given to women who are having local anesthesia, so that in an emergency the anesthesiologist can switch to general anesthesia without delay.

Some doctors instruct their patients to take an enema at home, and others have it administered to their patients in the hospital prior to surgery. Personally, I have found no difference in the degree of surgical difficulty between women who have had an enema and those who have not. Another point of minor controversy is whether or not to empty the urinary bladder with a rubber catheter immediately prior to surgery. An empty bladder is essential for adequate visualization of the uterus, but many doctors believe that it can be achieved simply by having a woman urinate immediately prior to the operation. A good laparoscopist should easily complete the procedure long before the bladder fills with urine again. For women with a history of chronic recurrent urinary tract infections, avoiding catheter use prevents the reintroduction of potentially infectious bacteria into the bladder.

The position assumed on the operating table is similar to that of a vaginal examination, except that your legs rest in stirrups that are far more comfortable than those found in most doctors' offices. The table is tilted at an angle so that your head is lower than the rest of your body. A metallic ground plate may be placed securely around the thigh and connected to the cautery machine via a wire. The newer bipolar cautery does not require a ground plate. Your abdomen, especially your navel, is throughly cleaned with an antiseptic solution.

An instrument is then attached to the cervix which, when moved in different directions during laparoscopy, allows visualization of the uterus, tubes, and ovaries. Though several instruments have been devised for this purpose, the Semm cannula, which creates a suction cup on the cervix, appears to be the safest and the least likely to traumatize the cervix or perforate the uterus (Figure 9–6). Unexplained light vaginal bleeding following laparoscopy is almost always due to the use of the cervical cannula and shouldn't alarm you.

The next step is the injection of novocaine or xylocaine, if local anesthesia is used. Liberal amounts are injected around the skin of the navel and the underlying tissues. Usually, the first needle stick will hurt but subsequent ones will not. If general anesthesia is preferred, an intravenous barbiturate rapidly puts you to sleep, and then the anesthesiologist administers a light anesthetic gas by mask. For maximum safety, a tube must be inserted into the trachea (windpipe) after sleep is induced; this allows the anesthesiologist to control respiration. The anesthesiologist can now be totally prepared to handle any heart and respiratory irregularities, which have in rare instances been reported when the abdomen is filled with the carbon dioxide gas. (Because of this possibility, it is wise to have an anesthesiologist standing nearby even when laparoscopy is performed under

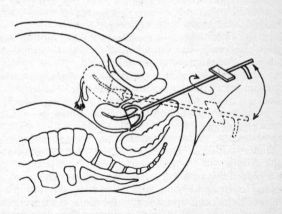

Figure 9-6.   Semm Cannula

local anesthesia.) You may experience a slight sore throat postoperatively when general anesthesia is given. This is due to the irritation of the tube placed in the trachea, and it usually subsides within two days.

After anesthesia is deep enough, a tiny incision is made at the lower border of the navel. Through it, a long, thin Verres needle is inserted into the abdominal cavity while the skin is elevated with towel clips. Elevating the skin in this manner prevents the Verres needle from injuring the intestine. It is the two towel clips which temporarily leave four tiny holes around the navel following laparoscopy.

The Verres needle is then attached to a tube, which in turn is connected to a machine containing either carbon dioxide or nitrous oxide gas. The gas is then run through the tubing and into the abdomen at a rate of one liter per minute. As the abdomen fills with gas, it becomes firm and tense and actually sounds like a drum when tapped. For a woman of average build, two liters is usually all that is required. (A third liter is usually needed for an obese woman.) If you are awake during laparoscopy, you are likely to experience mild to moderate discomfort and bloating as the gas fills the abdomen. In rare cases, the abdominal discomfort may be bothersome.

Following the injection of the gas, a large, sharp metal instrument called a trocar (Figure 9–7), encased in an electrically nonconductive sleeve, is inserted through the umbilicus and into the abdominal cavity.

Successful placement is confirmed by an audible rush of the previously injected gas when the trocar is removed and the sleeve is left in the abdominal cavity.

The laparoscope, which contains an electrocoagulating forceps, is then inserted through the sleeve. The light source is attached to the laparoscope, as is the tubing, which provides a constant flow of carbon dioxide or nitrous oxide from the machine (Figure 9–8).

Many doctors prefer the older, two-incision technique, in which the second incision is made in the lower abdomen with a smaller trocar and sleeve. The electrocoagulator is then inserted through the second incision (Figure 9–9).

If the two-incision technique is used, xylocaine must first be injected into the second site. Even with adequate local anesthesia, the second incision is often responsible for more discomfort than the first incision. At the present time, 70 percent of doctors doing laparoscopy prefer the two-incision

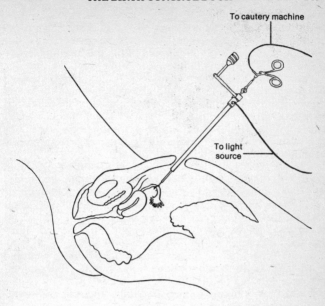

Figure 9-7.   Insertion of Trocar

technique, while 30 percent favor the newer, single-incision method. This is in sharp contrast to 1971, when the percentages were 90 and 10 respectively.

The Fallopian tube is then grasped with the coagulation forceps (Figure 9–10).

After the surgeon is sure that there is no intestine near the tube in danger of being accidentally burned, she or he presses on a foot pedal which activates an electrical current from the cautery machine. The current passes through the coagulation forceps and to the Fallopian tube (Figure 9–11). Repeated short bursts of electricity, initiated with each push of the foot pedal, cause the tube to burn and turn white. By applying slight upward traction on the forceps, the surgeon is then able to break the tube in half (Figure 9–12). Some doctors prefer to burn the tubes in one or several locations, rather than separate them.

After the tubes are coagulated, the surgeon checks that

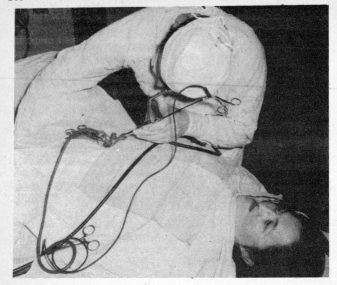

Figure 9-8.   Laparoscopy Using Single-Incision Technique

there is no bleeding from the arteries and veins in the mesosalpinx (see Figure 9–2). The surgeon then releases as much gas as possible from the abdomen by opening a valve on the sleeve and by manually compressing the abdomen. The instruments are removed, and the incision or incisions are closed with a chromic catgut absorbable suture and covered with one or two Band-aids.

Regardless of the type of anesthesia used, practically all women can leave the hospital within eight hours. The Band-aid may be removed on the day following surgery. Occasionally there will be a slight tenderness, redness, or leakage of fluid from the incision. Hot water soaks applied three times a day practically always clear up this minor infection.

What are the potential complications of laparoscopic sterilization?

Practically all of the complications associated with the procedure may be avoided if the person performing the surgery is a skilled, experienced, and conscientious surgeon. A doctor

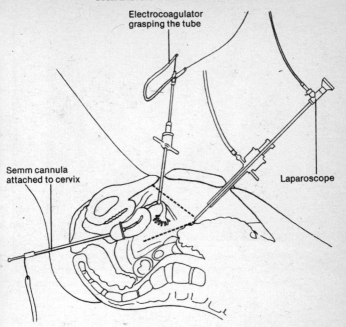

Figure 9-9. Two-Incision Laparoscopic Technique

with inadequate training, or one who performs laparoscopy only on rare occasions, never develops the facility for the procedure.

To achieve the best possible results, one also needs optimum surgical conditions—the best equipment, a competent anesthesiologist, and experienced nursing personnel.

Franklin D. Loffer and David Pent, in their excellent review of 32,719 laparoscopies, have analyzed possible complications of the operation in detail. The most common complication that they noted was cardiac irregularity resulting from the injection of gas into the abdomen. A total of 242 women, or 7.4 per 1,000 laparoscopies, had variations of this problem. Of this group, 85 women experienced changes in their pulse rate, 50 had alterations in their blood pressure, and 10 suffered cardiac arrest. Three of the 10 women died.

Figure 9-10.   Actual View of Fallopian Tube Being Grasped
with Coagulation Forceps as Seen Through the Laparoscope

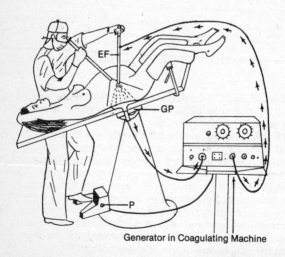

EF

GP

P

Generator in Coagulating Machine

Figure 9-11.   Electrical Circuit for Laparoscopic Coagulation

Figure 9-12.   Coagulated and Separated Ends of the Fallopian Tube as Seen Through the Laparoscope

All of these complications occur more often with carbon dioxide than with nitrous oxide. They are believed to be due to excessive amounts of the gas accumulating within the body and not being eliminated by the usual mechanism of rapid breathing.

Cardiac arrest caused by carbon dioxide accumulation may be prevented by the doctor's taking some very simple precautions. The first is not to instill excessive amounts of carbon dioxide in the abdomen. Two liters is usually sufficient, and anything more than three liters is excessive. Second, all patients should have their heartbeat monitored by the anesthesiologist throughout the procedure. This is indispensable for detecting early pulse irregularities, which occur long before the cardiac arrest. (It is interesting to note that in a 1975 survey of gynecologists performing laparoscopy, cardiac monitors were present in 91 percent of the operating rooms. However, a shocking 29 percent of these doctors did not make use of the monitor.)

When an irregularity of the pulse is noted in a patient

under general anesthesia, the anesthesiologist is usually able to correct the problem by increasing the respiratory rate, thus enabling the patient to breathe off the excessive amounts of carbon dioxide. The laparoscopist may also help correct these symptoms by releasing some of the carbon dioxide from the abdomen.

A fairly common and usually harmless complication may occur when the Verres needle is not placed correctly. If it lies above, rather than in, the abdominal cavity, the carbon dioxide may accidentally enter this area. It is more likely to happen in obese women and may be corrected by removing the needle and allowing fifteen minutes for the gas to absorb.

Very rarely, even with the needle in the correct location, the gas may dissect from the abdominal cavity into the chest cavity near the heart, resulting in an acute emergency. Gas may also find its way to the outside of the lung, causing it to collapse. Even rarer is the inadvertent injection of gas into a blood vessel. The gas may then be carried to the heart and lung as an embolus (see Pages 36–37) causing instant death. If your doctor adheres to those simple precautions, the likelihood of complications appears remote.

What is the incidence of bleeding complications?
Loffer and Pent reported 208 bleeding complications, or 6.4 per 1,000 women. Of those, 168 women experienced bleeding from the mesosalpinx. The bleeding was controlled with further coagulation in 101 women, but 67 required exploratory surgery to control the bleeding. This complication usually occurs when a doctor tries to break the tube before coagulating it thoroughly. In a similar, though smaller, study, it was noted that uncontrolled mesosalpinx bleeding was the most common complication requiring exploratory surgery. For this reason, many doctors coagulate the tube extensively in one or more areas without breaking it. The subsequent pregnancy rates following this coagulation-only method appear to be no higher than when the tube is coagulated and then broken.

Among the group who experienced bleeding, in 15 women the site was under the skin where the trocar was placed. It was easily controlled with a pressure bandage or a single suture.

Fatal or near-fatal bleeding, due to perforation of a major

blood vessel with a trocar, is usually reported as being very rare. When it does occur, the aorta and its large branch called the *iliac artery* are most likely to be damaged, and death from blood loss can be instant.

Dr. A. Jefferson Penfield, in a 1976 report, claims that major blood-vessel injury is not as rare as is generally believed. He questioned twenty-five experienced laparoscopists, and twelve of them reported knowledge of major vascular injury to nineteen patients. Three of those nineteen women died as a result of the hemorrhage. Of the nineteen injuries, the aorta was punctured eight times and the iliac artery seven. In sixteen of the nineteen injuries the procedure was performed by either a junior resident or a gynecologist doing one of his first cases.

Can the trocar ever cause perforation of the stomach or intestine?

Perforation may occur with both the Verres needle and the large trocar. Loffer and Pent report that it happens less than three times per one thousand operations. The stomach is usually the most common site of injury, followed by the large and small intestine. The stomach may be perforated when it is distended with swallowed air, or filled with gas breathed into it by the anesthesiologist when a tracheal tube is not inserted beforehand.

If the Verres needle perforates the stomach, and carbon dioxide or nitrous oxide is then injected, the elevated pressures on the gas gauge should arouse the doctor's suspicions that the needle is incorrectly placed. Often the anesthesiologist notes that the patient is passing tremendous amounts of gas out through her mouth. If perforation is suspected, the Verres needle may be removed and the procedure attempted again with a new sterile needle. Often the anesthesiologist can help the situation by first emptying the stomach and intestine of gas with a stomach tube.

The hole created in the stomach or intestine with a Verres needle will seal itself off and need not be sutured. However, when the larger trocar accidentally perforates, exploratory surgery is mandatory because a hole of that size is far too big to close by itself. It is a good idea for the doctor to leave the trocar in place rather than remove it prior to surgery. In this way, she or he can readily identify the exact perforation site as well as the extent of the damage.

Are accidental electrial burns a serious complication of laparoscopy?

In Loffer and Pent's study of 32,719 laparoscopies, there were 71 electrical accidents, or 2.2 per 1,000 tubal sterilizations. Burns resulting from cauterization usually damage either the skin of the abdomen, or the lining of the small or large intestine. In a 1975 survey conducted by the American Association of Gynecologic Laparoscopists, a total of 38 intestinal burns were recorded among 76,842 women, or .5 per 1,000 operations. In this study and others, a higher percentage of intestinal burns was noted when the single-incision technique was used. Burns of the skin, however, occur almost exclusively with the two-incision method.

Though Dr. Clifford Wheeless, in his excellent review, noted no increased incidence of intestinal injury while using local anesthesia, many doctors believe that a woman's slightest movement at the time of tubal coagulation may increase the chances of such injury. Skin burns are usually noted immediately at the time of surgery. However, most burns of the intestine are not detected until symptoms of bowel perforation appear. This may take anywhere from eighteen hours to fourteen days following the procedure. Early symptoms are vague lower abdominal pain and a low-grade fever, often misdiagnosed as tubal infection. Treatment consists of exploratory surgery and removal of the damaged segment of intestine.

How can the chance of burns be reduced?

A burn related to use of worn-out or faulty equipment is inexcusable. Otherwise, the best way to prevent burn injury is to retain an experienced and skillful laparoscopist.

Drs. Jacques-E. Rioux and Diogène Cloutier of Quebec have devised a safer coagulating system, named *bipolar cautery*. With their new method, the current travels from one prong of the coagulating forceps to the other. The only tissue destroyed is that which lies between the two prongs (Figure 9–3). In some experimental models the control switch is in the handle of the forceps, and cauterization is begun when the doctor pushes a button in the handle. This eliminates the possiblity of accidentally stepping on the foot pedal and causing an electrical burn. With bipolar cautery the amount of current used to achieve coagulation is only a fraction of that used by the standard method, and therefore adds to the

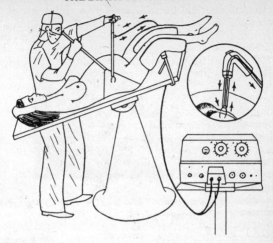

Figure 9-13. ˊ Bipolar Cautery

safety of this device. At the present time, bipolar cautery is available for both the one- and the two-incision laparoscopes.

Is there a laparoscope that can avoid all hazards of coagulation injury?

In 1974, Dr. In Bae Yoon of Johns Hopkins introduced the Falope Ring technique of tubal sterilization as a means of eliminating the hazards of electrocoagulation. The Falope Ring is actually a tiny silicone rubber band which is fitted over a special laparoscope. The forceps of this laparoscope grasp a segment of the tube and pull it up (Figure 9–14).

The Falope Ring is then pushed down over the segment of tube, causing occlusion (Figure 9–15).

By 1975, more than 350 Falope Ring sterilizations had been performed at Johns Hopkins, and 1,800 worldwide, without a single pregnancy reported. In addition to eliminating the thermal hazards, the Falope Ring also has the advantage of destroying less tubal tissue than the electrocoagulator. If you want corrective tubal surgery at a later date, because you decide you want more children, it appears

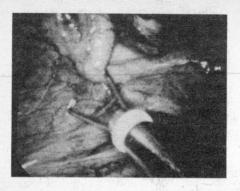

Figure 9-14. Grasping the Tube and Pulling It Up with the Falope Ring Laparoscope

that this method would have a greater reversibility rate than electrocoagulation. (The chances of successful pregnancy following surgery after electrocoagulation are less than 10 percent.) However, it is still too early to determine if this hypothesis is correct.

Many women erroneously believe that Falope Ring sterilization is definitely reversible. Never undergo the operation under this false assumption.

Are there any complications of Falope Ring surgery?

Three complications appear directly related to the procedure. The first is that 15 to 20 percent of women report a significant degree of lower abdominal cramping for twenty-four to forty-eight hours after the operation, a rare complaint following cauterization. The cramping is probably due to the cutting off of the blood supply at the site of the Ring. This problem may be alleviated if your doctor dips each Falope Ring in an anesthetic xylocaine jelly before putting it on the tubes.

Another, more serious problem related to the technique is bleeding in the mesosalpinx after inadvertent cutting of the tube while trying to pull it up with a forceps. There have been problems in which the tube has been pulled free from the mesosalpinx while the surgeon was trying to slide the

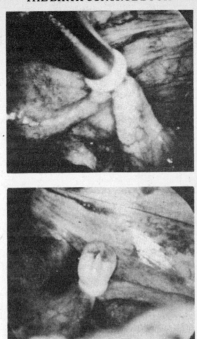

Figure 9-15.   Sliding the Falope Ring over the Tube and Final Result

Falope Ring into the correct position. Such bleeding can be quite serious but can usually be controlled with cauterization, the one method which users of the Falope Ring are trying to avoid. To date, the frequency of these complications has not been determined, but in one large study conducted by the American Association of Gynecologic Laparoscopists, the incidence of hemorrhage was 24 women per 1000 sterilizations. Of these, 5 per 1000 required exploratory surgery to control the bleeding. Comparison figures noted with standard tubal coagulation in this study were 4 per 1000 for tubal hemorrhage of which only .5 per 1000 necessitated exploratory surgery.

Though subsequent uterine pregnancy does not appear to be a serious complication following Falope Ring sterilization, it has been noted that the incidence of ectopic pregnancy in the Fallopian tube (see Page 90–91) may be significantly higher when compared to other methods. The incidence of this potentially serious complication has been reported at 2.3 per 1000 women having Falope Ring surgery.

You must remember that Falope Ring surgery has been used only by skilled physicians in several large medical centers. I worry about the number of bleeding problems that will be encountered when the Falope Ring reaches physicians with less dexterity and experience.

What is the chance of postoperative infection following laparoscopy?

Infection following laparoscopy is extremely rare, with 1.4 per 1,000 women. Most often it is only a minor inflammation at the navel where the suture was placed. Successful treatment consists of hot, wet compresses applied three times a day. Occasionally, antibiotics are also necessary.

Pelvic infections are even rarer and usually occur as a flare-up of an old infection already present in the tube at the time of the laparoscopy. Therefore many doctors prescribe postoperative antibiotics to those women noted to have evidence of chronic pelvic inflammation.

Why does pregnancy occur following laparoscopic sterilization?

As previously mentioned, less than one woman per one thousand undergoing the procedure subsequently become pregnant. As experience has been gained with the technique each year, the pregnancy rates have dropped significantly (Table 9–1). As noted in Table 9–1, the chances of subsequent pregnancy is lower when the two-incision technique is used.

Sixteen of the forty-four pregnancies following laparoscopic sterilization noted by Loffer and Pent were due to misidentification of structures by the novice laparoscopist, resulting in coagulation of the round ligament supporting the uterus rather than the tube. Rarely, despite the fact that the tube is adequately burned, a new opening is formed allowing the egg to pass through and become fertilized.

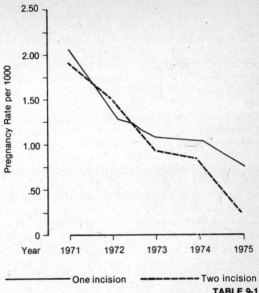

One incision ——————— Two incision

TABLE 9-1

Is local or general anesthesia preferred for laparoscopic sterilization?

In 1974, approximately 95 percent of all laparoscopic sterilizations were performed under general anesthesia. Though the current percentages are not available, I doubt that the number of doctors using local anesthesia has increased significantly.

The reason why most doctors prefer general anesthesia is that in the event of a rare cardiac or respiratory catastrophe, the respirations are more easily controlled with a tracheal tube already in place. Secondly, if emergency surgery is needed because of a problem such as hemorrhage, no delay is encountered. Many doctors fear that a woman may move when the tubes are grasped and coagulated under local anesthesia. Another advantage of general anesthesia—rarely mentioned by doctors, including myself—is that the doctor avoids a distracting conversation with an inquisitive or apprehensive patient while laparoscopy is being performed.

Though I am in full sympathy with all of a woman's questions and concerns, it would be irresponsible to answer questions during the operation if doing so might adversely affect my performance as a surgeon.

The one definite advantage of local anesthesia is the avoidance of the rare but definite risk that may be encountered with general anesthesia (see Page 173).

How often does a doctor's attempt at laparoscopic sterilization fail?

For a variety of reasons, a doctor may be unable to successfully accomplish the operation six or seven times per one thousand procedures attempted. The failed-laparoscopy rate depends primarily on the skill of the doctor as well as the presence of other conditions such as infection, endometriosis, extreme obesity, and adhesions secondary to previous surgery. Any of these may prevent safe visualization and isolation of the tubes for coagulation. If there is even the slightest risk of an intestinal burn, the procedure should be abandoned.

Though the likelihood of failure is minimal, you and your doctor must fully agree beforehand on the course of action to be taken in the event that it becomes a reality. Some women may want the doctor to proceed with the standard abdominal tubal ligation, but others elect not to undergo so formidable an operation, requiring several days of hospitalization and added expense.

How can I determine if a doctor is a good laparoscopist?

The most accurate source of information is a recommendation from an operating room nurse, a resident in obstetrics and gynecology at the particular hospital, or an anesthesiologist who works with each of the gynecologists on a daily basis. Unfortunately, not all women are lucky enough to have access to this inside information.

As in the case of selecting a doctor to perform an abortion (see Page 174), certification by the American Board of Obstetrics and Gynecology is no assurance of one's manual dexterity. However, the certificate demonstrates a certain amount of interest and determination on the part of the doctor in mastering the academic side of the specialty. There are surgeons and family practitioners who perform laparoscopy, but it is wise to investigate the frequency with which they do this. As with most surgical techniques, the experience of the operator is reflected in the ease with which the procedure is performed. The doctor who has performed several hundred laparoscopies at a rate of two or more a week is far more likely to be proficient than the occasional operator. The only way to find out is to ask your doctor how much experience he or she has had.

The American Association of Gynecologic Laparoscopists (AAGL) is a medical organization of physicians interested in laparoscopy. Members of AAGL receive periodic reprints of current literature in the area of laparoscopy. Case reports of serious laparoscopic complications are forwarded to members, and discussed at periodic meetings. Though the aims of the organization are admirable, membership is based not on a doctor's ability, but only on the completion of a short application form and a check for seventy-five dollars. Following acceptance into AAGL the performance of a member is not monitored, and there is no disciplining of doctors whose performance is less than adequate.

There is a book entitled *Directory of Medical Specialists* which is usually available at most local libraries. This valuable source of information lists those doctors who are Board-certified in all the various medical specialties and also provides the reader with the doctor's age, all previous medical training, and present hospital affiliations.

Are there any women who should not undergo laparoscopy?
Commonly listed contraindications to laparoscopy include intestinal obstruction, extensive abdominal malignancy or tuberculosis, previous abdominal surgery, cardiac and respiratory disease, obesity, and peritonitis (inflammation of the abdominal cavity). With the exception of the first two, the contraindications are relative rather than absolute, depending upon the severity of the disease and expertise of the laparoscopist.

For example, 11 to 33 percent of all women requesting sterilization have had previous abdominal surgery for Cesarean section, ovarian cyst, appendectomy, or ectopic pregnancy. Adhesions or scar tissue from such surgery usually should not discourage a doctor from successfully performing laparoscopy. However, if the previous surgery was for a ruptured appendix or extensive intestinal disease, such as advanced ulcerative colitis or regional ileitis, laparoscopy is best avoided.

If you have heart or respiratory disease that doesn't severely limit your activity, you'll usually tolerate laparoscopy well. Obviously, consultation with a cardiologist should precede all such laparoscopies. Personally, I believe that if you have a severe cardiac condition, laparoscopy is just too dangerous because of the potentially harmful effects of carbon dioxide on your heart and your restricted ability to breathe in a head-down position with the abdomen filled with gas.

Obesity is often listed as a contraindication to laparoscopy, but quite often doctors are pleasantly surprised at the ease with which it may be accomplished. Actually, the total weight is of less significance than the distribution of body fat, and a doctor may encounter more difficulty in a 180-pound woman with excess abdominal fat than in a 230-pound woman of the same height whose weight is more evenly distributed. An obese woman may wish to explore the possibility of laparoscopy before undergoing another method of tubal ligation.

Several reports from Scandinavia initially confirmed that laparoscopy may be safely performed on women with peritonitis confined to the lower abdomen. This may be helpful in differentiating between acute inflammation of the tubes and appendicitis. The former condition is best treated with antibiotics, and exploratory surgery for a mistaken diagnosis of appendicitis may thus be avoided. When peritonitis is more extensive and involves the upper abdomen, laparoscopy is contraindicated.

Is it dangerous for a woman with a hernia to undergo laparoscopy?

Many doctors and their patients are confused about the dangers of laparoscopy in the presence of a hernia or previous hernia repair. The three types of hernia—*umbilical, inguinal,* and *hiatal*—each present their own unique problems for the laparoscopist.

An umbilical hernia is an outward bulge of the navel caused by a weakness in the abdominal wall. These hernias are more common in females than in males, and are often associated with obesity and previous pregnancies. Umbilical hernias are potentially serious because they may contain intestinal contents in 60 percent of all cases. To avoid intestinal injury, the Verres needle and trocar should never be inserted into the umbilicus in the presence of a hernia. Instead, a safer site two inches below the navel may be selected.

Contrary to popular belief, the presence of a hernia in the inguinal area or groin area does not contraindicate laparoscopy. If a two-incision technique is used, the trocar should be placed on the side of the abdomen opposite the hernia.

Many doctors don't perform laparoscopy on women who have had previous corrective surgery for an inguinal hernia for fear that the pressure of the carbon dioxide will "blow out" the repair. It has been amply demonstrated that this reasoning is faulty, because the intraabdominal pressure produced by an ordinary sneeze is far greater than that caused by two to three liters of gas in the abdomen.

A hiatal hernia is a condition in which part of the stomach tends to slip through a small opening between the abdominal and chest cavities. It may be present in as many as 3 percent of the adult population, often without any symptoms. Confirmation of hiatal hernia is made by an upper gastrointestinal X-ray. When symptoms do exist, they include heartburn and upper abdominal and chest discomfort. When gas is injected into the abdomen, it can theoretically worsen the condition by forcing the stomach and abdominal contents into the chest cavity. That in turn may cause respiratory and cardiac distress. In reality, the only hiatal hernias of concern to the laparoscopist are those which are so large that they will always cause symptoms necessitating surgical repair. A hiatal hernia of this degree exists in less than one woman out of every two thousand requesting laparoscopy. Wheeless has performed laparoscopy without incident on thirty women with X-ray confirmation of hiatal hernia.

Can laparoscopic tubal coagulation be performed instead of traditional abdominal tubal ligation in the days immediately following childbirth?

Despite the impressive statistics from Cook County Hospital in Chicago and several other institutions, most doctors have never performed this operation postpartum. Some doctors even claim that it is hazardous. My own personal eperience with the technique on fifty postpartum women at Norwalk

Hospital has been excellent. There have been no complications, and all patients have experienced significantly less discomfort and a shorter hospitalization than those undergoing the abdominal procedure. There is also the added benefit of no visible scar. One great advantage of the procedure over the abdominal postpartum operation is that it may be performed on the second or third day following delivery rather than immediately after. This gives a woman more time to decide if she really wants the operation. Furthermore, if the newborn appears healthy at birth but develops serious complications after the first twenty-four hours, a hasty and tragic decision can be averted. With abdominal tubal ligation, both you and your doctor are rushed to have the surgery performed immediately following delivery in order to shorten the total time spent in the hospital.

Can laparoscopic sterilization be performed at the time of an abortion?
Several studies have demonstrated that combining the two procedures does not significantly increase the risk over that present when each is done separately. The abortion is always done first, followed by the sterilization.

It is unethical for a doctor to set any preconditions for your abortion. Too many doctors refuse to perform an abortion unless you also consent to tubal sterilization. Such conduct should be reported to the physician's county medical society.

How soon after laparoscopic tubal ligation can I resume intercourse?
Following an uncomplicated laparoscopic sterilization, it is okay to have intercourse the same day. Chest and shoulder-top pain appear to be the main factors limiting your enthusiasm for such activity. The cause of the pain is the presence of a small pocket of gas which remains in the abdomen following laparoscopy. Usually the gas dissolves within two days, but it can last for six or seven days. When the gas lies under the abdominal diaphragm, it stimulates a nerve that carries pain messages from the diaphragm to the chest and shoulders. This "referred" pain can be bothersome and may limit activity for as long as one week.

In their enthusiasm to "sell" this operation, gynecologists

often minimize the degree of postoperative discomfort. Though I have known patients who have actually played tennis or worked a full eight hours on the day following surgery, such rapid recovery is unusual. For the vast majority of women, some residual discomfort remains in the navel, shoulders, or chest for three to five days.

After what age should laparoscopic tubal coagulation no longer be performed?

Fertility greatly diminishes after the age of forty-seven, even if menses remain fairly normal. For this reason I prefer not to perform laparoscopic sterilization beyond this age. Instead I encourage use of safe contraceptive measures such as the diaphragm, condom, and foam. Though laparoscopy is a relatively safe procedure, I still believe that the risk is just too great for a woman beyond this age who most probably is unable to conceive.

VAGINAL TUBAL LIGATION

How is a vaginal tubal ligation performed?

Colpotomy refers to an incision made into the vagina at a point just behind the cervix. The lower part of the abdominal cavity, called the *cul-de-sac*, may be easily entered through such an incision (Figure 9–16).

When colpotomy is performed by a skilled gynecologist, the tubes may be easily brought out through the incision and tied (Figure 9–17).

The advantages of vaginal tubal ligation are that it may be performed under either local or general anesthesia, and it is cosmetically desirable because there is no abdominal scar. Postoperatively, the time spent in the hospital may be as little as one day, though the average stay is usually four days. Because the total hospital stay is shorter, the expense is less than that of the abdominal tubal ligation method. The postoperative time away from work has been reported as two to four weeks by some researchers, though as many as 50 percent of women undergoing the operation take longer to recover (Table 9–2).

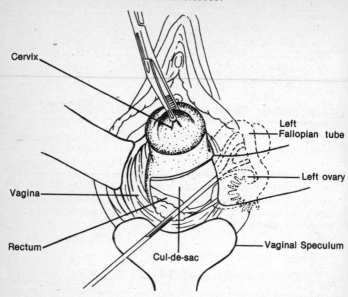

Figure 9-16. Entering the Abdominal Cavity Through the Vagina (Colpotomy)

Are there certain women who should not undergo vaginal tubal ligation?

This operation is contraindicated if you have an enlarged uterus, because the tubes are too far removed from the vaginal incision. For the same reason, vaginal tubal ligation is never performed immediately postpartum.

If you have had previous pelvic or abdominal surgery, scarring or adhesions may prevent easy entry into the cul-de-sac and adequate visualization of the tubes. A history of chronic and acute pelvic infection, as well as severe endometriosis (see Page 58), also increases the dangers of colpotomy.

Colpotomy is easier if you have experienced previous childbirth, because the ligaments supporting the uterus may be somewhat relaxed. This allows for easier manipulation of the uterus during the operation. For the woman who has

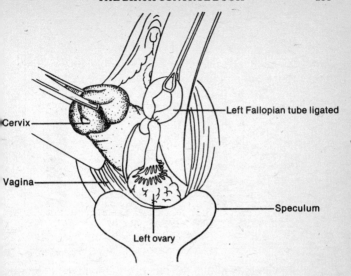

Figure 9-17. Tying the Tubes Through the Vagina (Colpotomy)

never borne children, the operation will often be less than satisfactory due to the lack of uterine relaxation and movement.

What are the complications of vaginal tubal ligation via colpotomy?

Several studies have demonstrated a significant number of serious postoperative pelvic infections and hemorrhage even when colpotomy is performed by a skilled gynecological surgeon. In the hands of a novice, the complication rate may be extremely high.

In one study of five-hundred tubal ligations, twenty-six women had complications in the immediate postoperative period. Of these twenty-six women, thirteen required hospitalization for either pelvic pain, vaginal bleeding, or pelvic infection. Late complications were present in a total of twenty-eight women, including eighteen with chronic pelvic infection and five with chronic pelvic pain and pain with intercourse.

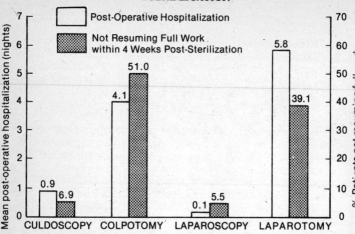

In another study of 800 women at the University of North Carolina, 4.9 percent experienced complications, while at the University of Michigan an alarming 20.9 percent of 340 women suffered immediate operative and postoperative complications such as excessive bleeding, bowel and bladder lacerations, hematoma at the operative site, and pelvic abscess. Two of the patients with pelvic abscess required hysterectomy and removal of both ovaries. Other investigators have reported similar complications with this procedure.

The point should be obvious: Vaginal tubal ligation via colpotomy may sound like an attractive operation, but it often isn't. Complications may develop 3 to 13 percent of the time, and when they do occur, they are potentially far more serious than those encountered with abdominal tubal ligation.

Finally, postoperative pregnancy rates of between .5 and 2 percent for vaginal tubal ligation are slightly higher than for the abdominal approach.

What is a culdoscopy?

A *culdoscope* is an instrument used for viewing the contents of the cul-de-sac. Vaginal tubal ligation may be performed using this instrument. The culdoscope is inserted in the same vaginal location used for colpotomy, but the incision is much smaller.

Tubal sterilization via culdoscopy (cull dos cup e) may be performed under either local or general anesthesia. Women are usually able to go home within six hours and return to work within one week following surgery. When performed by a skilled culdoscopist, the risks of infection, hemorrhage, and rectal and intestinal injury are far fewer than with colpotomy.

Though it sounds like an ideal method of surgical sterilization, very few doctors are skilled at performing it. Another disadvantage concerns the problems your doctor encounters while positioning you for surgery. The knee-chest position with the head down and buttocks facing up (Figure 9–19) may be quite difficult for you to maintain, especially if surgery is unusually prolonged. If you are asleep under general anesthesia, moving you and maintaining your correct position is often a strenuous job for the operating room personnel. With the introduction of the laparoscope, many doc-

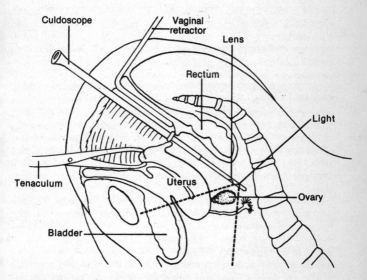

Figure 9-18.   Culdoscopy

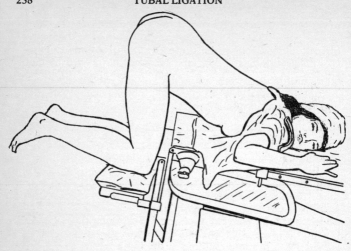

Figure 9-19.   Positioning the Patient for Culdoscopy

tors have abandoned culdoscopy as a means of tubal sterilization.

Is it true that some women experience irregular periods and abnormal vaginal bleeding following tubal ligation?
Regardless of the method of tubal sterilization used, if the blood supply to the ovary is reduced too much, irregular vaginal bleeding may result. This may happen to less than 10 percent of all women who undergo tubal sterilization. In rare cases, such bleeding may become a permanent condition which can only be remedied by hysterectomy.

One recent and very disturbing study from England has concluded that laparoscopic electrocoagulation may be responsible for delayed postoperative complications such as painful, heavy periods and pain with intercourse. In a 1975 report from the Royal Hampshire County Hospital, 257 women who underwent laparoscopic cauterization were sent a questionnaire ten to twenty-eight months following surgery. Of this group, 39 percent reported increased menstrual blood loss and 21 percent experienced greater menstrual pain. Some 10 women required hysterectomy. In a more recent follow-up report, one of the authors, Dr. A. D. Noble, said that 19 hysterectomies have now been performed. He attributes the postoperative problems to extensive disruption of the ovarian blood supply caused by cautery.

In the United States no such problems have been reported following laparoscopic sterilization of hundreds of thousands of women. Authorities in this country have questioned the validity of the Royal Hampshire Report, since it is based on too few women to be considered statistically valid.

Which method of tubal ligation involves the shortest hospital stay?

The dramatic differences between laparoscopic sterilization and other methods in terms of postoperative hospitalization and recovery times are noted in Table 9–2.

Postoperatively, is there any way to be absolutely sure that the tubes have been successfully blocked?

Twelve weeks following the procedure a hysterogram may be taken (see Page 93–94). Prior to surgery, when dye is injected through the cervix, it passes into the uterine cavity and out through the ends of the tubes and into the abdominal cavity.

Postoperatively, if surgery is successful, the dye fills the endometrial cavity and may pass a short distance up the tube. However, it should never pass to the end of the tube or into the abdominal cavity.

How am I legally protected against unwanted sterilization?

The Department of Health, Education, and Welfare has issued new regulations that state specifically that a man or woman undergoing sterilization must have a full and fair explanation of the procedure. This includes all its discomforts, risks, benefits, and alternatives. In addition, HEW regulations state that your informed consent must be documented on a special form in which all of these factors are mentioned. All consent documents must also explicitly indicate that the procedure is irreversible, that the patient was encouraged to ask questions, and that the sterilization request was voluntary. Another large restriction, which applies to all sterilizations supported by federal programs, is that the man or woman must be capable of giving effective legal consent to the procedure. That eliminates patients who are judged to be mentally incompetent, and those not of legal age. Finally, consent for sterilization must now be obtained at least seventy-two hours before the operation, so that you have ample time to reflect on your decision. For those under twenty-one, sterilization may not be performed with federal funds.

Until recently, HEW published a series of four pamphlets entitled "Your Sterilization Operation" in order to inform individuals about the procedures of laparoscopy, postpartum tubal ligation, vasectomy, and hysterectomy. One of the purposes of these pamphlets was to inform women what their legal rights are regarding these operations. The first three pamphlets are still for sale, and may be purchased by mailing thirty cents a copy to the Superintendent of Documents, Washington, D.C. 20401.

At the request of HEW Secretary Joseph Califano, the agency ceased publication and distribution of its hysterectomy booklet in November, 1977. The pamphlet had been a source of controversy because it suggested that hysterectomy solely for the purpose of sterilization was an acceptable procedure. Unfortunately, HEW has not moved to cut off funds paid to doctors who do hysterectomies in the absence of gynecological disease. In Chapter 10 we will discuss hysterectomy indications.

10

HYSTERECTOMY

Approximately 700,000 women underwent hysterectomy in the United States in 1975. By surpassing tonsillectomies, hysterectomies have now become the most frequently performed operation in the United States. It has been estimated that anywhere from 15 to 40 percent of these operations were unnecessary, though doctors have refuted this claim.

Those who accuse doctors of doing unnecessary surgery support their argument by the fact that twice as many hysterectomies are performed on insured women as on uninsured. In addition, hysterectomies are performed four times as often in the United States as in Sweden, and almost three times as often as in England and Wales. The standard explanation for the discrepancy is that medical care in these countries is paid for by the state, and doctors on a fixed salary gain no additional income by seeking unnecessary surgery. In the United States, on the other hand, the "fee-for-service" incentive and competition among too many surgeons for a limited number of patients supposedly bring out the worst in American doctors.

Gynecologists counter by saying that it is impossible for an outsider to understand the complex medical and personal relationships between patient and physician which may prompt the decision for hysterectomy. Second, they claim that the quality of life for women suffers in places like England because the doctors are too lazy to perform surgery needed to relieve distressing gynecological conditions. Finally, and rightly so, board-certified gynecologists point out that almost 35 percent of physicians practicing full-time gynecology in the United States are not certified by the American Board of Obstetrics and Gynecology. However, the noncertified physicians do three times as many operations as surgeons who are certified.

The controversy continues to rage, and as with most arguments of this magnitude, the truth undoubtedly lies somewhere in between these two extremes of opinion. The undeniable fact is that hysterectomy is a potentially dangerous procedure and responsible for the death of 600 to 1000 women per million undergoing this operation each year, or approximately 1 death per 1000 operations. Of greater concern is the fact that the number of hysterectomies performed in the United States between 1970 and 1975 rose from 602 per 100,000 women to 727 per 100,000 women. This represents an astounding increase of 21 percent (Table 10–1).

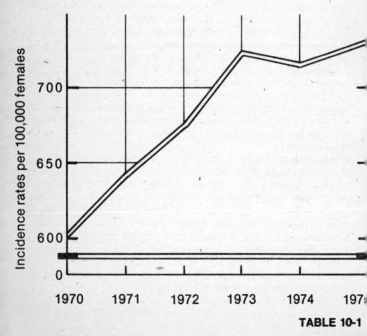

TABLE 10-1

What is a hysterectomy?
Hysterectomies are often incorrectly referred to as being *complete* or *incomplete* based on whether or not the ovaries are removed. Actually, total hysterectomy is the surgical removal of the entire uterus, including the cervix. On rare occasions, the surgeon may be unable to remove the cervix, in which case the operation is called a *supracervical* hysterectomy. Removal of both Fallopian tubes and both ovaries is termed a *bilateral salpingo-oophorectomy*, and if only the tube and the ovary on one side is removed, it is called a *unilateral salpingo-oophorectomy*.

Hysterectomy may be accomplished either with an abdominal incision or through the vagina, in which case no incision at all is required. An abdominal hysterectomy performed at the time of Cesarean section is called a *Cesarean hysterectomy*. A *postpartum hysterectomy* is one that is performed during the eight weeks following childbirth.

In the absence of gynecological disease, is hysterectomy ever justified as a method of permanent sterilization?
Sterilization is never a valid indication for either vaginal or abdominal hysterectomy. The rationale often cited for performing hysterectomy on a young woman is to prevent the 3.5 percent risk of her developing cancer of the cervix or uterus at a later date. Using the same reasoning, removal of the ovaries at the time of hysterectomy will preclude a combined cancer risk of 4.5 percent. If we continue with this deluded thinking, removal of both breasts at the age of thirty-five should prevent practically all cases of breast cancer.

Besides the risk of death, other complications of hysterectomy may be significant, including a major-complication rate estimated as high as 14 percent, and a minor-complication rate of approximately 50 percent. In one study at the University of Michigan, it was noted that 16 percent of women undergoing abdominal hysterectomy required a blood transfusion, and almost 50 percent needed antibiotics. Late complications of hysterectomy—such as depression, fatigue, painful intercourse due to scarring of the vaginal tissues, and sexual dysfunction related to emotional factors involved with the loss of the uterus—are rarely mentioned by doctors to their patients prior to surgery, though these problems do occur in a significant number of women. Your doctor's assurance that you will "bounce back" to your normal routine within a couple of weeks following surgery should be taken with a grain of salt. For some women the recuperative period will be two or three months.

Hysterectomy entails a hospital stay of seven to eight days, as well as an average of forty-two days away from work. Not to be forgotten is the doctor's fee, which may range from a low of $400 to as much as $1,500.

Is vaginal hysterectomy safer than abdominal hysterectomy?

Because a vaginal hysterectomy produces no visible scar, women are often led to believe that it is a safe, uncomplicated method of sterilization. Nothing could be further from the truth. If anything, for a young woman, the incidence of postoperative hemorrhage, pelvic infection, and urinary tract infection is probably higher than with abdominal hysterectomy. The reason for this is that the blood supply to the uterus of a menstruating woman is much greater than that following the menopause. As a result, there is less control of bleeding during surgery, which in turn predisposes the patient to secondary infection.

In 1975, Russell K. Laros, Jr. and Bruce A Work, Jr., from the University of Michigan, reported the results of 111 vaginal hysterectomies performed solely for the purpose of sterilization. When compared with other methods, such as laparoscopy, vaginal tubal ligation, and abdominal tubal ligation, the results were dismal. A total of 89 women, or 90 percent of the vaginal hysterectomy group, experienced postoperative fever. In more than 40 percent of these women the fever persisted for more than two days; 20 women suffered from pelvic infection, while 17 had urinary tract infections. Surgery was significantly prolonged and involved a blood loss greater than 500 cubic centimeters, or one unit of blood, in 18 of the 111 women. Finally, the average length of hospitalization was 9.5 days.

In summary, Laros and Work appropriately conclude, "Vaginal hysterectomy is not an ideal method of female sterilization. It is attended by significant morbidity, prolonged hospitalization, a long operating time, and significant blood loss. We feel that it should be used only in highly selected patients where there is a clear indication for hysterectomy alone and beyond the desire for sterilization."

When should a vaginal hysterectomy be performed?
The prime indication for vaginal hysterectomy should not be sterilization, but rather a condition called *uterine prolapse*. Uterine prolapse is a falling down of the entire uterus, so that the cervix actually drops into the lower vagina, and occasionally even out of the vagina. This condition usually occurs at or after the menopause, but milder degrees of prolapse are not uncommon in young women who have borne two or more children.

The cause of uterine prolapse is a loosening of the ligaments and muscles supporting the uterus. Symptoms may include pelvic pressure or heaviness, especially when standing; low backache; and the feeling that "something is falling out."

What is a cystocele?
A *cystocele* is a relaxation and bulging of the urinary bladder that often accompanies uterine prolapse (Figure 10–1).

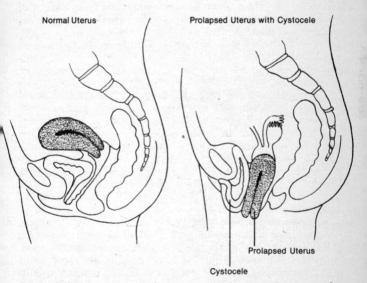

Normal Uterus

Prolapsed Uterus with Cystocele

Prolapsed Uterus

Cystocele

Figure 10-1.   Uterus in Normal and Prolapsed Position

Women with cystocele may experience recurrent urinary tract infections and frequent loss of urine while coughing, sneezing, and bearing down, such as with defecation. The loss of urine with such stress is called *stress incontinence.* Occasionally, a cystocele may be accompanied by a slight bulge below the urethral opening. This is called a *urethrocele* (Figure 10–2).

A *rectocele* is a bulge of the back wall of the vagina near the rectum and is also due to a weakening of the supporting tissues. If a woman has a hand mirror she may easily detect the presence of a cystocele or rectocele simply by bearing down while in a squatting position.

If I notice that I have a cystocele and experience rare episodes of stress incontinence, what should I do?

Many women who have given birth experience a slight degree of prolapse, cystocele, stress incontinence, or rectocele. However, it is rarely an indication for either vaginal hysterectomy, or urinary-bladder and rectocele repair. Instead, you can take steps to prevent the condition from becoming progressively worse. Obese women benefit greatly from weight reduction, while the heavy smoker who quits coughs less and thereby looses less urine. Muscle setting, or Kegel's

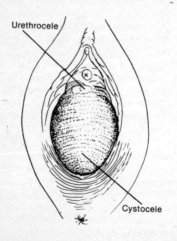

Figure 10-2.   Cystocele

exercises, are very useful in overcoming mild or moderate stress incontinence. The exercises are designed to strengthen and reeducate the muscles around the bladder and rectum. The simplest method of learning is to tighten the muscles of the buttocks as though trying to prevent the escape of feces from the anus. The same group of muscles is also used in trying to stop the flow of urine in midstream. After learning Kegel's exercises, you must practice them at least one hundred times per day for a minimum of six months. In addition, each time you pass urine, voluntarily interrupt the flow several times. If these exercises are diligently performed, you will note improvement in mild cases of stress incontinence within two months. For more severe cases, it may take at least six months or more. That is a small price to pay for avoiding major surgery.

What ulterior motives could lead doctors to prefer vaginal hysterectomy to abdominal hysterectomy?
One reason might be that all reputable hospitals have pathology departments and tissue committees that study the specimens removed during a surgical procedure. When an abdominal hysterectomy is performed, it is required that the uterus contain at least a minimal degree of pathological change to warrant its removal. If not, the physician performing the operation must explain his reasons for doing the surgery to both the tissue committee and members of his department. Repeated violations may cause the doctor to lose hospital and operating room privileges. However, a uterus removed vaginally is not reviewed by tissue committees because the presumed diagnosis is always "uterine prolapse." Sadly, it is for this reason that some doctors would attempt a difficult vaginal hysterectomy, rather than a more simple abdominal approach, when the amount of disease present is questionable.

If a woman requesting sterilization has a disease of the uterus, tubes, or ovaries, would hysterectomy then be indicated for sterilization?
That would depend upon the disease which was present, as well as its severity. In the presence of severe and incapacitating conditions such as endometriosis (see Page 58) or chronic pelvic infection, hysterectomy certainly would appear to be indicated. Preinvasive cancer of the cervix, or

carcinoma-in-situ, has a 33 percent chance of becoming the more-dangerous invasive carcinoma at a later date. Tying the tubes and leaving the cervix in a woman with that condition who has completed her childbearing appears to be less ideal than removal of the uterus.

The diagnosis of an ovarian cyst is too often used as an indication of removal of either the ovary containing the cyst, the other normal ovary, or even the uterus. Though there are many types of ovarian cysts, most of those which develop in menstruating women are not cancerous. In fact, the large percentage of those benign cysts form within the ovarian follicle or within the corpus luteum (see Pages 10–11), and are usually not larger than two inches in diameter. These cysts always disappear within one or two months. In the absence of symptoms such as severe abdominal pain, surgery is not indicated. Instead, a menstruating woman with a cyst should be reexamined after one month. If the cyst appears smaller, the chances are that it will be gone by the next month. If it is the same size or larger after one month, it usually means that it is not a follicle or corpus luteum cyst, and surgery is indicated. The one-month delay causes no harm, since practically all cysts in young women are benign. However, it avoids many unnecessary operations. Beware of the doctor who rushes to put you on his operative schedule for an ovarian cyst after only one vaginal examination.

What are fibroids?

By far the most common reason for hysterectomy in the United States is the presence of fibroid tumors of the uterus. Many of these operations could and should be avoided. Fibroids, or *leiomyomas*, are benign tumors of the uterus which have a firm to rock-hard consistency. They are found in as many as 40 percent of all women over the age of thirty-five, and their size ranges from that of a pea to that of a large grapefruit. More often than not, several fibroids are present within the same uterus (Figure 10–3).

More important than the size of these tumors is their location. A very small fibroid located just below the surface of the endometrium is often capable of causing profuse bleeding at the time of the menses, while a larger one in the uterine muscle may produce no symptoms at all.

The size of fibroids decreases, and the symptoms they produce disappear, after the menopause, since those tumors

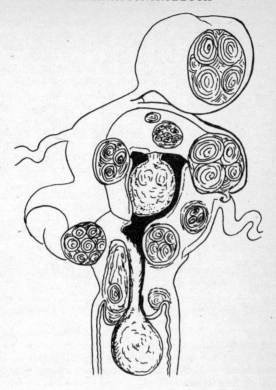

Figure 10-3.   Fibroid Tumors

are hormonally dependent. Birth control pills that contain estrogen are best avoided in a woman with a uterus enlarged with fibroids.

When fibroids cause symptoms, the most common one is heavy and prolonged menses with passage of blood clots. Occasionally when the bleeding is severe and lasts for several months, you may become anemic. Pain may accompany menstruation along with a feeling of heaviness in the pelvis which may be present throughout the entire month. Rectal pressure and urinary frequency and urgency may be caused by larger fibroids pressing on the rectum and urinary bladder.

When a hysterectomy is performed for fibroids that produce no symptoms, the requirements of the hospital's tissue committee will be met, though your best interests may not have been served. For this reason, have one or even two consultations before you undergo a hysterectomy for so-called asymptomatic fibroids. Happily, many insurance companies now pay for such consultations. In the absence of symptoms, most authorities agree that hysterectomy is indicated if the size of the enlarged uterus equals or exceeds the size of a twelve-week pregnancy. When the uterus is that big, symptoms are usually inevitable unless, of course, the menopause is imminent.

It is easy enough to determine if the size of your uterus is that of a twelve-week pregnancy or greater. With the urinary bladder emptied, a uterus of twelve week's size should be palpable above the pubic symphysis bone (see Chapter 1). Fibroid tumors of this size feel like hard, irregular bumps above the symphysis. If you can't feel the fibroids, ask your doctor to demonstrate them by pressing your hand on them during the examination.

If a fibroid suddenly grows rapidly in a young woman, what does it mean?

Assuming that you're not using birth control pills, the sudden increase in size of a fibroid may mean that you're pregnant. During pregnancy both the uterus and the fibroid grow substantially, though it is rare for a fibroid to interfere with the pregnancy.

A second possibility for the rapid fibroid growth may be that the fibroid has degenerated into a cancer. Some doctors have been known to use that argument as a scare tactic for performing hysterectomy. Actually, malignant change in a fibroid is an extremely rare event, occuring in less than one half of 1 percent of all women with fibroids. Characteristically, it occurs in the postmenopausal years and is so rare that most busy gynecologists have never seen a single patient with this type of malignancy.

Is there an alternative to hysterectomy for the young woman with fibroids who may want pregnancy at a later date?

Myomectomy, or removal of fibroids with preservation of the uterus, can usually be accomplished by making an incision over the fibroid, dissecting it out of the surrounding muscle, and then closing the defect.

Prior to myomectomy, you must be informed that there is a fibroid recurrence rate necessitating repair surgery 10 to 20 percent of the time. Furthermore, despite the fact that the uterus is not removed, the amount of bleeding at the time of surgery and the postoperative complication rate may be as high for myomectomy as for hysterectomy, or higher. Subsequent pregnancies must usually be delivered by Cesarean section due to weakening created in the uterine wall following myomectomy.

What other benign gynecological condition of the uterus is most likely to necessitate hysterectomy rather than tubal sterilization?

Adenomyosis is a benign, though progressively disabling, condition caused by endometrial glandular tissue being displaced into the muscle of the uterus. Unlike endometriosis, which is also caused by displaced endometrial glands, adenomyosis usually occurs in women who have given birth several times, with the onset of symptoms noted in the late thirties or after the age of forty. Though many women have never heard of the condition, adenomyosis is almost as common as fibroids, and is present in approximately 20 percent of all hysterectomy specimens. The incidence of adenomyosis at autopsy in women dying of other causes has been reported to be as high as 50 percent, and 50 percent of all women with adenomyosis also have fibroids.

The most common symptoms of the disorder are very heavy and frequent periods which become progressively more painful. Intercourse may also cause deep pelvic pain. On vaginal examination the findings may be variable, but usually the uterus is tender and slightly or moderately enlarged, with a globular shape.

A woman with minimal enlargement of the uterus may experience severe pain and be incorrectly diagnosed as neurotic. Characteristically, when hormones such as birth control pills and progesterone are given to relieve the pain, the stimulation to the displaced endometrial glands actually intensifies the discomfort.

The diagnosis of adenomyosis is often extremely difficult to make, because a D & C removes tissue from only the endometrium and not the muscle of the uterus. Study of the hysterectomy specimen by the pathologist is the only way to confirm a doctor's suspicion that adenomyosis exists. Adenomyosis, like fibroids, causes no further difficulties after the menopause. For this reason, a woman in her late forties with tolerable symptoms may best be treated in a homeopathic rather than a surgical manner.

If hysterectomy is performed for benign disease of the uterus, should a woman's healthy ovaries be removed?

If you were to ask ten gynecologists at what age they think normal ovaries should be removed at the time of hysterectomy, undoubtedly ten different answers would be received, ranging from "age thirty-five" to "never."

What are the facts? For one thing, of all malignancies that strike the genital tract, cancer of the ovary is the leading cause of death. Approximately ten thousand women in the United States die each year of this dreaded disease. Though it is less common than cancer of the cervix and endometrium, at the present time there are no adequate screening methods for detecting it, such as the Pap smear provides for cervical cancer. In addition, early symptoms are usually absent, and by the time they do appear the cancer usually has reached the incurable stage. For those two reasons, three of every four women afflicted with ovarian cancer die as a result of it.

Statistically, more than 90 percent of ovarian tumors discovered in women between the ages of twenty and thirty are benign. However, between the ages of fifty and seventy, the ratio of malignant to benign tumors is approximately 1 to 1. Based on those statistics, and prejudiced by the fact that I have known several wonderful women who have been afflicted with this terrible disorder, it is my policy to encourage women of forty and over to have their ovaries removed when surgery is performed for benign disease of the uterus. I have even made this suggestion to women of thirty-eight years of age without regretting it. It has been estimated that bilateral oophorectomy at the time of hysterectomy may reduce the total ovarian cancer risk by an estimated 20 percent.

Several studies have been conducted to determine whether or not the ovary retained at hysterecomy carries with it a greater potential for both malignant and nonmalignant disease at a later date. Such problems are referred to medically as the "residual ovary syndrome." It may occur in approximately 1 to 3 percent of all women undergoing hysterectomy while retaining either one or both ovaries.

The latest review of the "residual ovary syndrome" was in 1975 by J. E. Christ and E. C. Lotze from Baylor College of Medicine. Their findings are based on the study of 202 women who required repeat surgery due to problems associated with retained ovaries. Of the group, almost 54 percent required repeat surgery within five years of the hysterectomy. The most common complaint leading to reoperation was chronic pelvic and lower abdominal pain in 77 percent, and pain with intercourse in 67 percent of those women. Benign tumors were found in 23 percent, and malignancy was present in a surprisingly high 3 percent. Since the chance of developing cancer of the ovary is approximately 1 percent in women over forty who have never undergone hysterectomy, 3 percent represents a significant increase. Cancer of the retained ovary following hysterectomy has been studied by other groups, and practically all have found a significant potential for malignant change ranging between that low of 3 percent, and a high of 10.8 percent. The cause remains obscure, but it is a strong argument in favor of surgical removal of the ovaries at the time of hysterectomy.

Hormonal replacement with natural estrogens postoperatively is a safe and efficient method of controlling premature menopausal symptoms. In the absence of the uterus, you need not fear the only potentially serious problem associated with that medication: cancer of the endometrium. By taking estrogens in a three-weeks-on, one-week-off cycle, uncomfortably tender or engorged breasts should not be a problem.

Can hysterectomy be performed for the combined purpose of abortion and sterilization?

I am both amazed and appalled by the number of gynecologists who recommend this hazardous combined procedure.

One study of two hundred women who underwent vaginal hysterectomy for the purpose of abortion and vaginal hysterectomy clearly demonstrated the hazards inherent in the procedure. A significant postoperative temperature elevation was noted in 18 percent of the patients over a period of two days. If one includes those women with a temperature over 100.4° for one day, then the number with postoperative fever soars to ninety-five, or almost one half of the total number. In addition, three women required exploratory surgery, two suffered injury to the urinary bladder, and six experienced a significant blood loss of more than one and one-half units of blood.

Dr. Harold Schulman of the Albert Einstein College of Medicine has stated, "It is difficult to understand extending minor procedures (suction abortion and laparoscopic tubal sterilization) into major operative procedures. If a physician's guiding principle is to do no harm, then the reason for this conversion from a minor procedure should be compelling." Dr. Schulman goes on to say that when a hysterectomy is substituted for a simpler procedure, a doctor must also inform you that he or she is recommending a procedure which increases your risk of dying at least twenty times.

Is hysterectomy at the time of Cesarean section ever indicated?

Cesarean hysterectomy in the presence of an acute obstetrical emergency, such as uncontrolled hemorrhage or severe infection, is a valuable, life-saving procedure. However, when used as a means of sterilization at the time of a routine Cesarean section, it is unwarranted. Several studies have demonstrated that tubal ligation is a far safer procedure. Even in the presence of coexisting conditions such as a fibroid uterus or carcinoma-in-situ of the cervix, many gynecologists prefer to delay hysterectomy until at least eight weeks later, when the uterus and its blood vessels are more normal in size.

However, as with the situation of vaginal hysterectomy, the advocates of Cesarean hysterectomy continue to perform surgery even in the face of overwhelming evidence demonstrating that it is hazardous. Even in the best hands, 20 percent of patients operated upon need a blood transfusion. In one study from Columbia-Presbyterian Medical Center, 116 of 165 women undergoing Cesarean hysterectomy were transfused. Allergic reactions to transfused blood have in the past been responsible for the deaths of several patients, while the risk of hepatitis from a contaminated unit of blood is always a threat.

A postoperative complication rate of 30 to 50 percent is not uncommon. Some of those complications are quite serious, such as damage to the urinary bladder and ureter, which is the structure that carries urine from the kidney to the bladder. Severe pelvic infections have caused death in a small but significant number of women.

If, as Dr. Schulman says, the physician's guiding principle is to do no harm, one wonders why all doctors are not aware of that very simple message. How can a doctor in good conscience continue to use vaginal and Cesarean hysterectomy as a method of sterilization? It is obvious that the principle is not getting through to all doctors.

You must therefore approach health care with the same "buyer beware" skepticism you display when obtaining other goods and services. As a consumer of health care services, you must be able to distinguish between treatment which is good, not so good, and just plain deplorable.

The last chapter will be devoted to an analysis of the future of contraception, sterilization, and abortion techniques. Some of these ideas may never materialize, but others have a great deal of promise.

11
THE
FUTURE

Throughout the preceding chapters I have mentioned several of the newer techniques of contraception, sterilization, and abortion that are available to the general public on a limited basis. Many of the ideas that follow have not received approval for use from the FDA and remain at a stage of development which restricts their use to laboratory animals or very small experimental groups of men and women.

BIRTH CONTROL PILLS AND OTHER HORMONES FOR WOMEN

What new birth control pills will be available in the future?
Actually, very little is expected in the form of new oral contraceptive discoveries in the near future. One authority, Dr. Carl Djerassi, who first synthesized the progestins used in most of today's oral contraceptives, has estimated that it will take ten to seventeen years of testing at a cost of eighteen million dollars to introduce a major new contraceptive agent.

One hormonal preparation, *medroxyprogesterone acetate*, is a potent and effective contraceptive. When 150 milligrams is injected intramuscularly every three months, it successfully prevents pregnancy in 99.5 to 100 percent of all women who use it. A recent study has demonstrated that a 300 milligram dose given every six months is capable of achieving a pregnancy rate of only 1.73 per 100 woman-years. Medroxyprogesterone acetate is called *Depo-Provera* when used as an injection; in other applications (see Page 267) it is known simply as *Provera*. Depo-Provera is similar in chemical structure to progesterone and therefore produces very few of the unpleasant side effects associated with the estrogens and progestins found in birth control pills (see Chapter 2). Contraception is achieved by Depo-Provera's effect on the hypothalamus, preventing its release of those factors necessary for stimulating ovulation. In addition, medroxyprogesterone acetate alters the cervical mucus and inactivates the glands of the endometrium so that they are incapable of receiving an egg. Unfortunately, this beneficial effect is also one of its major drawbacks, since prolonged absence of menses may occur in as many as 70 percent of women given the medication. One year after the injections are stopped, 25 percent of previously fertile women remain infertile. Though it is believed that the infertility is not permanent, Depo-Provera is far too powerful a drug to use on individuals who may want to conceive at a later date.

Is Depo-Provera approved for use by the FDA?
Though the drug is currently used as a contraceptive in many other countries, at the present time it is not approved by the FDA for this purpose. Actually, its use was approved in September, 1974, following a long investigation. However, exactly one month later, the FDA reversed its decision, based upon claims that women who were treated with Depo-Provera in an experimental group had a higher incidence of cervical cancer. As a result, final approval of the drug will be delayed pending further investigation.

Is there a relationship between Depo-Provera and cervical cancer?
Based on current knowledge about cervical cancer, most authorities agree that Depo-Provera does not adversely influence the disease. Epidemiologists have amassed convincing evidence that cancer of the cervix is truly a venereal condition related to both early age at first coitus and exposure to multiple sexual partners. The invasive or potentially deadly form of cervical cancer does not suddenly appear, but

progresses slowly over several years from a microscopic pre-cancerous condition (dysplasia) to a harmless form of cancer limited to the upper layer of cells within the cervix (carcinoma-in-situ). Often there is a ten-year hiatus between the development of carcinoma-in-situ and invasive cancer, though in the majority of cases the disease never progresses beyond the stage of in-situ.

Doctors critical of the Depo-Provera—cervical cancer link point out that in the study under question by the FDA, the drug was given for so brief a period of time that it would be impossible to produce the spectrum of change from dysplasia to cancer, which usually takes several years.

There have been many theories as to the cause of cervical cancer, and a far more likely culprit than Depo-Provera appears to be the Type 2 herpes simplex virus. This virus is venereally transmitted and causes painful blisters in the genital area. Often it persists in its chronic form for months or years as a painless and asymptomatic, though highly contagious, condition. It is believed that the virus may initiate abnormal changes in the cells of the cervix. Support for this theory is based on the fact that a high percentage of women suffering from invasive cancer of the cervix are noted to have antibodies to herpes, indicating previous exposure to the virus. Women with in-situ carcinoma also have antibody titers to herpes, but of a lower frequency than those with invasive disease. Women with dysplasia are least likely to demonstrate herpes antibodies.

Ironically, Depo-Provera has been approved by the FDA as treatment for advanced stages of endometrial cancer, a disease known to be estrogen-dependent. Very high doses have been found to decrease the size of these cancers in as many as one out of every three patients with advanced disease. Depo-Provera has also been used extensively in treating a variety of conditions in both very young and old women without any reported increase in cervical cancer rates.

Which women could benefit from using Depo-Provera?

Depo-Provera appears to be an excellent contraceptive for a woman who has completed her childbearing and is unable to use birth control pills because of the problems caused by the estrogen they contain. In studies to date, there have been no apparent harmful changes in liver function, blood pressure, or lipid metabolism caused by medroxyprogesterone acetate.

One of the greatest uses of Depo-Provera is in providing contraception for the woman who is nursing her baby. Unlike birth control pills, which may decrease the milk supply and adversely affect the nursing infant, Depo-Provera has actually been found to increase the milk supply. In one study of 406 nursing women who received Depo-Provera, it was found that a greater percentage nursed longer and more successfully than a group of equally motivated women who did not receive this medication. In another study, investigators noted that the weight of infants of mothers given Depo-Provera was significantly greater after the third month of nursing when compared with a group not given this hormone. The composition of the breast milk appears to be altered under the influence of Depo-Provera. Concentrations of milk fat, lactose, and total solids are minimally increased, while those of milk protein are reduced. Thorough psychological and physical examination of over 100 babies at 12 and 18 months of age has demonstrated no developmental deficiencies among nursing infants who ingested Depo-Provera in their milk. Though this is encouraging information, greater numbers of infants must be studied before one can say with certainty that this hormone is harmless to the nursing infant.

In addition to treating cancer of the endometrium, Depo-Provera has been successfully used in treating endometriosis. It is also used to control heavy periods, often eliminating the need for hysterectomy. For some unknown reason, Depo-Provera works remarkably well in relieving the hot flashes of the menopause and, unlike estrogen, it is beneficial rather than harmful to the endometrium. Depo-Provera has also been used to halt premature breast development and menstruation in sexually precocious young girls who otherwise would experience these phenomena prior to the age of eight. It has been used with limited success in preventing the premature closure of the long bones of young girls destined to be abnormally short. If given before the adolescent growth spurt, it may affect the ultimate adult height by as much as two inches.

What are the disadvantages of using Depo-Provera?
During the three months after the first injection, the majority of women experience annoying bleeding between eight and thirty days in each thirty-day period. Thereafter, the in-

cidence decreases significantly, so that most women experience no periods at all after the first twelve months.

The absence of menses for prolonged periods of time affects individuals differently. For those women with previously heavy and prolonged menses accompanied by painful cramps, the absence of periods provides welcome relief. Many women who view the monthly menses as a sign that their reproductive system is healthy may understandably be concerned by the absence of periods. Others express concern that potentially harmful menstrual products are being retained within the uterus. It is important that those individuals be reassured that Depo-Provera prevents the formation of menstrual products by its action on the hypothalamus and endometrium. It is also comforting to know that normal menstrual function eventually returns in practically all women after the Depo-Provera is stopped.

Some evidence suggests that Depo-Provera may alter the glucose tolerance test and also cause abnormalities in plasma insulin levels. In one study, 15 percent of women with a previously normal glucose tolerance test converted to an abnormal test after taking Depo-Provera. In addition, a significant number of diabetics need more insulin while they are using this medication. Though this would not contraindicate the use of Depo-Provera in women with a family or personal history of diabetes, such individuals would certainly have to be watched more closely for any changes in their insulin requirements.

Despite the fact that Depo-Provera does not contain estrogen, it is best not taken by individuals with a previous history of thrombophlebitis or thromboembolism, since some evidence suggests that it causes a slowing or stagnation of blood flow to the extremities. When that happens, thrombophlebitis is more likely to occur.

Beagles treated with very high doses of Depo-Provera have had an increased incidence of benign and malignant breast tumors. Studies in both monkeys and humans, however, have not confirmed such a relationship. Obviously, until more is known about the subject, I would be hesitant to use Depo-Provera when there is a personal or familial history of either benign or malignant breast tumors.

Finally, practically all clinical studies to date have demonstrated a gradual increase in body weight among the majority of individuals who receive Depo-Provera injections.

The weight gain may vary from two to twenty pounds and tends to increase with longer use.

Is there any other long-acting contraceptive that causes less irregularity of the menstrual cycle?

Promising results have been achieved by adding either med-roxyprogesterone acetate (Provera) or norgestrel (the progestogen used in some birth control pills) to a synthetic plastic ring (Silastic) which is inserted into the vagina on the fifth day of the menstrual cycle and removed on the twenty-sixth day (Figure 11–1). Following removal of the ring, menstruation will occur within a few days. The ring is then inserted for another three weeks; the same ring can be used for up to six months. Insertion is identical to that of the diaphragm though the technique does not have to be as precise. Contraception is achieved by slow release of the Provera or the norgestrel through the vaginal wall and into the bloodstream. This circulating hormone prevents ovulation, alters the endometrium, and thickens the cervical mucus. The bodily effects caused by these agents are not quite as pronounced as when they are administered intramuscularly or orally.

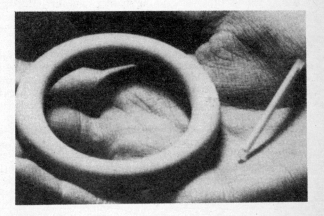

Figure 11-1. Silastic Vaginal Ring and Rod for Hypodermic Injection

In one study of 138 treatment cycles using a Provera ring, ovulation was prevented 136 times and there were no pregnancies. Periods resumed within one week after the ring was removed and, most importantly, ovulation resumed in 85 percent of all women within two post-treatment cycles after the ring was no longer used. The only side effects noted were superficial vaginal ulceration in four women (which healed quickly), 7 episodes of breakthrough bleeding, partial slippage of the ring in 7 women, and increased odorless vaginal discharge in 9 women. To date, women using the device have not found that it interferes with intercourse, but if there is discomfort, the ring can be removed before and replaced after intercourse without any loss of protection.

In a more recent study of 10 women, reported in the *American Journal of Obstetrics and Gynecology* in January, 1978, this same group of researchers added a natural estrogen, estradiol, to the norgestrel progestin in the vaginal ring. The beneficial effect of this has been to significantly diminish the incidence of breakthrough bleeding. However, this has been achieved at the expense of having low levels of estradiol absorbed into the bloodstream. Though the risk of circulating estradiol can't be compared to the dangers of the synthetic estrogens in birth control pills, it would appear that the beauty of the vaginal ring, namely the safety factor, is somewhat compromised by the addition of estrogen. As a result of this study, large-scale studies of this ring will be performed in several countries.

At the present time, clinical trials with the intravaginal ring are being conducted at the University of Southern California School of Medicine under the supervision and coordination of the Population Council's International Committee for Contraception Research. Approval for use by the FDA is still months or even years away.

Another area of research has been the implantation in the forearm or buttocks of one-inch-long Silastic rods containing norgestrel. The hormone is slowly released from its location under the skin, and its contraceptive effect is reported to last as long as ten years. Reversal to full fertility is achieved almost immediately by removing the Silastic rod through a small skin incision. The major side effect noted with these implants is unpredictable and occasionally prolonged bleeding. Formation of benign, though annoying, follicular cysts of the ovary are also fairly common. Figure 11–1 demonstrates both the Silastic vaginal ring and the Silastic rod.

Extensive use of various types of Silastic implants has taken place in Brazil and Chile. Hormones used have included Provera, norgestrel, and other progestins. In these studies, abnormal bleeding was noted by 30 percent of the women using this method of contraception. The incidence of lower abdominal pain, often associated with benign follicular ovarian cysts, was reported at three per one-hundred woman-years of use.

A more promising skin implant has been developed by Dr. Gopi N. Gupta of the Population Council. It is a pellet less than one-half inch long which contains a progestin, such as norgestrel and norethindrone, fused with a small amount of pure cholesterol. The addition of cholesterol makes the pellet totally bioabsorbable so that, unlike the Silastic rods, it does not have to be removed by incising the skin. Since it is not much bigger than a grain of rice, it can easily be injected under the skin at the time that it is inserted. Tests with the pellets to date suggest that they may prevent pregnancy for more than one year, and perhaps for as long as three. At the present time, tests are being conducted with various doses of progestins in Brazil, Chile, Finland, India, Jamaica, and Sweden. Dr. Gupta has also designed a birth control pellet for men (see Pages 289–290).

Preliminary testing has been conducted on snugly fitting Silastic contraceptive bracelets. Progestins contained in the bracelets are absorbed into the body through the skin. At the present time, experiments are being carried out with three different progestins and two different types of Silastic bracelets. The main problem has been in designing a bracelet which provides a constant rate of progestin release into the body over a prolonged period of time.

Studies have been conducted in Latin America with a once-a-month pill containing a long-acting estrogen and progestin. In one such study, the prenancy rate was a promising 2.9 per 100 woman-years. Irregular menstrual bleeding has been a definite obstacle to widespread use of the method.

Another once-a-month oral contraceptive, *aminoglutethimide*, and its derivatives, has been tested in experimental animals. Those compounds are referred to as *luteolytic agents*, because they bring about menstruation by suppressing the production of progesterone in the corpus luteum which is needed for implantation of the fertilized egg.

Are there any other promising hormonal preparations?

Danazol is a synthetic hormonal preparation similar in structure to the progestins. Used experimentally with great success in the treatment of endometriosis (see Page 58) and chronic systic mastitis (inflammation) of the breasts, preliminary data indicate that Danazol may also be an effective contraceptive. It acts by preventing the release of FSH and LH from the pituitary gland, thereby preventing ovulation. Its potential for use will be for those women who can't tolerate estrogen-containing contraceptives, and for those with such conditions as fibrocystic disease of the breasts, varicose veins, and phlebitis.

Danazol is chemically similar to progestins, and because of this the side effects it produces are also similar. These most commonly include weight gain, a decrease in breast size, and *moniliasis*. The latter is an infection caused by a microscopic yeast-like organism. Symptoms of this condition are a white, cheesy vaginal discharge accompanied by severe itching of the external genital area (see Chapter 2). Other less common Danazol side effects are acne, oily skin, voice changes, decreased libido, and increase of hair growth on the extremities and face, edema (fluid retention), and breakthrough bleeding. At the present time, Danazol has FDA approval only for use in treating endometriosis and not for use as a contraceptive.

A possible replacement for the pill, which would not have its side effects, is being studied at Rutgers University. This protein preparation, isolated from hamster embryos, will inhibit ovulation in unbred hamsters. The compound has been synthesized and has been tested on mice and rats with excellent results. Since this protein has a chemical structure totally unlike any oral contraceptive currently used, it may prove to be the beginning of successful research in finding a totally safe birth control pill.

Has anything been invented for the woman who can't swallow birth control pills?

Though oral contraceptives do not come in liquid form, the next best thing is now under trial in Britain. Actual chewable paper contraceptives, identical in appearance to a sheet of stamps, has been developed. The stamps are made of cellulose impregnated with estrogen and a progestin and have a taste similar to rice. At the present time, they are not available at any pharmacy or Chinese restaurants in the United States.

What is a progesterone receptor, and how is it related to contraception?

Progesterone prepares the endometrium for implantation of the fertilized egg, and it also creates a favorable environment for the developing fetus. However, before progesterone can exert these effects, it first must bind itself chemically to a specific substance in the endometrial cells called a *progesterone receptor*. Investigators at Baylor College of Medicine have isolated, for the first time, a receptor for progesterone. Future contraceptive research will be based on finding chemical substances similar to progesterone that are capable of binding with the progesterone receptors in the endometrium. This would prevent or block progesterone from reaching the receptor sites and establishing endometrial support for an implanting egg. R 2323 is an experimental chemical compound which shows the most promise as a progesterone blocker. In one study of 160 healthy, fertile women with regular menstrual cycles, R 2323 was given orally on the fifteenth, sixteenth, and seventeenth day after menses began. A total of 2,148 menstrual cycles were studied, with a pregnancy rate of 5 percent reported. It was noted that the treatment did not upset the normal menstrual cycle. In addition, the cycle length and menstrual flow were unusually regular. Spotting and abnormal bleeding occurred in less than 3 percent of the women studied. Unlike women using birth control pills, these women experienced a minimal amount of unpleasant side effects. Nausea or vomiting was noted in less than 8 percent of the total number of menstrual cycles recorded. Microscopic analysis of the endometriums of these individuals convincingly demonstrated a lack of progesterone effect, leading the investigators to conclude that R 2323 effectively competed with progesterone for the receptor-binding sites. Though the 5 percent pregnancy rate is unacceptably high, a pill of that type obviously has great potential. It is estimated that further testing and refinement of R 2323 and similar compounds will take at least six more years.

Similar studies have been conducted in an attempt to find

antagonists to the recently synthesized luteinizing hormone-releasing factor, or LRF (see Chapter 1). By blocking LRF, LH release by the pituitary gland will also be impaired. It is the release of LH which triggers ovulation and subsequent pregnancy. Other investigators have administered LRF to women as means of improving the accuracy of the rhythm method of contraception. By stimulating ovulation on a specific day each month, couples using rhythm will be better able to determine the days on which to avoid coitus.

Use of oral prostaglandins (Pages 182–183) as a once-a-month pill has been tested for several years with rather discouraging results. Despite the fact that prostaglandins are believed to have the capacity to disrupt the corpus luteum production of progesterone (Pages 10–11), in actual practice this does not always happen. When the level of progesterone stays high, pregnancy may result. Furthermore, the side effects of nausea, vomiting, and diarrhea make prostaglandins unacceptable as a birth control pill at the present time.

Is there a vaccine for women that will prevent pregnancy?

Intensive research has been aimed at developing safe and effective antifertility vaccines. Those vaccines are created by using one of several proteins found in sperm which scientists have been able to isolate. The capacity of sperm to fertilize an egg depends on each of these proteins. Immunization of a woman is theoretically possible following an injection of one of these male sperm proteins. Because the male protein, now called an *antigen*, is foreign to a woman's body, she reacts by producing substances called *antibodies* which destroy or inactivate the specific protein injected. At the present time, the feasibility of producing a local antibody reaction confined to the female genital tract is being evaluated. In the presence of high antibody levels in the organs of reproduction, sperm protein introduced through coitus could then be inactivated without producing a generalized or systemic body reaction. Some success has been achieved in rabbits and hamsters with an antibody which actually forms a coating around the egg thereby preventing the sperm from fertilizing it.

A *lactate dehydrogenase isoenzyme*, or LDH-X, is the most promising sperm antigen isolated to date. Experimental immunization of female mice and rabbits with LDH-X has reduced fertility with varying success ranging from 25 to 80 percent.

Hyaluronidase is a protein enzyme which has been purified from spermatozoa of birds, cattle, and rabbits. Antibodies to rabbit sperm hyaluronidase have been shown to immobilize and destroy sperm.

Acrosin is another sperm enzyme which, when injected as a foreign protein, has produced successful antibody formation in both sheep and humans. Researchers are encouraged by preliminary experiments on female sheep showing marked reduction in fertility following injection with purified ram acrosin.

Numerous other sperm antigens are under investigation, including two called S and T isolated from guinea pigs, and another called *aspermatogenic antigen*, or ASA. The latter, when injected into female guinea pigs, will induce infertility by immobilizing the sperm.

None of these vaccines have yet approached the stage where they are ready for widespread testing on humans.

Are there pregnancy hormones that might be used as antifertility vaccines?

Two hormones produced by the human placenta have been studied as potential antigens for antifertility immunization. One of those hormones—*human chorionic somatomammotropin*, or *HCS*–has met with little success. However, *human chorionic gonadotropin*, or *HCG*, shows much more promise as an antigen. This is the most important hormone of early pregnancy, and it is the elevated levels of this substance which are measured in the commonly performed urinary pregnancy test. Antibodies to a fraction of HCG, called its *beta-subunit*, or *B-HCG*, have been developed. When pregnant baboons are injected with antibodies to B-HCG, it results in complete disruption of the placenta and induction of abortion. Furthermore, when nonpregnant baboons are immunized with antibodies to B-HCG prior to mating, pregnancy does not result after they are mated.

Dr. Sheldon Segal of the Population Council predicts, "If everything goes well and no great problem of safety arises and we can test the vaccine for effectiveness quickly in subhuman primates, then we should have a vaccine for human use within a decade."

IUDS

What new developments are there with the IUD?
Currently, research has centered around prolongation of the amount of time that progesterone-containing IUDs can be left in the uterine cavity free of the risk of pregnancy. The present twelve-month limit of efficacy with the Progestasert device is its major drawback. Two preliminary studies using a T-shaped device containing an attached capsule of slow-releasing norgestrel appear promising (Figure 11–2). In one of these studies, one hundred women used this device for six months without one pregnancy reported. In both studies, the main problem was irregular menstrual bleeding. To date, the unanswered question is how long those devices can safely prevent pregnancy. Another area of concern is the potentially harmful effect of norgestrel on a developing fetus if

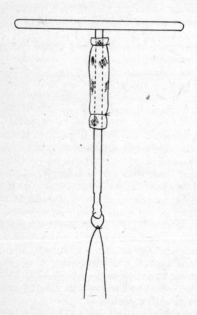

Figure 11-2.   T-Shaped Device with Attached Norgestrel

accidental pregnancy occurs. Since the medication is identical to the norgestrel in Ovral, the danger appears to be real (see Page 48–49).

Since abnormal vaginal bleeding is one of the major drawbacks of IUD use, researchers have attempted to correct this by adding an antifibrinolytic substance to experimental IUDs. This chemical, named tranexamic acid (AMCA) is released slowly from the surface of the IUD and prevents breakdown of blood in the endometrium. This in turn decreases blood loss caused by the IUD. In a comparative study involving 450 women over a period of 6 months it was noted that the IUD removal rate for bleeding or pain was 1.1 per 100 AMCA-IUD users compared to 9.9 per 100 women using a standard IUD.

Are there any other promising IUDs?
Probably the most promising is a fluid-filled device which is inserted into the uterine cavity in its deflated form and then filled with a saline solution so as to fit the contour of the endometrial cavity (Figure 11–3).

This IUD is made of a silicone polymer pouch reinforced with a Dacron mesh. The results of one study of 697 women, with a total of 6,672 woman-months of use, appear in Table 11–1. Efforts are being made to modify the design of that IUD in order to decrease the unacceptably high expulsion and medical removal rates.

What is the Ypsilon?
The Ypsilon is a Y-shaped IUD specifically designed to adjust to the uterine cavity. It has a frame of medical-grade stainless steel wire that is completely covered by silicon rubber and a short web of silicon which prevents overspreading of the two arms of the Y (Figure 11–4). At the present time, the Ypsilon comes in a nulliparous (never having had a baby), or small, size and a standard size.

The Ypsilon is currently under investigation in such diverse areas as the United States, Brazil, and Thailand. In this country practically all the research on the device has been carried out at the New York Hospital—Cornell Medical Center. Table 11–2 shows the results for 628 women with the nulliparous-size IUD inserted.

The pregnancy rate was only .77 per hundred woman-years among the 125 nulliparous women out of the group of

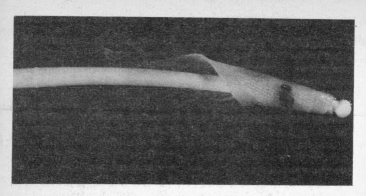

Figure 11-3A. Fluid-Filled IUD

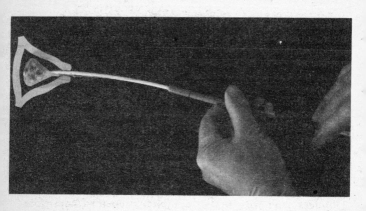

Figure 11-3B. Filling with Saline Following Insertion

TABLE 11-1 — FLUID-FILLED IUD CUMULATIVE RESULTS PER 100 WOMAN-YEARS

	NULLIPAROUS (390 WOMEN)	MULTIPAROUS (307 WOMEN)
Pregnancy Rate	4.3	1.5
Expulsions	19.4	10.5
Medical removal for bleeding	14.3	10.9
Cumulative continuation rate	58	68

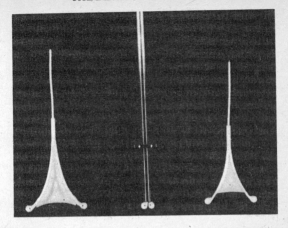

Figure 11-4.   Standard and Nulliparous Ypsilon IUDs

628. The higher pregnancy rate of 2.4 per hundred woman-years, among multiparous women, those who had previously borne children, was attributed to the fact that the small Ypsilon size could not adequately cover the larger uterine cavity of these women. Today clinical trials with Ypsilons of different sizes are in progress.

A remarkable safety feature of this IUD has been the total absence of uterine perforation even when the device has been inserted at the time of an abortion, when the uterus is softer and more likely to be perforated.

TABLE 11-2—YPSILON IUD RESULTS PER 100 WOMAN-YEARS

	NULLIPAROUS (628 WOMEN)
Expulsion Rate	3.2
Medical Removals	5.1
Nonmedical Removals	3.2
Pregnancy Rate	2.2

What is the Antigon-F?

The Antigon-F is a kite-shaped IUD with a polyethylene frame bridged by a thin membrane, and a magnet embedded in one side (Figure 11–5).

Insertion is facilitated by compressing it into a 10-millimeter-wide plastic inserter. The purpose of the magnet is to permit detection of the device with a special instrument, thereby eliminating the need for a pelvic examination.

The Antigon-F was first used in Denmark. As in the case of the Ypsilon, practically all testing in this country has been conducted at New York Hospital—Cornell Medical Center. Another similarity between the Antigon-F and the Ypsilon is that both are extremely unlikely to perforate the uterus. To date, the Antigon-F has been responsible for only one perforation despite thousands of insertions. Unlike the Ypsilon, this device fares poorly among nulliparous women, as it has a very high expulsion and medical removal rate. For multiparous women, the results appear to be excellent (Table 11–3).

In Table 11–3, the Antigon-F was tested in only 14 nul-

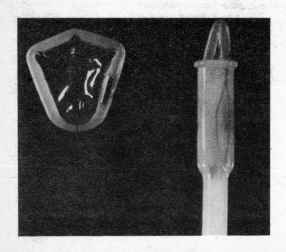

Figure 11-5.   Antigon-F IUD

TABLE 11-3—RESULTS OF ANTIGON-F USE PER 100 WOMAN-YEARS

	NULLIPAROUS (14 WOMEN)	MULTIPAROUS (470 WOMEN)
Expulsions	23.5	5.1
Medical Removals	17.6	10.6
Nonmedical Removals	0	6.1
Pregnancies	0	.85

liparous women. In a more recent followup of 24 nulliparous women using the device for two years, the expulsion rate diminished very slightly to 20.6 per 100 woman-years, while the medical-removal rate was cut in half.

What is the Anderson Leaf?

The Anderson (Latex) Leaf is made of silicone rubber mixed with a zinc and copper solution (Figure 11–6). Tests conducted in several countries since 1972 have demonstrated pregnancy rates ranging between 1.4 and 3.2 per 100 woman-years. The expulsion rate of 2.7 to 6.2 per 100 woman-years is also acceptable. However, in one study the medical removal rate because of bleeding was an unacceptable 24 per 100 woman-years.

Figure 11-6. Anderson (Latex) Leaf

What is the TCu-220C?

The latest and most promising copper-containing IUD is the TCu-220C. This device is unique in that it has fine solid copper sleeves on both the vertical and horizontal arms of a T-shaped plastic device. The copper T in its present form, called the TCu-200 (see IUDs), only has copper on its vertical arm and the copper is a wrapped around wire rather than a copper sleeve. As a result, the TCu-200 tends to lose copper too fast. Based on preliminary data, it would appear that the TCu-220C is capable of maintaining slow copper release and contraceptive efficiency for 20 to 30 years.

The TCu-220C has not been approved for general use by the FDA.

DIAPHRAGMS

Can we expect any improvements in the diaphragm?

Very interesting research has been done at the University of Arizona on a diaphragm made of collagen (a protein substance) sponge. When dry, the sponge feels somewhat like felt. When it is wet, the device is very soft and can be squeezed to 10% of its original size, which is approximately 2½ inches in diameter.

The researchers working on this diaphragm, known as the CSC (Collagen Sponge Contraceptive) hope that eventually the device can be inserted and left in the vagina for an entire month. A woman wearing the CSC should be able to remove it at any time, rinse it with tap water, and reinsert it. The CSC will be inserted with applicators similar to those used with tampons; it can also be placed manually.

Unlike the rubber diaphragm, the collagen sponge should not be subject to displacement during intercourse. Though it is believed that spermicidal agents will not have to be used with the CSC, animal studies from the University of Arizona in 1978 confirmed that the addition of zinc to the CSC enhanced its contraceptive effect. The research was performed by placing the zinc in contact with sensitive tissues of rabbits and hamsters. No toxic effects were noted in the animals, though many more studies must be performed before such a device is tested on women.

THE RHYTHM METHOD

What new procedures will be available in the near future for improving the accuracy of the rhythm method?
Extensive research is being directed at improving the accuracy of the rhythm method. Many women, for either religious or personal reasons, will continue to rely solely on rhythm as a means of contraception.

In addition to studying the cervical mucus for glucose concentration (see Page 136), investigators at Wayne State University School of Medicine have analyzed the changes in the concentration of two enzymes: *esterase* and *amino peptidase*. A sharp decrease in the concentration of both of these enzymes has been noted in the cervical mucus immediately prior to ovulation, followed by a return to normal values after ovulation. The aim of future investigation will be to devise a simpler technique for the testing of these enzymes so that they may be used as a method of predicting ovulation.

Luteinizing hormone-releasing factor, or LRF (see Page 11), has been synthesized in the laboratory and may have great potential for the woman using the rhythm method. Since ovulation is caused by a sudden increase of LH secondary to LRF stimulation, a woman taking LRF at a specific time each month may be able to stimulate ovulation on a definite predictable day and therefore avoid coitus at that time. This will be potentially helpful if you can't use the rhythm method because your periods are too irregular.

Speaking of LH, it has been noted that this hormone has a chemical structure similar to the pregnancy hormone produced by the placenta and called HCG, or *human chorionic gonadotropin*.

The recent pregnancy blood test developed by Dr. Brij B. Saxena of Cornell Medical Center (see Page 160) is capable of accurately detecting slight elevations of either hormone. This fact may have great application for users of the rhythm method, since LH levels are highest immediately before ovulation. If the new blood test can be developed for use as a urinary exam as well, you will be able to check your urine daily and to detect the LH elevation which precedes ovulation.

One new, simple, and inexpensive saliva method of predicting ovulation is now undergoing investigation. It is based on the principle that the concentration of a chemical named *alkaline phosphatase* in the saliva is greatest at the time of ovulation.

In this test, a woman chews a small piece of paraffin in order to stimulate saliva production. She then puts in her mouth a filter-paper test strip saturated with material which gives a visual color change from white to blue in the presence of alkaline phosphatase.

At the present time, this method has been able to predict ovulation within a period of one to seven days, which still makes it too inaccurate for widespread use.

In a very recent study, another salivary chemical—*salivary phosphate*—has been studied in fourteen ovulating women on a daily basis throughout two consecutive menstrual cycles. All women demonstrated a significant peak in salivary phosphate concentration exactly at the time of ovulation.

Other experiments with saliva have been used to determine the approximate day of ovulation. Just as the cervical mucus increases in glucose concentration at the time of ovulation (see Chapter 5), so does the saliva. By observing color changes on glucose test paper mixed with saliva, investigators were able to determine the approximate day of ovulation in seven of ten women.

The cyclic ferning pattern clearly demonstrated in cervical mucus (see Chapter 5) also occurs in other secretions, such as nasal mucus, tears, spinal fluid, and saliva. Maximum ferning at the time of ovulation is due to high concentrations of sodium and chloride following estrogen stimulation. Attempts at determining ovulation by studying salivary ferning have been unsuccessful because the fern pattern is not as distinct as it is in the cervix.

Sialic acid is a substance found in saliva. Preliminary studies have demonstrated that the sialic acid concentration begins to decrease one to two days prior to ovulation, and reaches its lowest levels at the time of ovulation. Development of a simple salivary test to anticipate impending ovulation would be of great benefit for couples using rhythm. (Sialic acid is also found in the cervical mucus, and its concentration also decreases in the cervix prior to ovulation.)

The newest and most exciting method for determining ovulation, based on the consistency of the cervical mucus, is an instrument called the viscometer, or "Ovutimer" (Figure 11–7).

It was introduced in April, 1976, by three Boston medical researchers and will soon be available for use by gynecologists as an office test. In addition, a tampon-size consumer version of the Ovutimer is under development for use by women at home. It will be an inexpensive and compact piece of equipment which, when inserted into the vagina against the cervix, will enable you to tell if you are in your fertile period.

How does the Ovutimer work?
A disposable probe is applied daily against the cervical os and a small sample of mucus is obtained. The probe is then

Figure 11-7.   Ovutimer

inserted into the ring with the indicator arm elevated (Figure 11–7). Before ovulation, when there is little mucus, the indicator arm will not move from the 3 position. However, during the fertile period—when the mucus is thin and not viscous—the arm will fall to the 0 or 1 position. That drop of the indicator arm may take place over four, five, or six days in succession, beginning with the first day of the fertile period. At the end of the fertile period, when the mucus becomes thick, the reading rises to between 2.5 and 4. Figure 11–8 demonstrates the results obtained from 81 observations on 9 women.

The decline of the indicator arm from 3 to 0 over a three-day period is clearly seen, as is the rise to the 2 position on the day following ovulation.

The manufacturers of the Ovutimer predict that it will be available to the public by early 1979. The predicted cost of the tampon-size device is ten dollars, while the disposable probes should sell for less than twenty-five cents.

What is a Tachmeter?

A Tachmeter is another device used for measuring the consistency of cervical mucus. It is being tested by the same

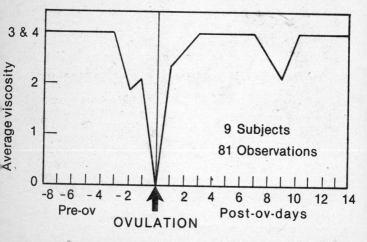

Figure 11-8.   Ovutimer Readings during the Menstrual Cycles

research group in Boston which has studied the Ovutimer. "Tachiness" of cervical mucus is defined by Dr. Harold Kosasky as the cohesive force of cervical mucus which must be overcome to pull the fluid apart. The thicker the mucus, the more difficult it is to pull it apart. To operate the Tachmeter, a sample of cervical mucus is placed between two plastic grid plates. After 20 seconds the plates are drawn apart and an electronic readout gives a measure of the "tachiness" at the point of maximum pulling force. Mucus at the time of ovulation shows very little "tachiness." At the present time, the device is at least a year away from being commercially available, and no estimated costs to the consumer have been determined.

What is an Ovulometer?

The Ovulometer is a simple battery-run device that measures changes in the electrostatic current or voltage naturally present in the body. A woman using the Ovulometer gets an instant reading on a pocketsize meter by touching two electrodes to the index finger of each hand. According to Doctor Howard Lutz, one of its developers, the charge reads positive in all men throughout the month. Women, however, usually give a negative reading, but become positive 3 to 6 days prior to ovulation. Conversion back to negative occurs 24 to 48 hours after ovulation. The Ovulometer is now being tested among women with a variety of illnesses to see if certain medical conditions will alter the results obtained. The device is expected to cost $49.

Are there newer ways to improve the temperature method of rhythm?

Yes, if the man you're living with takes *his* daily temperature! This suggestion is not as strange as it may appear. Dr. Margaret Henderson of Australia recently reported her findings to the Royal Australasian College of Physicians. Dr. Henderson studied the daily basal body and evening temperatures of twenty-five healthy men between the ages of twenty and fifty-six. She found that ten of these men, who were living with a particular woman for a prolonged period of time, had temperature cycles synchronous with those of the women with whom they lived. They actually experienced a midcycle temperature drop just prior to the woman's ovulation. Even more amazing, the men experienced a two- to five-day temperature elevation coinciding with the woman's ovulation and the subsequent rise in her body temperature.

Another recent development that may improve the temperature method is a special heat-sensitive transmitter that has been developed by the National Aeronautics and Space Administration. This device can measure the intravaginal temperature prior to and after ovulation extremely accurately. Though it is not currently available, there may be a great future for such a sensitive device in pinpointing the more subtle temperature changes during the menstrual cycle.

POSTCOITAL CONTRACEPTION

Are there any new postcoital contraceptives?
Most of the work on postcoital contraception has centered around the use of newer natural and synthetic prostaglandins, as well as the standard $PGF_2\alpha$ and PGE_2 (see Page 183). In addition to stimulating uterine contractions, prostaglandins also appear capable of disrupting the corpus luteum. The eventual goal is to develop a prostaglandin compound, with minimal unpleasant side effects, that will destroy the corpus luteum and cause very early pregnancy termination.

One synthetic prostaglandin compound, 15(s)K-methyl-$PGF_2\alpha$ -methyl-ester—or 15-methyl $PGF_2\alpha$ for short—appears to show the most promise. In a 1975 study in Sweden, this compound was given as a vaginal suppository to sixteen women, all between thirty-one and forty-three days after their last period. Ten of the sixteen were confirmed to be pregnant at the time the medication was administered. Following insertion of a suppository every three hours, bleeding began within three to six hours in all women and lasted an average of eight days. The confirmed pregnancies were successfully terminated at that early stage with bleeding equal in amount to, or only slightly heavier than, that of normal menses. Prostaglandin side effects, such as nausea and vomiting, were minimal. Whether the primary action of the 15-methyl prostaglandin is on the uterine muscle or the corpus luteum has not been determined, but the future of a self-administered suppository, when your period is late, appears promising. It seems a safer alternative than menstrual extraction. At the present time the suppositories are not available for widespread use.

Dr. Niels H. Lauersen, of the New York Hospital—Cornell Medical Center, has recently reported success with the use of an intravaginal silicone plastic disc impregnated with a solution of 15-methyl PGF$_2\alpha$. Unlike prostaglandin suppositories, the device requires no repeated insertions, provides a steady release of prostaglandin, and can be held in place over the cervix with either a diaphragm or a tampon. Successful menstrual induction, as well as first- and second-trimester abortions, has been accomplished using the new device.

A prostaglandin pellet has also been devised which can be inserted through the cervix and into the uterine cavity with an applicator similar to that of an IUD. The pellet dissolves at body temperature and has an effect equal to that of the prostaglandin solutions. The one disadvantage is that it can't be self-administered.

Finally, extracts from the exotic African endod plant have been successfully instilled into the uterine cavities of experimental rats on the sixth day of pregnancy. The plant has the ability to prevent the endometrium from retaining the implanting embryo.

ABORTION

Which of the new prostaglandins may be used to terminate pregnancies beyond the menstrual-extraction stage?
Both the standard prostaglandin compounds and the newer 15-methyl PGF$_2\alpha$ have been tried experimentally for termination of first- and second-trimester pregnancies. A similar compound *15-methyl PGE$_2$*, has also been used successfully for this purpose, either as a vaginal suppository or as an intramuscular injection. When given intravenously, prostaglandins are responsible for too many unpleasant side effects, such as nausea, diarrhea, vomiting, and fever.

All these compounds show great promise for use between the twelfth and sixteenth weeks of pregnancy, when the uterus is too large for safe suction curettage and too small for intraamniotic injection (see Chapter 7). If developed to the point of extensive clinical use, prostaglandins should make this emotionally upsetting four-week waiting period obsolete.

In one study at New York Hospital, 120 patients were given intramuscular injections of 15-methyl $PGF_2\alpha$. Abortion was successfully induced in 117 women in an average time of less than fifteen hours. Of great interest was the fact that 53 women were between the crucial thirteenth and sixteenth weeks of pregnancy, and 52 of them aborted successfully. The one failure was related not to the procedure, but to a fibroid tumor which blocked the cervical canal and prevented passage of the fetus. The New York Hospital investigators noted that pregnancies of sixteen weeks or less were aborted in significantly less time than those of seventeen weeks or more. Complications noted in this study were vomiting in more than half of the women, nausea in 17 percent, and diarrhea in 7 percent.

In another study, one of thirty women between the fifteenth and twenty-first weeks of pregnancy, intramuscular 15-methyl PGE_2 was 100 percent successful in inducing abortion. Of those thirty women, two retained their placenta following expulsion of the fetus. The injection-to-abortion interval averaged eighteen hours in nulliparous women and twelve hours in those who had previously given birth. Side effects included transient episodes of vomiting in twenty-two of the thirty women. In this study as well as others, a significant number of women experienced a temperature elevation of 2° F. or greater following the intramuscular injection of prostaglandins. Often the fever was accompanied by chills, but both subsided following expulsion of the fetus.

PGE_2 has been the most popular prostaglandin developed for use as a vaginal suppository. In a second New York Hospital study, involving seventy women, the suppositories were inserted every one to two hours. The results were impressive: all seventy women aborted in an average time of less than twelve hours. Nineteen women in this group were between the thirteenth and sixteenth weeks of their pregnancies, and eight who were aborted successfully were less than twelve weeks pregnant. Complications were similar to those obtained with other prostaglandin preparations —vomiting in thirty-six women, diarrhea in thirteen, and temperature elevation in fifty. Surgical removal of the placenta was required in only one patient.

From these experimental data I must conclude that use of

intraamniotic saline and prostaglandins will become obsolete in the near future. Intramuscular and intravaginal prostaglandin administration is safer, is less painful, and appears to have a shorter abortion-to-induction interval. Furthermore, it requires no special skill on the part of the person inducing the abortion. The side effects, though unpleasant, are not dangerous, and with slight modification of the prostaglandin dose, the incidence of those complications will eventually be significantly reduced.

Are there any solutions which are safer for intraamniotic injection than saline and prostaglandins?
Various solutions have been tried experimentally in an attempt to find one which is as effective as either saline or prostaglandins, but safer. Urea, a substance used in making plastics, appears to be the chemical which best fulfills that description, though it, too, has its shortcomings.

The one great advantage of intraamniotic urea is that even if it is accidentally injected into a vein, it will cause no unpleasant side effects. Its main drawbacks are that the injection-abortion interval may be longer than twenty-four hours, and it fails to induce abortion 20 percent of the time.

Attempts have been made to use intraamniotic urea in combination with lesser quantities of prostaglandins than those normally used. By doing so, investigators have hoped for a reduction of the unpleasant side effects noted when prostaglandins are used alone. Results of several studies document abortion to induction intervals of less than twenty hours, but surprisingly, the incidence of vomiting actually increases. In one study combining urea with $PGF_2\alpha$, and another with PGE_2, the incidence of vomiting was 73 and 70 percent respectively.

FEMALE STERILIZATION

What are the newest laparoscopic sterilization techniques?
Much research has been directed toward the improvement and refinement of the methods of laparoscopic sterilization. Almost as popular as the Falope Ring is a spring-loaded plastic clip developed at the University of North Carolina (Figure 11-9).

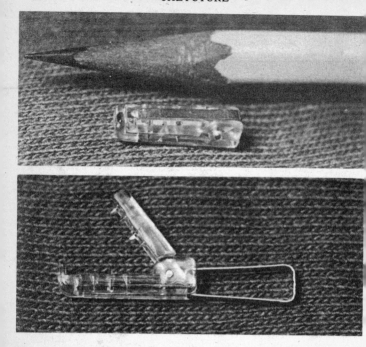

Figure 11-9.   Plastic Spring Clip of Laparoscopic Sterilization

Of one thousand women undergoing this laparoscopic technique, twenty-four became pregnant within six months following surgery. However, when the number was corrected for factors such as imperfect clips or inaccurate application of the clips, the rate was two per one thousand women. In another study of four hundred women at the University of Virginia, six pregnancies occurred following the use of the clips. Of these, five were due to errors by the doctors performing the procedure, and only one was due to failure of the technique. As with the Falope Ring, a major complication of the clip is pain at application. Lower abdominal pain lasting an average of forty-eight hours may occur in one of every four women.

The North Carolina group has also investigated the possibility of reversing the procedure for individuals who may want pregnancy at a later date. Experiments with animals are promising; of eight pigs sterilized with those clips, six became pregnant following their removal at the time of reconstructive surgery.

Two other noncoagulating laparoscopic devices are being studied in West Germany. One is a self-tying nonabsorbable suture applied to the center of the tube (Figure 11–10).

A disadvantage of the method is that it can only be performed through a two-incision technique. In addition, it also appears to require a high degree of manual dexterity on the part of the operator.

What does the future hold for laparoscopic coagulation techniques?

Many doctors think that endocoagulation is the method of the future. This technique is even better, newer, and safer

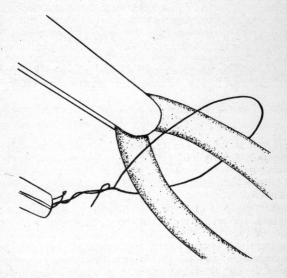

Figure 11-10.   Simulated Laparoscopic Tubal Ligation with Nonabsorbable Suture

than the bipolar system. With endocoagulation, the necessary heat for coagulation comes from heating bars at the lower part of special forceps called *crocodile forceps*. The crocodile forceps may move along the tube and safely destroy it in several different locations (Figure 11–11). The heating bars in the crocodile forceps are powered by a very low voltage for added safety.

Included in the new device are ingenious acoustic signals, so that the surgeon hears a different sound as the tissue in the tube is heated and cooled. If the tissue is getting too much heat for too long, the surgeon will instantly be aware of it because of the sound produced. The amount of heat can be adjusted to the type of tissue being coagulated. The one disadvantage of the instrument in its present form is that it has been developed only for a two-incision laparoscope.

Promising research has been applied to the development of a miniaturized laparoscope. The Needlescope is a laparoscope having a diameter not much larger than a needle. By using a two-puncture technique at a point at least two inches below the umbilicus, successful tubal coagulation has been accomplished among several volunteers. The advantages of this instrument over the standard laparoscope are a minimal danger of organ damage; the skin puncture sites are self-closing and require no stitches; and the electrical current used for coagulating the tubes is so low that there is practically no danger of accidental intestinal or skin burns.

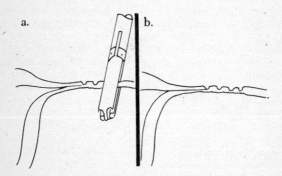

Figure 11-11.   Crocodile Forceps Coagulating the Tube, and Final Results

The disadvantages of the Needlescope are that using it requires greater skill than the standard laparoscope, the field of vision is narrowed, and the amount of light produced within the abdomen is not adequate at the present time.

Can tubal sterilization be achieved in any other way?

In an attempt to simplify tubal sterilization, doctors have instilled various caustic solutions and pastes through the cervix and into the uterine cavity. Those substances create inflammatory scar tissue in the endometrium and at the point where the tube enters the uterine cavity, thereby occluding (blocking) it. Chemicals used for the purpose have included silver nitrate, quinicrine (a drug used in the treatment of malaria), zinc chloride, phenol, plastic occlusives, and tissue adhesives.

Success following these methods has been unpredictable, and to date they have not been found to be practical for widespread use. In one recent study in which silver nitrate paste was used, fourteen of eighteen women, or 78 percent, showed successful closure of both tubes when tested with a hysterogram eight weeks later (see Page 94). However, the remaining four women had blockage of only one tube. In another study, in which quinicrine was instilled into the uterine cavities of thirty-seven women, an unacceptably low number of twenty-four women had subsequent closure of both tubes.

MCA (methyl cyanoacrylate) is a clear liquid substance which solidifies upon contact with moist body tissues. When injected into the Fallopian tubes it has the capacity to produce closure. In one study from England, MCA was tested on 41 volunteers. Following the procedure, 70 percent of the women studied had tubal closure proven by hysterogram. Re-injection of MCA in those women not demonstrating X-ray evidence of tubal closure is now under investigation. Another group from England has been experimenting with ceramic plugs similar to those used in orthodontic and orthopedic surgery. Preliminary tests in 15 women have not been totally successful, and much more research appears necessary.

If these methods can ever be developed to the point of achieving a greater percentage of tubal occlusions, sterilization would then be possible as an inexpensive office procedure performed with paracervical block anesthesia. However, it appears that use of the *hysteroscope* holds greater promise for success than any other technique.

What is a hysteroscope?

A hysteroscope is a viewing instrument with a powerful light source which is used to look into the uterus *(hystero)*, through the cervix. A separate operating channel is provided for introduction of such instruments as biopsy forceps, scissors, and a cautery probe for burning the opening of the tube as it enters the uterine cavity.

This instrument, though still in its experimental stages, is in the words of one of its chief researchers, Dr. Robert S. Neuwirth of Columbia University, "the fastest, simplest, safest, and least expensive sterilization method ever to reach the clinical testing stage." Hysteroscopic sterilization can be performed under general anesthesia or as an office precedure with mild sedation and paracervical block. At the present time, Dr. Neuwirth has a success rate of 95 percent, though others using the technique have been less successful.

Other research projects being conducted with hysteroscopy involve the insertion of substances into the tubes—such as plastic occlusives, tissue adhesives, and splints—which may be removed at a later date in order to achieve reversible sterilization.

The question which remains unanswered is whether or not pregnancy rates following hysteroscopic sterilization can be reduced to a level equal to that of a laparoscopic sterilization, or only slightly greater. Obvious advantages of hysteroscopy would be low cost, safety, and applicability for women who would otherwise be denied laparoscopy because of previous extensive abdominal surgery, obesity, and cardiac and respiratory disease.

MALE CONTRACEPTION AND STERILIZATION

In the eight fiscal years prior to 1975, the Agency for International Development allotted over $35 million for fertility research. Of this total, only 5 percent went for male contraceptive study.

However, it is encouraging to note a recent positive trend toward a more equal distribution of contraceptive research funds. Fiscal 1974 was the first year that the federal government put more funds into male fertility studies than female fertility studies.

How would a birth control pill for men work?

The pituitary gland of a man contains FSH and LH (see Chapter 1). If those hormones are suppressed, sperm production by the testes is successfully prevented. However, a problem arises here, because FSH and especially LH are needed for production of the male hormone testosterone. Without testosterone, a man's libido and sexual potency are lost. To date, the problem has been to find a contraceptive which suppresses FSH and LH without causing loss of libido and potency. Danazol (see Page 264) may eventually become the ideal male contraceptive, because it inhibits FSH and LH and, if anything, causes masculinizing rather than feminizing side effects.

Drs. Rodney D. Skoglund and C. Alvin Paulsen of the University of Washington have found that Danazol combined with testosterone was a potentially effective and reversible male contraceptive. Sperm counts below 2 million (the normal average is between 40 million and 400 million) were noted in eleven of their thirteen patients given these two medications over a six-month period. The men noted no loss of potency, and fertility returned within five months after treatment was stopped.

Because LH is more important than FSH for testosterone production by the testes, an ideal contraceptive would be one that inhibits FSH without impairing LH release. Phenytoin is a drug with such an effect. In one study of twenty-four men using Phenytoin at the University of Southern California, one third had low FSH levels and the majority had low sperm counts.

Inhibin, a newly confirmed hormone produced by the testes, may eventually prove to be the perfect male contraceptive. After forty years of work, endocrinologists were finally able to isolate inhibin in 1977. Preliminary data suggest that inhibin can effectively lower FSH levels without altering LH or testosterone release.

Dr. Gopi N. Gupta of the Population Council has developed a bioabsorbable birth control pellet which is injected under the skin. The pellet for men is identical to that used for women and contains a progestin combined with

cholesterol (see Page 263). The former helps to diminish
sperm count, while the latter allows the medication to be
released into the body over a period of one to three years. To
prevent a lowering of a man's testosterone levels by the
progestin, Dr. Gupta injects a second pellet armed with testosterone which releases a small dose each day. This contraceptive is now undergoing evaluation in several countries
throughout the world.

Another promising and reversible birth control pill for
men is *5-thio-dextro-glucose*. Though this has only been
tested in mice, it has proven to be both safe and capable of
totally inhibiting the sperm count within four weeks. The
pill acts by preventing real glucose from being taken up by
the sperm cell, thereby inactivating it. Fertility is usually
restored within four weeks after the pill is stopped.

What mechanical methods have been devised to reduce a man's fertility?

Various researchers have inserted plugs, valves, and clips
into the vas deferens of dogs, guinea pigs, and a few men
—all with uniformly poor results. The devices have been of
various sizes, shapes, and materials. One rather ingenious
device contains a magnetic ball which can be moved from
on to off simply by passing a magnet over the scrotum (Figure 11–12).

The newer valves have been made mainly of gold and
plastic. Silicone rubber implants have also been inserted
into the vas deferens as a means of reversible sterilization.
For now, most investigators agree that these devices are far
from being ready for use by the general public.

A problem with many of these devices is that the tissues
around them react with inflammation and scarring following their insertion. Such reactions prevent reversibility and
speak unfavorably for the future of such devices.

A few investigators have attempted vas deferens occulu-
sion by injecting strong chemicals directly into the lumen,
or cavity, of the vas. The most successful solution used to
date has been a mixture of 90 percent alcohol and 4 percent
formaldehyde. Preliminary studies on rats, dogs, and a small
number of volunteers have been encouraging. However,
these chemicals produce an inflammatory reaction and the
formation of scar tissue within the vas, and will therefore
never be practical as a reversible method of sterilization.

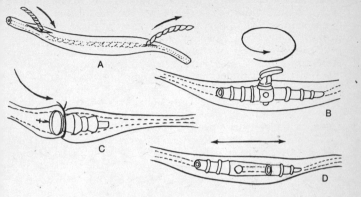

Figure 11-12. Types of Experimental Reversible Plugs and Valves Used for Vasectomies

Another chemical, alpha-chlorohydrin, when injected into the epididymis of rats prevents normal maturation of sperm. The immature sperm that are produced are incapable of achieving fertilization.

The most recent and fascinating method of decreasing sperm counts was reported at the University of Missouri School of Medicine, where sperm formation was suppressed in dogs and five men by use of ultrasound. The subjects sat on a special chair with their testes resting in a Plexiglass cup filled with water (Figure 11–13), and the water served as a conductor for the high-frequency sound emanating from the ultrasonic transducer (Figure 11–13).

Following the treatment, both the dogs and the men had suppressed sperm counts. The effect is believed to be reversible, though it may last for one to two years. The advantage of ultrasound is that there are no harmful side effects, it is painless, and the procedure is even reported to be pleasurable. In this study, the libido of the men undergoing treatment actually improved.

Is there an operation that reverses vasectomy?
Approximately 1 out of 2,000 vasectomy patients at a later date decide to undergo surgery in order to have more chil-

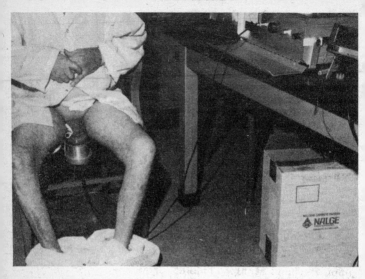

Figure 11-13.   Reducing Sperm Counts with Ultrasound

dren. This usually happens when a man remarries following either divorce or the death of his wife. The unforeseen death of a child may also precipitate this decision.

The operation for reuniting the cut ends of the vas deferens is called *vasovasotomy*. To perform this operation, an incision is made over the previous vasectomy site. The ends of the vas are located, opened, and sewn together with very fine suture material (Figure 11–14).

Though it looks easy in the illustration, the destruction to the lumen or the opening of the vas deferens may be quite extensive, and the caliber of one end may be different from that of the other, making repair difficult. Following surgery, reappearance of sperm in the semen may be noted in as few as 35 percent, and as many as 84 percent, of all men. However, sperm in the ejaculate does not guarantee success in achieving pregnancy. In the above study, in which 84 percent—or 78 of 93 men—demonstrated viable sperm, only 31 men—or 33 percent of the total—were capable of impreg-

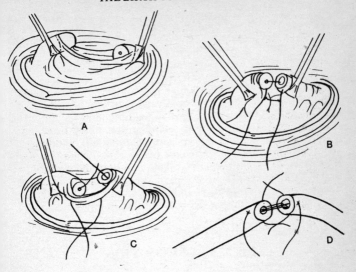

Figure 11-14.   Vasovasotomy Technique

nating their partners. The reasons appeared obscure, but until recently most people believed it was due to the antibody formation that those men produced against their own sperm.

In 1976, Dr. Sherman J. Silver and Dr. Earl Owen astounded the medical world by reporting thirty vasovasotomies, performed in both San Francisco and Australia, in which they used a specialized operating microscope. Both doctors had had training in microvascular surgery. They were able to perform the surgery using special miniature instruments and extremely fine, almost invisible surgical suture while viewing the operative area under the microscope. By meticulously suturing the free ends of the vas deferens in two layers rather than the standard one layer, they reported active sperm in all postoperative ejaculates studied. A most impressive seventeen pregnancies have already occurred, and in the other thirteen the time elapsed since surgery has been too short to evaluate the pregnancy potential of these men. However, even if none of the remaining men achieve conception, the results of Silver and Owen are already far better than any achieved by using the standard surgical approach.

Naturally, these two doctors have been inundated with calls from men requesting surgery. Other doctors in this country seek training in that delicate surgical technique, but it will be quite a while before many become proficient at using it. Mastering microscopic vasovasotomy surgery takes at least three months of intensive training, and few practicing physicians are willing to sacrifice that much time from their busy practices for a procedure they would be doing infrequently. In addition, the cost of the microscope and special surgical instruments is at least ten thousand dollars.

The current fee for a standard vasovasotomy may range from four hundred dollars to two thousand dollars. Clearly, with the new technique the cost will be greatly increased.

SEX PRESELECTION

Are there any new methods which will allow a couple to predict the sex of their child?
Sex selection prior to conception was first suggested by Hippocrates, the father of medicine. It was his theory that boys developed in the right side of the uterus, and girls in the left. Aristotle, believing in the theory, suggested that to conceive a male, a woman should lie on her right side after intercourse, "for therein is the greatest generative heat, which is the chief procuring cause of male children."

Several population studies have demonstrated that the main motivation of American men and women seems to be for a sex-balanced family, usually in the male chauvinistic order of boy first and girl second. When this is achieved, a couple will be more likely to seek effective contraception or permanent sterilization. This fact has great significance for ecologists concerned with population control, since it has been noted that a greater percentage of couples with children of the same sex are willing to try for a third child than couples with one child of each sex. This attitude is especially prevalent in many other countries of the world, where couples will try repeatedly until a much-preferred male heir is produced. It is obvious that zero population growth will not be achieved in some of these countries if family planning continues in such a haphazard and unscientific manner.

Scientists have now been able to accurately identify and separate X- and Y-bearing spermatozoa (see Chapter 1) based on differences in size, weight, and motility. The most popular method used to achieve separation has been *centrifugation*, or spinning, of semen specimens at high speeds. This causes settling of the heavier X-bearing spermatozoa to the bottom of the test tube, while the lighter Y-bearing spermatozoa stay suspended. To date, successful separation and insemination of the upper layer of Y-bearing spermatozoa has been achieved. However, a method has not yet been devised for preventing damage to the X-bearing spermatozoa as a result of the separation procedure. As a result, artificial insemination with the certainty of producing a female is still not possible.

It has been noted that Y-bearing sperm are faster swimmers than X-bearing sperm. Based on that information, Dr. Ronald J. Ericsson has developed a special filter which separates the male-producing sperm. Artificial insemination should produce an abundance of males, though the success of his method is still considered controversial. Recently, fertility clinics at the University of California Hospital in Berkeley and Michael Reese Hospital in Chicago have begun artificially inseminating women with their partner's semen after it has undergone that special processing.

Following conception, the sex of the fetus may be determined—with accuracy approaching 100 percent—by *amniocentesis*, the sampling of amniotic fluid from the gestational sac. The fluid is obtained in the same manner as it is when midtrimester abortion is performed (see Pages 178–179). The cells of the amniotic fluid are then examined and cultured in the laboratory. This process may take two to three weeks. If the sex of the fetus is not the one the parents want, abortion by use of protaglandins or saline may then be performed.

The one great application of sex preselection based on amniocentesis has been in the therapeutic termination of pregnancies in which there is a considerable risk of giving birth to an infant having a sex-linked disease. Diseases such as hemophilia and a common type of muscular dystrophy are carried on one of the two X chromosomes of the healthy mother (see Chapter 1). All male fetuses inheriting the disease-carrying X will be afflicted with the disease, while those inheriting the other X chromosome will be normal. The odds, therefore, of a mother who is a carrier of a sex-linked disease passing it to her male offspring are 50 percent. Unfortunately, amniocentesis does not allow us to tell a healthy X from an unhealthy one, but can determine whether a fetus is female or male. If the fetus is a male, a woman has the option of terminating the pregnancy.

Important ethical questions have been raised as to whether or not modern technology should be used to abort potentially healthy offspring merely on the basis of a couple's sex preference for their child. Opinions among theologians and geneticists have varied from those who readily accept the procedure to those voicing strong disapproval, such as "a ghastly misuse of technology." Anthropologist Margaret Mead, on the other hand, strongly favors sex determination and says, "If we could determine sex, and couples could say what sex they wanted, for the first time in human history girls would be as wanted as boys."

Other factors to be considered when amniocentesis is used are the 1 percent risk of accidental abortion due to trauma caused by the procedure itself, the added cost of at least $150 for culturing the cells, and the increased medical hazards incurred by the woman who elects to undergo a midtrimester prostaglandin or saline abortion.

It is known that fetal cells may actually pass into the maternal bloodstream during pregnancy. Based on this fact, researchers in Switzerland have successfully predicted the fetal sex 86 percent of the time. The drawback to this method is that it, too, only becomes accurate between the fourteenth and eighteenth weeks of pregnancy, when the more dangerous prostaglandin or saline abortion will be necessary to terminate the unwanted pregnancy.

It is possible that the repugnance that some people feel toward this type of abortion may be lessened somewhat if the fetal sex could be determined at an early stage of pregnancy, when a safe menstrual extraction could be performed. Successful studies have been carried out in the People's Republic of China by sampling cells that are shed into the endocervical canal from the placenta. The cells are obtained in the same manner as a Pap smear, and the accuracy of sex prediction to date has been 94 percent. Of fifty-three women carrying males, only one chose to terminate her pregnancy, while the majority carrying females opted for a therapeutic abortion.

There is great practical significance for offering these facilities to pregnant women in the People's Republic of China and other countries experiencing explosive population growth. Where there is a strong tradition and age-old desire for sons, a couple usually persists in their efforts until they succeed, regardless of the personal or economic consequences.

If sex preselection became readily available and totally safe, what would be its effect on future offspring?

Questionnaires sent to married couples about their gender preference in planning their families indicate that 80 percent prefer a male first-born and female second-born. Though Margaret Mead may see no apparent harm in the trend, other authorities predict potentially serious consequences resulting from that kind of family planning.

Three members of the department of psychology at California State University recently addressed themselves to the problem in a letter published in the *American Journal of Obstetrics and Gynecology*. They note, as others have, the first-born children of either sex tend to be achievement-oriented, conscientious, creative, self-controlled, and serious. They are also more likely to attend college and achieve a high position in their chosen work. Second-born children, on the other hand, are more cheerful, popular, and easy-going, and less likely to achieve those goals which society judges important. The psychologists point out that first-born children resemble society's masculine sex-role stereotype while second-born children resemble the feminine one. They conclude that if sex preselection follows the expected male first-born preference, it will unfortunately create "more masculine men and feminine women than are currently seen."

The fight for equality has been difficult enough for women without adding to it the burden of being the second child in a preselected family. In my opinion, family planning by sex preselection is the worst form of sex discrimination because the second-born child will know for her lifetime that she was not the favored one.

A final practical point is that women are naturally older when giving birth to their second child. As a result, those usually female offspring will be at greater risk of suffering the genetic risks and pregnancy complications which increase with maternal age.

Old ways die hard, especially in many countries of the world where custom and religion place great emphasis on and preference for male offspring. Luckily, the good old U.S.A. isn't a society with such deep-rooted tradition. The macho desire of some American men for young male superstars in their own image should not be accepted as a fact of life, to go unchallenged. The feminist movement has made great inroads in denouncing and eradicating stereotypic and sexist thinking. More important than sex preselection is sex education of the type which grants equal opportunity based on ability and not on gender.

PLANNED PARENTHOOD CHAPTERS

ALABAMA

BIRMINGHAM
Planned
  Parenthood-Birmingham Area
2301 Arlington Ave. *(M)* (35205)
(205) 933–8444

HUNTSVILLE
Planned Parenthood Assn. of
  Madison County
125 Earl St. *(M)* (35805)
(205) 539–2746

ARIZONA

PHOENIX
Planned Parenthood Assn. of
  Phoenix
1301 South Seventh Ave. *(M)*
  (85007)
(602) 257–1515

TUCSON
Planned Parenthood Center of
  Tucson, Inc.
127 South Fifth Ave. *(M)* (85701)
(602) 624–7477

CALIFORNIA

EUREKA
Planned Parenthood of
  Humboldt County
P.O. Box 6272 *(P) (M)* (95501)
(707) 442–5709

FRESNO
Planned Parenthood of Fresno
416 West McKinley *(M)* (93728)
(209) 486–2411

LOS ANGELES
Planned Parenthood/World
  Population Los Angeles
3100 West Eighth St. *(M)*
  (90005)
(213) 380–9300

ORANGE
Planned Parenthood Assn. of
  Orange County
704 North Glassell *(M)* (92667)
(714) 639–3023

(M) Medical   (E) Educational   (P) Provisional

PACIFIC GROVE
Planned Parenthood of
  Monterey County, Inc.
229 17th St. *(M)* (93950)
(408) 373–1691

PASADENA
Pasadena Planned Parenthood
  Committee, Inc.
1045 North Lake Ave. *(M)*
  (91104)
(213) 798–0708

SACRAMENTO
Planned Parenthood Assn. of
  Sacramento
1507 21st St., Suite 100 *(M)*
  (95814)
(916) 446–5034

SAN DIEGO
Planned Parenthood of San
  Diego County
2100 Fifth Ave. *(M)* (92101)
(714) 231–1282

SAN FRANCISCO
Planned Parenthood
  Alameda-San Francisco
1660 Bush St. *(M)* (94109)
(415) 441–0555

SAN JOSE
Planned Parenthood Assn. of
  Santa Clara County
17 North San Pedro *(M)* (95110)
(408) 287–7526

SAN MATEO
Planned Parenthood Assn. of
  San Mateo County
2211–2215 Palm Ave. *(M)*
  (94403)
(415) 574–2622

SAN RAFAEL
Planned Parenthood Assn. of
  Marin County
710 C St., Suite 9 *(M)* (94901)
(415) 454–0471

SANTA BARBARA
Planned Parenthood of Santa
  Barbara County, Inc.
322 Palm Ave. *(M)* (93101)
(805) 963–4417

SANTA CRUZ
Planned Parenthood of Santa
  Cruz County
427 Ocean St. *(M)* (95060)
(408) 426–5550

STOCKTON
Planned Parenthood of San
  Joaquin County
116 W. Willow *(M)* (95202)
(209) 464–5809

WALNUT CREEK
Planned Parenthood of Contra
  Costa County, Inc.
1291 Oakland Blvd. *(M)* (94596)
(415) 935–3010

WOODLAND
Planned Parenthood Assn. of
  Yolo County
327 College St., Suite 102 *(M)*
  (95695)
(916) 662–4646

COLORADO

DENVER
Rocky Mountain Planned
  Parenthood
2030 East 20th Ave. *(M)* (80205)
(303) 388–4215

Boulder Chapter
Boulder Planned Parenthood
  (M)
2760 29th St., Boulder (80302)
(303) 447–1040

(M) Medical   (E) Educational   (P) Provisional

Colorado Springs Chapter
Colorado Springs Planned
  Parenthood *(M)*
1619 West Colorado Ave.,
  Colorado Springs (80904)
(303) 475-7162

Denver Chapter
Denver Planned Parenthood *(M)*
Central Denver Clinic 2030 East
  20th Ave., Denver (80205)
(303) 388-4777

Fort Collins Chapter
Larimer County Planned
  Parenthood *(M)*
149 West Oak St., #8, Fort Collins (80521)
(303) 456-0517

Pueblo Chapter
Pueblo Planned Parenthood *(M)*
151 Central Main, Pueblo
  (81003)
(303) 545-0246

CONNECTICUT
NEW HAVEN
Planned Parenthood League of
  Connecticut, Inc.
129 Whitney Ave. *(M)* (06510)
(203) 865-0595

Bridgeport Chapter
Bridgeport Planned Parenthood
  (M)
1067 Park Ave., Bridgeport
  (06604)
(203) 366-0664

Danbury Chapter
Danbury Planned Parenthood
  (E)
240 Main St., Danbury (06810)
(203) 743-2446

Hartford Chapter
Hartford Planned Parenthood
  (M)
297 Farmington Ave., Hartford
  (06105)
(203) 522-6201

Meriden Chapter
Meriden/Wallingford Planned
  Parenthood *(E)*
Box 2119, Meriden (06450)
(203) 235-3231

Middletown Chapter
Middlesex Planned Parenthood
  (M)
79–81 Crescent St., Middletown
  (06457)
(203) 347-5255

New Britain Chapter
New Britain Planned
  Parenthood *(E)*
Box 292, New Britain (06050)
(203) 225-9811

New Haven Chapter
New Haven Planned Parenthood
  (M)
129 Whitney Ave., New Haven
  (06511)
(203) 865-4250

New London Chapter
Southeast Chapter, Planned
  Parenthood *(M)*
420 Williams St., New London
  (06320)
(203) 443-5820

Stamford Chapter
South Fairfield Planned
  Parenthood *(M)*
259 Main St., Stamford (06901)
(203) 327-2722

(M) Medical   *(E) Educational*   *(P) Provisional*

Torrington Chapter
Northwest Chapter, Planned
  Parenthood *(M)*
27 Pearl St., Torrington (06790)
(203) 489–5500

Waterbury Chapter
Waterbury Planned Parenthood
  (M)
115 Prospect St., Waterbury
  (06702)
(203) 757–1955

4Willimantic Chapter
Northeast Chapter, Planned
  Parenthood *(M)*
791 Main St., Willimantic
  (06226)
(203) 423–1500

DELAWARE
WILMINGTON
Delaware League for Planned
  Parenthood
825 Washington St. *(M)* (19801)
(302) 655–7293

DISTRICT OF COLUMBIA
WASHINGTON
Planned Parenthood of
  Metropolitan Washington,
  D.C.
1109 M St., N.W. *(M)* (20005)
(202) 387–4711

Washington, D.C. Chapter
Washington, D.C. Chapter
Planned Parenthood *(M)*
1120 M St., N.W., Washington
  D.C. (20005)

Landover, Maryland Chapter
Planned Parenthood of Prince
  George's County *(M)*
Landover Mall East Tower
  Building, #203, Landover
  (20785)
(301) 773–5601

Wheaton, Maryland Chapter
Planned Parenthood of
  Montgomery County *(M)*
1141 Georgia Ave., Wheaton
  (20902)
(301) 933–2300

Falls Church, Virginia Chapter
Planned Parenthood of
  Northern Virginia *(M)*
5622 Columbia Pike, Falls
  Church (22041)
(804) 820–3335

FLORIDA
GAINESVILLE
Planned Parenthood of North
  Central Florida
P.O. Box 12385 *(P) (E)* (32604)
(904) 377–0881

JACKSONVILLE
Planned Parenthood of
  Northeast Florida, Inc.
305 East Church St. *(M)* (32202)
(904) 354–7796

OPA LOCKA
Planned Parenthood Assn. of
  South Florida, Inc.
3400 N.W. 135th St. *(P) (E)*
  (33054)
(305) 949–4196

ORLANDO
Planned Parenthood of
  Mid-Florida, Inc.
118 East Robinson *(P) (E)*
  (32801)
(305) 843–4280

SARASOTA
Planned Parenthood of
  Southwest Florida
Sarasota Memorial Hospital,
  P.O. Box 2532,
1224 S. Tamiami Tr. *(M)* (33578)
(813) 959–4648

(M) Medical   (E) Educational   (P) Provisional

Naples Chapter
Planned Parenthood-Naples
  Center *(M)*
482 Tamiami Tr. N., Naples
  (33940)
(305) 649-5484

WEST PALM BEACH
Planned Parenthood Palm
  Beach Area
120 South Olive Ave. Suite 555
  (M) (33401)
(305) 655-7984

Boca Raton Chapter
South County Center Planned
  Parenthood *(M)*
162 West Palmetto Park Rd.,
  Boca Raton (33432)
(305) 737-7455

GEORGIA
ATLANTA
Planned Parenthood Assn. of the
  Atlanta Area
118 Marietta St., N.W. *(M)*
  (30303)
(404) 688-9302

AUGUSTA
Planned Parenthood of East
  Central Georgia, Inc.
P.O. Box 3293, Hill Station *(M)*
  (30904)
(404) 736-1161

HAWAII
HONOLULU
Hawaii Planned Parenthood,
  Inc.
1164 Bishop St., 12th Floor *(M)*
  (96813)
(808) 521-6991

IDAHO
BOISE
Planned Parenthood Assn. of
  Idaho, Inc.
P.O. Box 264 *(M)* (83701)
(208) 345-0760

ILLINOIS
BLOOMINGTON
Planned Parenthood of McLean
  County
210 East Washington St. *(M)*
  (61701)
(309) 829-3028

CHAMPAIGN
Planned Parenthood of
  Champaign County
314 S. Neil St. *(M)* (61820)
(217) 359-8022

CHICAGO
Planned Parenthood
  Assn.-Chicago Area
55 East Jackson Blvd. *(M)*
  (60604)
(312) 322-4200

DECATUR
Planned Parenthood of Decatur,
  Inc.
988-990 S. Main St. *(M)* (62521)
(217) 429-9211

PEORIA
Planned Parenthood Assn. of
  Peoria Area
313 S.W. Jefferson *(M)* (61602)
(309) 673-6911

SPRINGFIELD
Planned Parenthood-Springfield
  Area
624 South Second *(M)* (62704)
(217) 544-2744

(M) Medical   *(E) Educational*   *(P) Provisional*

INDIANA

BLOOMINGTON
Planned Parenthood of South
  Central Indiana
421 South College Ave. *(M)*
  (47401)
(812) 336-0219

EVANSVILLE
Planned Parenthood of
  Evansville, Inc.
1610 South Weinbach Ave. *(M)*
  (47714)
(812) 479-1466

GARY
Planned Parenthood of
  Northwest Indiana, Inc.
740 Washington St. *(M)* (46402)
(219) 883-0411

INDIANAPOLIS
Planned Parenthood Assn. of
  Indianapolis, Inc.
615 North Alabama St. *(M)*
  (46204)
(317) 634-8019

LAFAYETTE
Planned Parenthood Assn. of
  Tippecanoe County
P.O. Box 1114 *(E)* (47902)
(317) 742-9073

MUNCIE
Planned Parenthood of East
  Central Indiana, Inc.
303 Johnson Building *(M)*
  (47305)
(317) 282-8011

SOUTH BEND
Planned Parenthood of North
  Central Indiana
201 South Chapin *(M)* (46625)
(219) 289-7027

Elkhart Chapter
Elkhart County Health Unit *(M)*
315 S. Second St., Elkhart
  (46514)
(219) 293-7715

Warsaw Chapter
Kosciusko County Planned
  Parenthood *(M)*
P.O. Box 555, Warsaw (46580)
(219) 267-3889

Plymouth Chapter
Marshall County Planned
  Parenthood *(M)*
218 LaPorte St., Plymouth
  (46563)
(219) 936-8680

TERRE HAUTE
Planned Parenthood Assn. of the
  Wabash Valley, Inc.
330 South 6th St. *(M)* (47807)
(812) 232-3578

IOWA

DES MOINES
Planned Parenthood of Iowa
P.O. Box 4557 *(M)* (50306)
(515) 280-7000

MT. PLEASANT
Planned Parenthood of
  Southeast Iowa
125½ W. Monroe *(M)* (52641)
(319) 385-8322

Burlington Chapter
Planned Parenthood of Des
  Moines County *(M)*
521 N. 5th, Burlington (52601)
(319) 753-2281

Fort Madison Chapter
Planned Parenthood of North
  Lee County *(M)*
631 Ave. H, Fort Madison
  (52627)
(319) 372-1130

(M) Medical   (E) Educational   (P) Provisional

Keokuk Chapter
Planned Parenthood of South
  Lee County *(M)*
927 Exchange St., Keokuk
  (52632)
(319) 524-2759

Mt. Pleasant Chapter
Planned Parenthood of Henry
  County *(M)*
125½ W. Monroe, Mt. Pleasant
  (52641)
(319) 385-4310

Wapello Chapter
Planned Parenthood of Louisa
  County *(E)*
407 Washington, P.O. Box 182,
  Wapello (52653)
(319) 523-8297

Washington Chapter
Planned Parenthood of
  Washington County *(M)*
Clara Barton & 4th, P. O. Box
  44, Washington (52353)
(319) 653-3525

SIOUX CITY
Planned Parenthood of Sioux
  City
2825 Douglas St. *(M)* (51101)
(712) 258-4019

WATERLOO
Planned Parenthood of
  Northeast Iowa
1825 Logan Ave. *(P) (E)* (50703)
(319) 235-3731

KANSAS
WICHITA
Planned Parenthood of Kansas
158 North Grove St. *(M)* (67214)
(316) 686-3356

KENTUCKY
BEREA
Mountain Maternal Health
  League
P.O. Box 429 *(M)* (40403)
(606) 986-4677

LEXINGTON
Lexington Planned Parenthood
  Center, Inc.
331 West Second St. *(M)* (40507)
(606) 252-0448

LOUISVILLE
Planned Parenthood Center, Inc.
843-845 Barrett Ave. *(M)*
  (40204)
(502) 584-2471

MARYLAND
BALTIMORE
Planned Parenthood Assn. of
  Maryland, Inc.
610 North Howard St. *(M)*
  (21201)
(301) 752-0131

LANDOVER CHAPTER
(see District of Columbia)

WHEATON CHAPTER
(see District of Columbia)

MASSACHUSETTS
CAMBRIDGE
Planned Parenthood League of
  Massachusetts
99 Bishop Richard Allen Dr. *(E)*
  (02139)
(617) 492-0518

MICHIGAN
ANN ARBOR
Washtenaw County League for
  Planned Parenthood
912 N. Main St. *(M)* (48104)
(313) 769-8530

(M) Medical   (E) Educational   (P) Provisional

BENTON HARBOR
Planned Parenthood Assn. of Southwestern Michigan
785 Pipestone *(M)* (49022)
(616) 925–1306

DETROIT
Planned Parenthood League, Inc.
Professional Plaza Concourse Bldg.
3750 Woodward Ave. *(M)* (48201)
(313) 832–7200

FLINT
Flint Community Planned Parenthood Assn.
310 E. Third St., Y.W.C.A. *(M)* (48503)
(313) 238–3631

Owosso Chapter
Shiawassee County Planned Parenthood Assn. *(E)*
P.O. Box 542, Owosso (48867)
(517) 723–6420

GRAND RAPIDS
Planned Parenthood Assn. of Kent County, Inc.
425 Cherry, S.E. *(M)* (49502)
(616) 459–3101

Big Rapids Chapter
Mecosta County Family Planning *(M)*
P.O. Box 1156, Big Rapids (49307)
(616) 796–8644

Grand Haven Chapter
Planned Parenthood of Ottawa County *(M)*
Box 728, Grand Haven (49417)
(616) 842–4569

Ionia Chapter
Planned Parenthood of Ionia County *(M)*
111 Kidd, Ionia (48846)
(616) 527–3250

KALAMAZOO
Planned Parenthood Assn. of Kalamazoo County
612 Douglas Ave. *(M)* (49007)
(616) 349–8631

MUSKEGON
Muskegon Area Planned Parenthood Assn., Inc.
1095 Third St. *(M)* (49440)
(616) 722–2928

PETOSKEY
Northern Michigan Planned Parenthood Assn.
316½ N. Mitchell *(M)* (49770)
(616) 347–9692

Alpena Chapter
Planned Parenthood-Alpena County *(E)*
2330 Sandy Lane, Alpena (49707)
(517) 356–1137

Cadillac Chapter
Cadillac Planned Parenthood *(E)*
c/o Ms. Kathy Tunney 110 North Park St., Cadillac (49601)
(616) 775–4956

Marquette Chapter
Marquette-Alger Family Planning Assn. *(E)*
225 E. Michigan Ave., Marquette (49855)
(905) 255–5070

(M) Medical   (E) Educational   (P) Provisional

Petoskey Chapter
Petoskey Planned Parenthood
  (E)
316½ N. Mitchell St., Petoskey
  (49770)
(616) 347–9692

Sault St. Marie Chapter
Sault St. Marie Planned
  Parenthood *(E)*
P.O. Box 246A, Route 1, Sault
  St. Marie (49783)
(906) 632–8103

MINNESOTA
ST. PAUL
Planned Parenthood of
  Minnesota, Inc.
1965 Ford Parkway *(M)* (55116)
(612) 646–9603

Bemidji Chapter
Planned Parenthood of Bemidji
  Area *(E)*
722 15th St., Box 822, Bemidji
  (56601)
(218) 751–8683

Brainerd Chapter
Central Minnesota Planned
  Parenthood *(M)*
502 Front St., Brainerd (56401)
(218) 829–1469

Duluth Chapter
Planned Parenthood of
  Northeast Minnesota *(M)*
504 East Second St., Duluth
  (55805)
(218) 722–0833

Mankato Chapter
South Central Planned
  Parenthood *(E)*
Room 203, Liberty Bldg.,
  Mankato (56001)
(507) 378–5581

Minneapolis Chapter
Planned Parenthood of
  Metropolitan Minneapolis *(M)*
230 Walker Bldg.
803 Hennepin Ave., Minneapolis
  (55403)
(612) 336–8931

Rochester Chapter
Planned Parenthood of
  Rochester Area *(M)*
116½ South Broadway,
  Rochester (55901)
(507) 228–5186

St. Paul Chapter
Planned Parenthood of St. Paul
  Metropolitan Area *(M)*
408 Hamm Bldg.
408 St. Peter Street, St. Paul
  (55102)
(612) 224–1361

MISSOURI
COLUMBIA
Planned Parenthood of Central
  Missouri
800 North Providence Rd., Suite
  5 *(M)* (65201)
(314) 449–2475

KANSAS CITY
Planned Parenthood Assn. of
  Western Missouri/Kansas
1001 E. 47th St. *(M)* (64110)
(816) 756–2277

KIRKSVILLE
Planned Parenthood of
  Northeast Missouri, Inc.
P.O. Box 763 *(M)* (63501)
(816) 665–5672

ROLLA
Planned Parenthood of the
  Central Ozarks
Box 359, 1032B Kings Highway
  (M) (65401)
(314) 364–1509

(M) Medical   (E) Educational   (P) Provisional

SPRINGFIELD
Planned Parenthood of
  Southwest Missouri, Inc.
1918 E. Meadowmere *(M)*
  (65804)
(417) 869–6471

ST. LOUIS
Planned Parenthood Assn. of St.
  Louis
2202 South Hanley Rd. *(M)*
  (63144)
(314) 781–3800

MONTANA
BILLINGS
Planned Parenthood of Billings
2718 Montana Ave. *(M)* (59101)
(406) 252–2131

MISSOULA
Planned Parenthood of Missoula
  County
301 Alder *(M)* (59801)
(406) 728–5490

NEBRASKA
LINCOLN
Planned Parenthood of Lincoln
3830 Adams St. *(M)* (68504)
(402) 466–2387

OMAHA
Planned Parenthood of Omaha
2916 North 58th St. *(M)* (68104)
(402) 554–1045

NEVADA
LAS VEGAS
Planned Parenthood of
  Southern Nevada, Inc.
601 S. 13th St. *(M)* (89101)
(702) 385–3451

RENO
Planned Parenthood of
  Northern Nevada
406 Elm St. *(M)* (89503)
(702) 329–1781

NEW HAMPSHIRE
LEBANON
Planned Parenthood Assn. of the
  Upper Valley
1 Foundry St. *(M)* (03766)
(603) 448–1214

NEW JERSEY
CAMDEN
Planned Parenthood-Greater
  Camden Area
590 Benson St. *(M)* (08103)
(609) 365–3521

HACKENSACK
Planned Parenthood Center of
  Bergen County
485 Main St. *(M)* (07601)
(201) 489–1140

JERSEY CITY
Planned Parenthood Assn. of
  Hudson County
777 Bergen Ave., Room 218 *(M)*
  (07303)
(201) 332–2565

MORRISTOWN
Planned Parenthood of
  Northwest New Jersey, Inc.
197 Speedwell Ave. *(M)* (07960)
(201) 539–1364

NEWARK
Planned Parenthood-Essex
  County
15 William St. *(M)* (07102)
(201) 622–3900

(M) Medical   *(E) Educational*   *(P) Provisional*

NEW BRUNSWICK
Planned Parenthood League of
 Middlesex County
84 Carroll Pl. *(M)* (08901)
(201) 246-2404

PATERSON
Passaic County Planned
 Parenthood Center
145 Presidential Blvd.,
 Riverview Terrace *(M)* (07522)
(201) 274-3883

PLAINFIELD
Planned Parenthood of Union
 County Area, Inc.
234 Park Avenue *(M)* (07060)
(201) 756-3736

SHREWSBURY
Planned Parenthood of Mon-
 mouth County, Inc.
69 Newman Springs Rd. *(M)*
 (07701)
(201) 842-9300

TRENTON
Planned Parenthood Assn. of the
 Mercer Area
437 E. State St. *(M)* (08608)
(609) 599-3736

NEW MEXICO
ALBUQUERQUE
Bernalillo County Planned
 Parenthood Assn., Inc.
113 Montclaire, S.E. *(M)* (87108)
(505) 265-3722, Ext. 21

LAS CRUCES
Dona Ana County Planned
 Parenthood Assn.
302 West Griggs Ave. *(M)*
 (88001)
(505) 524-8516

SILVER CITY
Planned Parenthood of
 Southwest New Mexico
524 Silver Heights Blvd. *(M)*
 (88061)
(505) 388-1553

NEW YORK
ALBANY
Planned Parenthood Assn. of
 Albany
225 Lark St. *(M)* (12210)
(518) 434-2182

BINGHAMTON
Planned Parenthood of Broome
 County, Inc.
710 O'Neill Bldg. *(M)* (13901)
(607) 723-8306

BUFFALO
Planned Parenthood Center of
 Buffalo
210 Franklin St. *(M)* (14203)
(716) 853-1771

EAST MEADOW
Planned Parenthood of Nassau
 County
1940 Hempstead Turnpike *(M)*
 (11554)
(516) 292-8380

ELMIRA
Planned Parenthood of the
 Southern Tier
200 East Market St. *(M)* (14901)
(607) 734-3313

GENEVA
Planned Parenthood of Ontario
 County
435 Exchange St. *(M)* (14456)
(315) 394-0310

(M) Medical   *(E) Educational*   *(P) Provisional*

GLENS FALLS
Southern Adirondack Planned
  Parenthood Assn.
126 Warren St. *(M)* (12801)
(518) 792–0994

HUNTINGTON
Planned Parenthood Center of
  North Suffolk
17 East Carver St. *(M)* (11743)
(516) 427–7154

ITHACA
Planned Parenthood of
  Tompkins County
512 East State St. *(M)* (14853)
(607) 273–1513

NEWBURGH
Planned Parenthood Center of
  Orange & Sullivan Counties
91 DuBois St. *(M)* (12550)
(914) 562–5748

NEW YORK
Planned Parenthood of New
  York City, Inc.
300 Park Ave. South *(M)* (10010)
(212) 777–2002

NIAGARA FALLS
Planned Parenthood of Niagara
  County
906 Michigan Ave. *(M)* (14305)
(716) 282–1223

Lockport Chapter
Lockport Planned Parenthood
  (M)
555 Pine St., Lockport (14094)
(716) 433–4464

ONEONTA
Planned Parenthood Assn. of
  Delaware & Otsego Counties,
  Inc.
48 Market St. *(M)* (13820)
(607) 433–2890

PATCHOGUE
Planned Parenthood of East
  Suffolk, Inc.
127 South Ocean Ave. *(M)*
  (11772)
(516) 475–5705

PLATTSBURGH
Planned Parenthood of Clinton
  County
94 Margaret St. *(M)* (12901)
(518) 561–4430

POUGHKEEPSIE
Planned Parenthood of
  Dutchess-Ulster, Inc.
85 Market St. *(M)* (12601)
(914) 471–1540

ROCHESTER
Planned Parenthood of
  Rochester & Monroe
  Counties, Inc.
24 Windsor St. *(M)* (14605)
(716) 546–2595

SCHENECTADY
Planned Parenthood of
  Schenectady & Affiliated
  Counties, Inc.
414 Union St. *(M)* (12305)
(518) 374–5353

SYRACUSE
Planned Parenthood Center of
  Syracuse, Inc.
1120 E. Genesee St. *(M)* (13210)
(315) 424–8260

UTICA
Planned Parenthood Assn. of the
  Mohawk Valley, Inc.
1424 Genesse St. *(M)* (13502)
(315) 724–6146

(M) Medical   (E) Educational   (P) Provisional

WATERTOWN
Planned Parenthood of
  Northern New York, Inc.
161 Stone St. *(M)* (13601)
(315) 782-0481

Canton Chapter
St. Lawrence County Planned
  Parenthood *(M)*
15 Main St., Canton (13617)
(315) 386-2441

Lowville Chapter
Lewis County Planned
  Parenthood *(M)*
7552 State St., Lowville (13367)
(315) 376-2741

Malone Chapter
Franklin County Planned
  Parenthood *(M)*
109 East Main St., Malone
  (12953)
(518) 483-7150

Watertown Chapter
Jefferson County Planned
  Parenthood *(M)*
161 Stone St., Watertown
  (13601)
(315) 788-8065

WEST NYACK
Planned Parenthood of
  Rockland County
37 Village Square *(M)* (10994)
(914) 358-1145

WHITE PLAINS
Planned Parenthood of
  Westchester, Inc.
149 Grand St. *(M)* (10601)
(914) 428-7876

NORTH CAROLINA
CHARLOTTE
Planned Parenthood of Greater
  Charlotte
East Independence Plaza Bldg.
951 S. Independence Blvd. *(M)*
  (28202)
(704) 377-0841

OHIO
AKRON
Planned Parenthood Assn. of
  Summit County, Inc.
137 South Main St., Room 218
  (M) (44308)
(216) 535-2671

ATHENS
Planned Parenthood of
  Southeast Ohio
306 Security Bldg.
8 North Court St. *(M)* (45701)
(614) 593-3375

CANTON
Planned Parenthood of Stark
  County
626 Walnut Ave., N.E. *(M)*
  (44702)
(216) 456-7191

CINCINNATI
Planned Parenthood Assn. of
  Cincinnati
2406 Auburn Ave. *(M)* (45219)
(513) 721-7635

CLEVELAND
Planned Parenthood of
  Cleveland, Inc.
2027 Cornell Rd. *(M)* (44106)
(216) 721-4700

(M) Medical   (E) Educational   (P) Provisional

Elyria Chapter
Maternal Health Assn. of Lorain
    County *(M)*
266 Washington Ave., Elyria
    (44035)
(216) 245–4712

Painsville Chapter
Family Planning Assn. of Lake
    & Geauga Counties
1499 Mentor Ave., Painsville
    (44077)
(216) 352–0608

COLUMBUS
Planned Parenthood of Central
    Ohio, Inc.
206 East State St. *(M)* (43215)
(614) 224–8423

Circleville Chapter
Pickaway Family Planning Assn.
    (M)
Berger Hospital
600 N. Pickaway, Circleville
    (43113)
(614) 374–5143

DAYTON
Planned Parenthood Assn. of
    Miami Valley
224 N. Wilkinson St. *(M)* (45402)
(513) 226–0780

HAMILTON
Planned Parenthood Assn. of
    Butler County, Inc.
305 South Front St. *(M)* (45011)
(513) 894–3875

MANSFIELD
Planned Parenthood Assn. of
    Mansfield Area
25 North Park St. *(M)* (44902)
(419) 525–3075

Galion Chapter
Planned Parenthood Assn. of
    Crawford County
200 Harding Way E., Galion
    (44833) *(M)*
(419) 468–9926

Wooster Chapter
Planned Parenthood of Wayne
    County *(M)*
111 South Buckeye, Wooster
    (44691)
(216) 262–4866

NEWARK
Planned Parenthood Assn. of
    East Central Ohio
17 North First St. *(M)* (43055)
(614) 345–5450

SPRINGFIELD
Planned Parenthood of West
    Central Ohio
401 N. Plum St. *(M)* (45504)
(513) 325–7349

TOLEDO
Planned Parenthood League of
    Toledo
Hillcrest Hotel, 16th &
    Madison, P.O. Box 10003 *(M)*
    (43699)
(419) 246–3651

YOUNGSTOWN
Planned Parenthood of
    Mahoning Valley
105 East Boardman St. *(M)*
    (44503)
(216) 746–5662

OKLAHOMA
OKLAHOMA CITY
Planned Parenthood Assn. of
    Oklahoma City
10 N.E. 23rd St. *(M)* (73105)
(405) 528–2157

(M) Medical   (E) Educational   (P) Provisional

TULSA
Planned Parenthood Assn. of
Tulsa
808 South Peoria Ave. (M)
(74120)
(918) 587–8419

OREGON
CORVALLIS
Planned Parenthood of Benton
County, Inc.
Family Planning Clinic
610 Van Buren (E) (97330)
(503) 753–3348

EUGENE
Planned Parenthood Assn. of
Lane County
134 East 13th Ave. (M) (97401)
(503) 344–9411

MEDFORD
Planned Parenthood of Jackson
County
11 Myrtle St. (M) (97501)
(503) 773–8285

PORTLAND
Planned Parenthood Assn., Inc.
1200 S.E. Morrison (M) (97214)
(503) 234–5411

PENNSYLVANIA
ALLENTOWN
Planned Parenthood Assn. of
Lehigh County
806 Hamilton St., 2nd Floor (E)
(18101)
(215) 439–1033

BRISTOL
Planned Parenthood Assn. of
Bucks County
721 New Rodgers Rd. (M)
(19007)
(215) 785–4591

EASTON
Planned Parenthood of
Northampton County, Inc.
275 S. 21st St. (M) (18042)
(215) 253–7195

EAST STROUDSBURG
Monroe County Planned
Parenthood Assn.
162 E. Brown St. (M) (18301)
(717) 421–4000, Ext. 630

LANCASTER
Planned Parenthood of
Lancaster
37 S. Lime St. (M) (17601)
(717) 394–3575

PHILADELPHIA
Planned Parenthood Assn. of
Southeastern Pennsylvania
1220 Sanson St. (M) (19107)
(215) 574–9200

PITTSBURGH
Planned Parenthood Center of
Pittsburgh
102 9th St. (M) (15222)
(412) 434–8950

READING
Planned Parenthood Center of
Berks County
48 South 4th St. (M) (19602)
(215) 376–8061

SCRANTON
Planned Parenthood
Organization of Lackawanna
County
207 Wyoming Ave., Suite 322
(M) (18503)
(717) 344–2626

(M) Medical   (E) Educational   (P) Provisional

WEST CHESTER
Planned Parenthood of Chester
    County
113 West Chestnut St. *(M)*
    (19380)
(215) 692–1770

WILKES-BARRE
Planned Parenthood Assn. of
    Luzerne County
63 North Franklin St. *(M)*
    (18701)
(717) 824–8921

YORK
Planned Parenthood of Central
    Pennsylvania
710 S. George St. *(M)* (17403)
(717) 845–9681

Johnstown Chapter
Cambria/Somerset Planned
    Parenthood *(M)*
423 Main St., Johnstown
    (15901)
(814) 535–5545

York Chapter
York Chapter Planned
    Parenthood *(M)*
710 South George St., York
    (17403)
(717) 845–9681

RHODE ISLAND
PROVIDENCE
Planned Parenthood of Rhode
    Island
187 Westminster *(M)* (02903)
(401) 421–9620

SOUTH CAROLINA
CLEARWATER
Planned Parenthood of Aiken
    County
P.O. Box 277 *(M)* (29822)
(803) 593–9283

COLUMBIA
Planned Parenthood of Central
    South Carolina, Inc.
2719 Middleburg Dr., Suite 202
    (M) (29204)
(803) 256–4908

TENNESSEE
KNOXVILLE
Planned Parenthood Assn. of
    Knox County
114 Dameron Ave., N.W. *(E)*
    (37917)
(615) 524–7487

MEMPHIS
Memphis Planned Parenthood
    Assn., Inc.
Suite 1700, Exchange Building
9 North Second St. *(M)* (38103)
(901) 525–0591

NASHVILLE
Planned Parenthood Assn. of
    Nashville
University Plaza 112 21st Ave.
    South *(M)* (37203)
(615) 327–1066

OAK RIDGE
Planned Parenthood Assn. of the
    Southern Mountains, Inc.
162 Ridgeway Center *(M)*
    (37830)
(615) 482–3406

TEXAS
AMARILLO
Panhandle Planned Parenthood
    Assn.
604 West Eighth St. *(M)* (79101)
(806) 372–8731–2

AUSTIN
Planned Parenthood Center of
    Austin
1823 E. 7th St. *(M)* (78702)
(512) 477–5846

(M) Medical   (E) Educational   (P) Provisional

BROWNSVILLE
Planned Parenthood of Cameron
    County
1158 E. Elizabeth Rd. *(M)*
Room 310—Security Building
    (78520)
(512) 546–9288

CORPUS CHRISTI
South Texas Planned
    Parenthood Center
1220 S. Staples, Room 205 *(E)*
    (78404)
(512) 884–4352

DALLAS
Planned Parenthood of Northeast Texas
2727 Oak Lawn, Suite 228 *(M)*
    (75219)
(214) 522–0290

EL PASO
Planned Parenthood Center of
    El Paso
214 West Franklin St. *(M)*
    (79901)
(915) 542–1919

FORT WORTH
Planned Parenthood Center of
    Fort Worth
301 S. Henderson *(M)* (76104)
(817) 332–9101

HOUSTON
Planned Parenthood of Houston
3601 Fannin *(M)* (77004)
(713) 522–3976

KINGSVILLE
Planned Parenthood Assn. of
    Chaparral Country
117 South Fifth St., P. O. Box
    1134 *(M)* (78363)
(512) 592–2649

LAREDO
Planned Parenthood of Webb
    County, Inc.
2000 San Jorge *(M)* (78040)
(512) 723–4606

LUBBOCK
Planned Parenthood Center of
    Lubbock
3821 22nd St. *(M)* (79410)
(806) 795–7123

MISSION
Planned Parenthood Assn. of
    Hidalgo County
P.O. Box 1069 *(M)* (78572)
(512) 585–4575

ODESSA
Permian Basin Planned
    Parenthood, Inc.
American Bank Commerce
    Bldg.
Suite 401 *(M)* (79761)
(915) 563–2530

SAN ANGELO
Planned Parenthood Center of
    San Angelo
122 West Second St. *(M)* (76901)
(915) 655–9141

SAN ANTONIO
Planned Parenthood Center of
    San Antonio
106 Warren St. *(M)* (78212)
(512) 227–2227

WACO
The Central Texas Planned
    Parenthood Assn.
P.O. Box 6308 *(M)* (76706)
(817) 754–2392

(M) Medical   *(E) Educational*   *(P) Provisional*

UTAH
SALT LAKE CITY
Planned Parenthood Assn. of
  Utah
Chapman Bldg.
28 East 2100 South *(M)* (84115)
(801) 487–8914

VERMONT
BURLINGTON
Planned Parenthood Assn. of
  Vermont
158 Bank St. *(M)* (05401)
(802) 862–9637

VIRGINIA
HAMPTON
Peninsula Planned Parenthood
1520 Aberdeen Rd., Room 314
  (P) (M) (23666)
(804) 826–2079

NORFOLK
Planned Parenthood of Norfolk
  & Chesapeake, Inc.
222 W. 19th St. *(E)* (23517)
(804) 625–5591

RICHMOND
Virginia League for Planned
  Parenthood
1218 W. Franklin St. *(M)* (23220)
(804) 353–5516

Chase City Chapter
Mecklenburg County Chapter
  Planned Parenthood
313 High St., Chase City (23924)
  (E)
(804) 372–4631

Suffolk Chapter
Tri-County Area Planned
  Parenthood *(E)*
P.O. Box 1400, Suffolk (23434)
(804) 539–3456

ROANOKE
Planned Parenthood of Roanoke
  Valley, Inc.
920 S. Jefferson St. *(P) (E)*
  (24016)
(703) 342–6741

WASHINGTON
BELLINGHAM
Planned Parenthood of
  Whatcom County
P.O. Box 4 *(M)* (98225)
(206) 734–9095

EVERETT
Planned Parenthood of
  Snohomish County
2730 Hoyt Ave. *(M)* (98201)
(206) 259–0096

KENNEWICK
Planned Parenthood of
  Benton-Franklin Counties
P.O. Box 6842 *(P) (M)* (99336)
(509) 586–2164

SEATTLE
Planned Parenthood of
  Seattle-King County
2211 East Madison *(M)* (98112)
(206) 447–2350

SPOKANE
Planned Parenthood of Spokane
N. 507 Howard St. *(M)* (99201)
(509) 624–3271

TACOMA
Planned Parenthood of Pierce
  County
312 Broadway Terrace Bldg. *(M)*
  (98402)
(206) 572–6955

WALLA WALLA
Center for Family Planning
329 South Second St. *(M)*
  (99362)
(509) 529–3570

(M) Medical   (E) Educational   (P) Provisional

YAKIMA
Planned Parenthood Assn. of
  Yakima County
208 N. 3rd Ave. *(M)* (98901)
(509) 248–3625

WEST VIRGINIA
VIENNA
Planned Parenthood Assn. of
  Parkersburg
210 Fifth St. *(E)* (26101)
(304) 485–1144

WISCONSIN
MILWAUKEE
Planned Parenthood Assn. of
  Wisconsin
1135 West State St. *(M)* (53233)
(414) 271–8181

Appleton Chapter
Planned Parenthood Assn. of
  Fox Valley *(M)*
128 Durkee St., Appleton
  (54911)
(414) 731–6304

Green Bay Chapter
Planned Parenthood of Green
  Bay *(M)*
Bellin Bldg.
130 East Walnut St., Green Bay
  (54301)
(414) 432–0031

Jefferson Chapter
Planned Parenthood of
  Dodge-Jefferson Counties
159 West Garland St., Jefferson
  (53549) *(M)*
(414) 674–2233

Kenosha Chapter
Planned Parenthood of Kenosha
  (M)
5621 18th Ave., Kenosha (53140)
(414) 654–0491

Madison Chapter
Planned Parenthood of Madison
  Dane County *(M)*
Regent Mills Professional Bldg.
1051 Regent St., Madison
  (53715)
(608) 256–7257

Manitowoc Chapter
Planned Parenthood of
  Manitowoc-Two Rivers *(M)*
910A South 8th St., Manitowoc
  (54220)
(414) 684–1332

Oshkosh Chapter
Planned Parenthood of Oshkosh
  (M)
Washington Bldg., 105
  Washington, Oshkosh (54901)
(414) 235–0015

Sheboygan Chapter
Planned Parenthood of
  Sheboygan *(M)*
635 West Center St., Sheboygan
  (53081)
(414) 458–9401

West Bend Chapter
Planned Parenthood of
  Washington County *(M)*
320 South 5th Ave., West Bend
  (53095)
(414) 338–1303

(M) Medical   (E) Educational   (P) Provisional

Reprinted courtesy of:
Planned Parenthood-World Population
(Planned Parenthood Federation of America, Inc.)
810 Seventh Avenue
New York, N.Y. 10019

GLOSSARY

Abortion—The expulsion of the products of conception, or fetus, from the uterus.

Adenomyosis—A benign though progressively disabling condition caused by endometrial glandular tissue being displaced into the muscle of the uterus.

Adenosis—A benign condition in which glands shift to areas other than their usual locations. *Vaginal adenosis* occurs when glands that are normally located within the cervix find their way into the vagina.

Amenorrhea—The absence, or abnormal stoppage, of the menstrual period.

Amniocentesis—The insertion of a needle into the fluid-filled amnionic sac surrounding the fetus, thus making possible injection of various chemical solutions or withdrawal of amniotic fluid. This fluid can be analyzed to determine the sex of the fetus, or chromosomal abnormalities.

Asherman's Syndrome—Destruction and scarring of the endometrium caused by previous infection or as a result of a D & C performed to remove infected pregnancy tissue. Symptoms include scanty or absent periods and infertility.

Bilateral salpingo-oophorectomy—The surgical removal of both Fallopian tubes and both ovaries.

Billings Method—An application of the rhythm method in which ovulation is determined by noting daily changes in the consistency of the cervical mucus.

Bipolar cautery—A method of cauterizing (burning) the Fallopian tubes when performing laparoscopic sterilization.

Bounce Test—A technique that may help a woman determine the day of ovulation. Starting six days before the day that ovulation is expected, the woman should sit down abruptly three to four times every morning and evening on a hard surface such as a wooden chair. Occasionally, lower abdominal pain can be noted when bouncing on the day of ovulation.

Cannula—Plastic or metal tubing of various sizes used during abortion and laparoscopy.

Carcinoma-in-situ (of the cervix)—The presence of cancer cells confined to the upper, surface layer of the cervix. If left untreated for a period of months or years, this condition may progress to a more dangerous invasive form of cervical cancer.

Cauterization—The destruction of tissues by burning.

Cholestasis—The stoppage of the flow of bile. When this occurs the accumulating bile salts may be responsible for itching and jaundiced skin.

Coitus Interruptus—A method of contraception practiced during intercourse, in which the penis is withdrawn from the vagina before ejaculation.

Colposcope—An instrument used for viewing the cervix under magnification. It is helpful in diagnosing and treating diseases of the vagina and vulva. The colposcope is most useful in the detection of cancerous and precancerous conditions.

Colpotomy—A surgical incision made in the upper part of the vagina through which the abdominal cavity can be entered and the uterus, Fallopian tubes, and ovaries examined.

Corpus luteum—A yellow structure formed in the ovary after ovulation. If the egg is fertilized, the corpus luteum will grow and produce hormones that will support the pregnancy for several months. In the absence of pregnancy, the corpus luteum degenerates.

Culdoscopy—The visual inspection of the pelvic organs with a viewing instrument called a culdoscope.

Curette—An instrument used to remove tissue from the uterine cavity.

Cryosurgery—A treatment of various surgical conditions in which diseased tissues are destroyed by freezing them at temperatures ranging between −60 and −90 degrees centigrade.

Cystocele—A protrusion of the urinary bladder into the vagina.

Danazol—A new, synthetic medication that is similar in structure to the male hormone testosterone. Danazol has been used successfully in the treatment of endometriosis, and it also has potential as a contraceptive for both men and women.

Depo-Provera—Trade name for *medroxy-progesterone acetate*, a synthetic progesterone-like hormone, given as an intramuscular injection. Though Depo-Provera has proven to be a valuable contraceptive medication when administered every three months, it has not yet been approved by the FDA for this purpose.

Diethylstilbesterol (DES)—A synthetic estrogen hormone that may be used as a "morning-after" pill following unprotected intercourse. DES was formerly prescribed during pregnancy to prevent miscarriage. As a result, a significant percentage of male and female offspring of such pregnancies have developmental abnormalities of the genital tract. A number of vaginal and cervical cancers in young women have also been attributed to in utero exposure to DES.

Dilatation and curettage (D&C)—A surgical procedure in which the cervix is gradually opened with instruments called dilators. Tissue is then removed from the surface of the endometrium and cervix with another instrument called a curette.

Douche—A stream of fluid directed into the vagina either through a bulb syringe or tubing attached to a bag.

Dysmenorrhea—Painful menstruation.

Dyspareunia—Painful intercourse.

Dysplasia (of the cervix)—Changes in the cells of the upper surface layer of the cervix. If left untreated, this condition can progress over a period of months or years to carcinoma-in-situ.

Ectopic pregnancy—A pregnancy that develops outside of the normal location within the uterus. Ectopic pregnancies are usually located in the Fallopian tube, although they have occurred in the ovary, the abdominal cavity, and even the cervix.

Electrocauterization—The destruction of tissue by burning, using an instrument attached to an electrical circuit.

Electrocoagulation—Refers to the dehydration and destruction of tissue cells subjected to intense heat. Electrocauterization and electrocoagulation are used synonymously when referring to the burning of the Fallopian tubes during laparoscopic sterilization.

Embolus—A clot that travels through the blood stream, and obstructs a distant blood vessel. *Pulmonary embolus* occurs when a blood vessel that carries oxygen to the lung is blocked.

Endocoagulation—A very promising and extremely safe method of coagulating the Fallopian tubes during laparoscopic sterilization. At the present time, this method is not available for general use.

Endometriosis—A fairly common and often painful condition caused by the presence of pieces of endometrium in areas other than the normal location within the uterus.

Endometrium—The inner lining of the uterus.

Epididymitis—An inflammation of the *epididymis*, the tubular structure through which sperm pass after leaving the testes. This type of inflammation may occur as a postoperative complication of vasectomy.

Estrogen—A female hormone produced mainly in the ovary. Estrogen has also been synthesized in various forms in chemical laboratories.

Falope Ring—A band made of silicon rubber known as Silastic. When placed around the Fallopian tube during laparoscopy a Falope Ring can

successfully produce tubal sterilization.

Fallopian tubes—The two structures that transport the egg from the ovary to the uterine cavity.

Fern test—A method of determining the approximate day of ovulation by examination of the cervical mucus under the microscope.

Fibroids—see *Leiomyomas*

Fimbria—Finger-like projections located at the ends of the Fallopian tubes.

Follicle—A fluid-filled sac that is located in the ovary and that contains the developing egg. At the time of ovulation, the egg is released when the follicle breaks through the surface of the ovary.

Frenulum—A ridge of skin on the under-surface of the penile glans adjacent to the shaft of the penis.

Galactorrhea—The flow of milk from the nipples.

Hepatoma—A benign though potentially dangerous tumor of the liver.

Hypertonic Saline—A strong solution of salt or sodium chloride. When injected into the amniotic sac after the first three months of pregnancy, hypertonic saline will induce abortion.

Hysterectomy—The surgical removal of the uterus.

Hysterogram—An X-ray of the uterine cavity taken immediately after a special dye solution is injected into the cavity through the cervix.

Hysteroscopy—A procedure in which a viewing instrument called a *hysteroscope* is inserted into the uterine cavity through the cervix.

Hysterotomy—A surgical incision into the muscle of the uterus.

Incompetent cervix—A cervix that is too weak to carry the weight of a growing intrauterine pregnancy. An incompetent cervix dilates prematurely and may be responsible for miscarriage after the third month of pregnancy.

Interval sterilization—Surgical sterilization procedure carried out at a time not associated with a recent pregnancy.

Intrauterine pregnancy—A pregnancy developing in its normal location within the uterine cavity.

Irving sterilization—Refers to one of many methods of tying the Fallopian tubes, named after the man who first described this technique.

Laminaria digitata—Dried sea weed that can be inserted into the cervix prior to an abortion, causing the cervix to dilate.

Laparoscopy—A procedure in which a viewing instrument called a *laparoscope* is inserted into the abdominal cavity, usually in the area of the navel. Laparoscopy allows a doctor to examine the inner organs and to perform a variety of operations without having to make surgical incisions.

Leiomyomas—Benign growths of muscle of the uterus, also known as *fibroids*.

Menstrual Extraction—The removal of tissue from the lining of the uterus through a small flexible plastic cannula attached to a source of suction. Menstrual extraction is usually performed on a woman who is fearful of pregnancy and who is three weeks or less beyond her missed period.

Minilaparotomy—An operation to accomplish sterilization in which a small incision is made in the lower abdomen through which the Fallopian tubes may be tied.

Minipill—A type of birth control pill that contains a progestin but no estrogen. Unlike birth control pills that contain both estrogen and progestins, minipills are taken every day without interruption.

Mittelschmerz—A term used to describe the lower abdominal pain experienced by some women at the time of ovulation.

Multiparous—Having previously given birth.

Myomectomy—An operation in which *leiomyomas* (fibroids) are removed from the uterus.

Myometrium—The muscular layer of the uterus.

Neuroleptics—A group of anaesthetic agents that have been used for minor surgical procedures.

Nulliparous—Having never given birth.

Os—A Latin word meaning "mouth" or "opening." The os of the cervix is the small opening leading into the uterine cavity.

Ovulometer—An experimental, battery-run device that can determine the day of ovulation by measuring changes in body voltage.

Ovutimer—An experimental instrument that determines the day of ovulation by measuring changes in the consistency of the cervical mucus.

Pampiniform plexus—A network of veins in the penis.

Phlebitis—The inflammation of a vein.

Pomeroy technique—One of many methods of tying the Fallopian tubes, named after the man who first described it.

Postcoital—Referring to events that follow intercourse.

Postpartum—Referring to events that occur after delivery or childbirth.

Premarin—The trade name for an estrogen preparation that is mainly used in the treatment of menopausal and postmenopausal disorders. Premarin also has other applications, including use as a postcoital contraceptive.

Prepuce—The fold of skin, often called the foreskin, that covers the glans penis. The prepuce is removed at the time of circumcision.

Progesterone—The hormone that is responsible for the endometrium preparing for the reception and development of the fertilized egg. Progesterone is produced by the corpus luteum.

Progestin—The term used to describe a variety of synthetic hormonal preparations having some chemical similarities to natural progesterone.

Progestogen—A general term used to describe a variety of synthetic progesterone-like hormonal preparations. Progestogen is used synonymously with progestin.

Prolactin inhibitory factor (PIF)—A hormone produced in the hypothalamus that travels to the pituitary gland where it prevents the release of another hormone named prolactin. In the absence of PIF, prolactin stimulates milk secretion from the nipples.

Prostaglandins—A group of chemical substances that occur naturally in the body and that can also be synthesized in the laboratory. When injected or used as vaginal suppositories, prostaglandins produce strong uterine contractions resulting in abortion.

Provera ring—An experimental contraceptive device in which a silastic ring containing Provera is placed in the vagina throughout most of the month. The Provera is released slowly through the vaginal wall and into the bloodstream. The circulating hormone prevents ovulation, alters the endometrium, and thickens the cervical mucus so that sperm can't pentrate it.

Puerperal sterilization—Surgical sterilization performed within the first few days following childbirth.

Rectocele—A bulge of the rectum into the vagina due to a weakening of the supporting tissues around the rectum.

Residual ovary syndrome—A variety of diseases, including a higher incidence of cancer of the ovary, noted following hysterectomies in which the ovaries were not removed.

Rho GAM—Trade name for a medication given to women

with RH negative blood type immediately after abortion or fullterm delivery.

Saxena blood test—A new pregnancy test discovered by Brij B. Saxena that appears to be extremely accurate in detecting pregnancy as early as 6 to 8 days after conception, or on the first day after a missed period.

Sequential pills—A type of birth control pill that is no longer marketed. Estrogen pills were ingested during the first part of the cycle, followed by pills containing estrogen and a progestin toward the end of the cycle.

Silastic ring—An experimental ring-shaped contraceptive device made of silicone rubber and impregnated with a variety of progestins. The Silastic ring is inserted in the vagina like a diaphragm, and the progestins are slowly released from the device into the blood stream.

Silastic rod—An experimental contraceptive device. A rod-shaped silicone capsule about one-inch long is impregnated with one of several hormones and is injected below the skin surface. Hormones are released slowly from the rods; their contraceptive effect lasts over a period of months or even years.

Speculum—An instrument that allows one to view a passage or cavity of the body. In gynecology, vaginal speculums are routinely used to view the vagina and cervix, while specially designed speculums have been developed for surgical procedures such as minilaparotomy.

Spinnbarkeit—A term that refers to the stretchability of the cervical mucus, which is most pronounced at the time of ovulation.

Squeeze technique—Delaying ejaculation by withdrawing the penis from the vagina during intercourse and exerting pressure at the coronal ridge.

Stilbesterol—Synonymous with diethylstilbesterol or DES.

Suction curettage—The process of emptying the contents of the uterine cavity with a plastic or metal curette attached to a source of suction.

Tenaculum—An instrument used to grasp the cervix prior to gynecological procedures such as IUD insertion, menstrual extraction, and suction currettage.

Testosterone—A hormone produced mainly by the testes that is responsible for the development and maintenance of male sex characteristics. Small amounts of testosterone are also found in women.

Thrombophlebitis—An inflammation in the wall of a vein to which a blood clot is attached.

Thrombus—A plug, or clot, in a blood vessel.

Trocar—A sharp-pointed instrument used for piercing the abdominal wall prior to laparoscopy, or the vaginal wall prior to culdoscopy.

Tubal ligation—Surgical sterilization achieved by tying surgical string around a segment of the Fallopian tubes. This general term is sometimes used even when the tubes are cauterized, cut, or blocked with a clip or band.

Tubal pregnancy—An ectopic pregnancy occuring in the Fallopian tube.

Unilateral salpingo-oophorectomy—Surgica removal of one Fallopian tube and the ovary adjacent to it.

Uterine Prolapse—The falling down of the uterus from its normal position, caused by a weakening of the ligaments and tissues that support it.

VACTERL—An acronym used to describe a pattern of anomalies noted in offspring of mothers given hormonal preparations either early in pregnancy or in the months immediately preceding pregnancy.

Vacurette—An instrument made of plastic tubing which, when attached to a suction source, can be used to induce a menstrual extraction or an abortion.

Vaginal hysterectomy—An operation in which the uterus is removed through the vagina.

Vaginal spermicides—Chemicals in the form of tablets, creams, jellies, and aerosols that are inserted into the vagina prior to intercourse in order to kill sperm.

Vas deferens—The tubular duct that carries sperm from the testes.

Vasectomy—A surgical sterilization procedure in which the vas deferens is cut and the ends are separated so that sperm can no longer pass through.

Vasovasotomy—A surgical procedure designed to re-establish fertility in a man who previously had a vasectomy.

Verres needle—An instrument that is inserted into the abdominal cavity prior to laparoscopy through which carbon dioxide or nitrous oxide is injected.

Woman-years—A term used to determine the relative effectiveness of a particular contraceptive based on the number of women who use it over a specific length of time. For example, if one type of IUD is responsible for 4 pregnancies among 100 women using it for a period of one year, then the pregnancy rate would be 4 per 100 woman-years.

BIBLIOGRAPHY

Chapter 2—BIRTH CONTROL PILLS

Andrews, W.C., Larsen, G.D.: Endometriosis: Treatment with hormonal pseudopregnancy and/or operation. *American Journal of Obstetrics and Gynecology*, 121:643–649, 1974.

Ariel, I.M.: Enovid therapy for fibrocystic disease. *American Journal of Obstetrics and Gynecology*, 117:453–459, 1973.

Barsivala, V.M., Virkar, K.D.: The effects of oral contraceptives on various components of human milk. *Contraception*, 7:307, 1973.

Baum, J.K., Bookstein, J.J., Holtz, F., et al.: Possible association between benign hepatomas and oral contraceptives. *Lancet*, 2:926–929, 1973.

Baumblatt, M.J., Winston, F.: Pyridoxine and the pill. *Lancet*, 1:832–833, 1970.

Bennion, L.J., Ginsberg, R.L., Garnick, M.B., et al.: Effects of oral contraceptives on the gallbladder bile of normal women. *The New England Journal of Medicine*, 294:189–192, 1976.

Beral, V.: Mortality among oral-contraceptive users. *Lancet*, 2:727–731, 1977.

Borglin, N.E.: Oral contraceptives and liver damage. *British Medical Journal*, 1:1289–1290, 1965.

The Boston Collaborative Drug Surveillance Program of Boston University Medical

Center. Surgically confirmed gallbladder disease, venous thromboembolism, and breast tumors in relation to postmenopausal estrogen therapy. *New England Journal of Medicine*, 290:15–19, 1974.

Bragonier, J.R.: Influence of oral contraception on sexual response. *Medical Aspects of Human Sexuality*, pp. 130–143, October, 1976.

Dialogues in Oral Contraception, The pill and female reproduction. Vol. 2, No. 1: pp. 7–8, 1977.

Diamond, S., Medina, J.L.: Migraine can be treated. *The Female Patient*, pp. 11–13, October, 1976.

Faloon, W.W.: Ileal bypass for obesity: postoperative perspective. *Hospital Practice*, pp. 73–82, January, 1977.

Fasal, P., Paffenberger, R.S.: Oral contraceptives as related to cancer and benign lesions of the breast. *Journal of the National Cancer Institute*, 55:767–773, 1975.

Gambrell, D.R., Bernard, D.M., Sanders, B.I., et al.: Changes in sexual drives of patients on oral contraceptives. *The Journal of Reproductive Medicine*, 17:165–171, 1976.

Heinonen, O.P., Slone, D., Monson, R.R., et al.: Cardiovascular birth defects and antenatal exposure to female sex hormones. *The New England Journal of Medicine*, 296:67–70, 1977.

Jain, A.K.: Cigarette smoking, use of oral contraceptives, and myocardial infarction. *American Journal of Obstetrics and Gynecology*, 126:301–307, 1976.

Janerich, D.T., Piper, J.M., Glebatis, D.M.: Oral contraceptives and congenital limb-reduction defects. *The New England Journal of Medicine*, 291:697–700, 1974.

Johansson, E.D.B., Krai, J.G.: Oral contraceptives after bypass operations. *Journal of the American Medical Association*, 236:2847, 1977.

Kent, S.: Authorities evaluate low-dose estrogen pills. *Contemporary OB/GYN*, 9:37–43, 1977.

Kistner, R.W.: Observations on the effects of new synthetic progestogens on endometriosis in the human female. *Fertility and Sterility*, 16:61, 1965.

Lyon, F.A.: The development of adenocarcinoma of the endometrium in young women receiving long-term sequential oral contraception. *American Journal of Obstetrics and Gynecology*, 123:299–301, 1975.

Mann, J.I., Inman, W.H.W.: Oral contraceptives and death from myocardial infarction.

British Medical Journal,
2:245–248, 1975.

Mann, J.I., Vessey, M.P.,
Thorogood, M., et al.:
Myocardial infarction in
young women with special
reference to oral
contraceptive practice. *British
Medical Journal,* 2:241–245,
1975.

Medical World News. Birth
defects after the pill. p. 73,
October 17, 1977.

Medical World News. Does pill
affect IQ of offspring? p. 55,
October 4, 1974.

Medical World News. Milder
genital herpes with the pill. p.
90, April 4, 1977.

Mumford, J.P.: Drugs affecting
oral contraceptives. *British
Medical Journal,* pp. 333–334,
May 11, 1974.

Nelson, J.H.: Selecting the
optimum oral contraceptive.
*Journal of Reproductive
Medicine,* 11:135–141, 1973.

Nissen, E.D., Kent, D.R., and
Nissen, S.E.: Liver tumors
and the pill: analyzing the
data. *Contemporary Ob/Gyn,*
8:103–111, 1976.

Nora, J.J., Nora, A.H.: Birth
defects and oral
contraceptives. *Lancet,*
1:941–942, 1973.

Novak, E.R.: Ovulation after
fifty. *Journal of Obstetrics and
Gynecology,* 36:903, 1970.

Oral Contraceptives and Health.
*Report of the Royal College of
General Practitioners,* Pitman
Medical, London, 1974.

Ory, H., Cole, P., MacMahon, B.,
et al.: Oral contraceptives and
reduced risk of benign breast
diseases. *The New England
Journal of Medicine,*
294:419–422, 1976.

Osman, M.M., Toppozada, H.K.,
Ghanem, M.H., et al: The
effect of an oral contraceptive
on serum lipids.
Contraception, 5:105, 1972.

Pritchard, J.A., Scott, D.E.,
Whalley, P.J.: Maternal folate
deficiency and pregnancy
wastage. *American Journal of
Obstetrics and Gynecology,*
109:341–346, 1971.

Ramcharan, S., Sponzilli, E.E.,
Wingerd, J.C.: Serum protein
fraction—Effects of oral
contraceptives and
pregnancy. *Journal of
Obstetrics and Gynecology,*
48:211–214, 1976.

Roe, D.A.: How the pill affects a
woman's nutritional status.
Medical Opinion, pp. 58–61,
September, 1976.

Rothman, K.J.: Fetal loss,
twinning, and birth weight
after oral contraceptive use.
*The New England Journal of
Medicine,* 297: 468–471, 1977.

Sandmire, H.F., Austin, S.D.,
Bechtel, R.C.: Carcinoma of
the cervix in oral
contraceptive steroid and IUD

users and nonusers. *American Journal of Obstetrics and Gynecology*, 125:339–345, 1976.

Silverberg, S.G., Makowski, E.L.: Endometrial carcinoma in young women taking oral contraceptive agents. *Journal of Obstetrics and Gynecology*, 46:503–506, 1975.

Skolnick, J.L., Stoler, B.S., Katz, D.B., et al.: Rifampin, oral contraceptives, and pregnancy. *Journal of the American Medical Association*, 236:1382, 1976.

Spellacy, W.N.: Metabolic effects of oral contraceptives. *Clinical Obstetrics and Gynecology*, 17:53–63, March, 1974.

Spellacy,, W.N., Buhi, W.C., Birk, S.A.: Effects of norethindrone on carbohydrate and lipid metabolism. *Obstetrics and Gynecology*, 46:560–563, 1975.

Spellacy, W.N., Buhi, W.C., Birk, S.A.: The effects of norgestrel on carbohydrate and lipid metabolism over one year. *The American Journal of Obstetrics and Gynecology*, 125:984–986, 1976.

Stern, E., Forsythe, A.B., Youkeles, L., et al.: Steroid contraceptive use and cervical dysplasta: Increased risk of progression. *Science*, 196: 1460–1462, 1977.

Streiff, R.R.: Folate deficiency and oral contraceptives. *Journal of the American Medical Association*, 214:105–108, 1970.

Theuer, R.C.: Effect of oral contraceptive agents on vitamin and mineral needs. *The Journal of Reproductive Medicine*, 8:13–18, 1972.

Tietze, C., Bongarts, J., Schearer, B.: Mortality associated with the control of fertility. *Family Planning Perspectives*, 8:6–14, 1976.

Vessey, M., Doll, M., Peto, R., et al.: A long-term follow-up study of women using different methods of contraception—an interim report. *Journal of Biosocial Science*, 8:373–427, 1976.

Vessey, M.P., Doll, R.: Investigation of relation between use of oral contraceptives and thromboembolic disease. *British Medical Journal*, 2:199, 1968.

Vessey, M.P., Weatherall, J.A.C.: Venous thromboembolic disease and the use of oral contraceptives: a review of mortality statistics in England and Wales. *Lancet*, 2:94, 1968.

Weinberger, M.H.: Oral contraceptives and hypertension. *Hospital Practice*, pp. 65–75, May, 1975.

Chapter 3—IUDs

Barrie, H.: Congenital malformation associated with intrauterine contraceptive device. *British Medical Journal*, 1:488–490, 1976.

Beling, C.G., Cederqvist, L.L., Fuchs, F.: Demonstration of gonadotropin during the second half of the cycle in women using intrauterine contraception. *American Journal of Obstetrics and Gynecology*, 125:855–858, 1976.

Cederqvist, L.L., Fuchs, F.: Cervical perforation by the Copper T intrauterine device. *American Journal of Obstetrics and Gynecology*, 119:854–855, 1974.

Connell, E.B.: The uterine therapeutic system: a new approach to female contraception. *Contemporary OB/GYN*, 6:49–55, 1975.

Davis, H.J.: The shield intrauterine device. *American Journal of Obstetrics and Gynecology*, 106:455–456, 1970.

Dawood, M.Y., Birnbaum, S.J.: Unilateral Tubo-ovarian abscess and intrauterine contraceptive device. *Journal of Obstetrics and Gynecology*, 46:429–432.

Dowie, M., Johnston, T.: A case of corporate malpractice. *Mother Jones*, p. 36, November, 1976.

Drill, V.A., O'Brien, F.B., Jr.: Cervical and uterine perforations by copper-containing intrauterine devices. Letter to the editor, *American Journal of Obstetrics and Gynecology*, 122:535, 1975.

Hallatt, J.G.: Ectopic pregnancy associated with the intrauterine device: A study of seventy cases. *American Journal of Obstetrics and Gynecology*, 125:754, 1976.

Jain, A.K., Moots, B.: Fecundability following the discontinuation of IUD use among Taiwanese women. *Journal of Biosocial Science*, 9:137–151, 1977.

Kahn, H.S., Tyler, C.W.: IUD-related hospitalizations. *Journal of the American Medical Association*, 234:53–56, 1975.

Kahn, H.S., Tyler, C.W.: Mortality associated with use of IUDs. *Journal of the American Medical Association*, 234:57–59, 1975.

Kent, S.: Therapeutic effects of Progestasert. *Contemporary OB/GYN*, 10:33–40, 1977.

Lehfeldt, H., Wan, L.S.: Unusual uterine perforation with a new intrauterine device. *Journal of Obstetrics and Gynecology*, 37:826–831, 1971.

Nariyandada, G.S., Lane, M.E., Sobrero, A.J.: A comparative randomized double-blind study of the copper-T200 and copper-7 intrauterine devices with modified insertion techniques. *American Journal of Obstetrics and Gynecology*, 120:110–116.

Newton, J., Elias, J., McEwan, J., et al.: Intrauterine contraception with the Copper-7: evaluation after two years. *British Medical Journal*, 2:447, 1974.

Perlmutter, J.F.: Experience with the Dalkon Shield as a contraceptive device. *Journal of Obstetrics and Gynecology*, 43:443–446.

Tatum, H.J., Schmidt, F.H.: Contraceptive and sterilization practices and extrauterine pregnancy. *Fertility and Sterility*, 28:401–421, 1977.

Tatum, H.J., Schmidt, F.H., Jain, A.K.: Management and outcome of pregnancies associated with the Copper T intrauterine contraceptive device. *American Journal of Obstetrics and Gynecology*, 126:869–879, 1976.

Tatum, H.J., Schmidt, F.H., Phillips, D., et al.: The Dalkon Shield controversy. *Journal of the American Medical Association*, 231:711–717, 1975.

Taylor, S.E., McMillan, J.H., Greer, B.E., et al.: The intrauterine device and tubo-ovarian abscess.

American Journal of Obstetrics and Gynecology, 123:338–342.

Tredway, D.R., Umezaki, C.U., Mishell, D.R., Jr., et al.: Effect of intrauterine devices on sperm transport in the human being: Preliminary report. *American Journal of Obstetrics and Gynecology*, 123:734–735, 1975.

Westrom, L., Bengtsson, L.P., Mardh, P.: The risk of pelvic inflammatory disease in women using intrauterine contraceptive devices as compared to non-users. *Lancet*, 2:221–224, 1976.

Chapter 4—DIAPHRAGMS, SPERMICIDES, AND CONDOMS

Bernstein, G.S.: Clinical effectiveness of an aerosol contraceptive foam. *Contraception*, 3:37, 1971.

Melamed, M.R., Koss, L.G., Flehinger, B.J., et al.: Prevalence rates of uterine cervical carcinoma in situ for women using the diaphragm or contraceptive oral steroids. *British Medical Journal*, 3:195–200, 1969.

Tietze, C., Dingle, J.T.: Comparative study of three contraceptive methods: vaginal foam tablets, jelly alone, and diaphragm with jelly or cream. *American Journal of Obstetrics and Gynecology*, 85:1012–1022, 1961.

Vessey, M., Wiggins, P.:
Use-effectiveness of the
diaphragm in a selected
family planning clinic
population in the United
Kingdom. *Contraception*, 9:15,
1974.

**Chapter 5—COITUS INTER-
RUPTUS AND RHYTHM**

Biel, K.:
Ginekologiczno-Polozniczej,
Krakow, Poland, Folia Med
Cracov 1969, 11(1) 17–34
(Polish) in *Population and
Reproduction Research
Abstracts*, Experimental Issue
Number 4, 1970, U.S.
Department of Health,
Education, and Welfare.

Billings, E.L., Billings, J.J.,
Brown, J.B., et al.: Symptoms
and hormonal changes
accompanying ovulation.
Lancet, 1:282, 1972.

How physicians can help make
rhythm work, *Contemporary
OB/GYN*, 7:107–108, 1976.

Lane, M.E., Arceo, R., and
Sobrero, A.J.: Successful use
of the diaphragm and jelly by
a young population: Report of
a clinical study. *Family
Planning Perspectives*, 8:81–86,
1976.

Marshall, J.: A field trial of the
basal-body temperature
method of regulating births.
Lancet, 2:8, 1968.

Masters, W.H., Johnson, V.E.:

Human Sexual Response,
Little, Brown and Company,
pp. 103–104, 1966.

Natural Family Planning,
Proceedings of a research
conference, Edited by William
A. Uricchio and Mary Kay
Williams, The Human Life
Foundation, Washington, D.C.

Saxena, B.B., Hasan, S.H.,
Haour, F., et al.:
Radioreceptor assay of
human chorionic
gonadotropin in detection of
early pregnancy. *Science*,
184:793–795, 1974.

Semans, J.H.: Premature
ejaculation: A new approach.
Southern Medical Journal,
49:353–357, 1956.

Tredway, D.R.: Rapidity of
sperm transport in female
reproductive tract.
Contemporary OB/GYN,
7:89–90, 1976.

Vorherr, H.: Contraception after
abortion and post partum.
*American Journal of Obstetrics
and Gynecology*,
117:1002–1025, 1973.

Westoff, C.F., Jones, E.F.:
Contraception and
Sterilization in the United
States 1965–1975. *Family
Planning Perspectives*, 9: No. 4,
153–157, 1977.

Westoff, C.F., Jones, E.F.: The
secularization of United
States Catholic birth control
practices. *Family Planning*

Perspectives, 9: No. 4, 153–157, 1977.

Zuspan, K.J., Zuspan, F.P.: Thermogenic alterations in the woman. *American Journal of Obstetrics and Gynecology*, 120:441–445.

Chapter 6—POSTCOITAL CONTRACEPTION

Bley, R.P.: The use of estrogens as postcoital contraceptive agents. *American Journal of Obstetrics and Gynecology*, 116:1044–1050, 1973.

DES in utero—Managing the consequences. *Contemporary OB/GYN*, 5:103–132, 1975.

Gill, W.B., Schumacher, G.F.B., Bibbo, M.: Structural and functional abnormalities in the sex organs of male offspring of mothers treated with diethylstilbesterol (DES). *The Journal of Reproductive Medicine*, 16:147–153, 1976.

Gore, B.Z., Caldwell, B.V., Speroff, L.: Estrogen-induced human luteolysis. *Journal of Clinical Endocrinology and Metabolism*, 36:615, 1973.

Haspels, A.A., Andriesse, R.: *European Journal of Obstetrical and Gynecological Reproductive Biology*, 3:113, 1973.

Herbst, A.L., Kurman, R.J., Skully, R.E.: Vaginal and cervical abnormalities after exposure to stilbesterol in utero. *Journal of Obstetrics and Gynecology*, 40:287, 1972.

Herbst, A.L., Robboy, S.J., Scully, R.E., et al.: Clear-cell adenocarcinoma of the vagina and cervix in girls: Analysis of 170 Registry cases. *American Journal of Obstetrics and Gynecology*, 119:713–728, 1974.

Herbst, A.L., Ulfelder, H., Poskanzer, D.C.: Adenocarcinoma of the vagina: association of maternal stilbesterol therapy with tumor appearance in young women. *The New England Journal of Medicine*, 284:878, 1971.

Jukes, T.H.: Estrogens in beefsteak. *Journal of the American Medical Association*, 229:1920–1921, 1974.

Kaufman, R.H., Binder, G.L., Gray, P.M., et al.: Upper genital tract changes associated with exposure in utero to diethylstilbestrol. *American Journal of Obstetrics and Gynecology*, 128:51–56, 1977.

Kuchera, L.K.: Postcoital contraception with diethylstilbesterol-updated. *Contraception*, 10:47, 1974.

Lehfeldt, H.: Postcoital contraception. *OB/GYN Digest*, pp. 28–30, 1976.

Medical World News, p. 37, Dec. 1, 1975.

Medical World News, Mamography for DES mothers? pp. 7–8, Jan. 9, 1978.

Morris, J.M.: Mechanisms involved in progesterone contraception and estrogen interception. *American Journal of Obstetrics and Gynecology*, 117:167–176, 1973.

Morrow, C.P., Townsend, D.E.: Management of adenosis and clear-cell adenocarcinoma of vagina and cervix. *The Journal of Reproductive Medicine*, 15:25–26, 1975.

The New York Times, January 26, 1977.

Sonek, M., Bibbo, M., Wied, G.L.: Colposcopic findings in offspring of DES-treated mothers as related to onset of therapy. *The Journal of Reproductive Medicine*, 16:65–70, 1976.

Yalom, I.D., Green, R., Fish, N.: Prenatal exposure to female hormones. Effect on psychosexual development in boys. *Archives of General Psychiatry*, 28:554, 1973.

Chapter 7—ABORTION

ACOG *Technical Bulletin*, Hypertonic saline amnioinfusion for termination of second trimester pregnancy. Number 37, Feb., 1976.

Anderson, G.G., Steege, J.F.: Clinical experience using prostaglandin $F_2\alpha$ for midtrimester abortion in 600 patients. *Journal of Obstetrics and Gynecology*, 46:591–595, 1975.

Athanasiou, R.: Psychological effects of abortion? *Contemporary OB/GYN*, 3:54–55, 1974.

Berger, G.S., Bourne, J.P., Tyler, C.W., et al.: Termination of pregnancy by "super coils": Morbidity associated with a new method of second-trimester abortion. *American Journal of Obstetrics and Gynecology*, 116:297, 1973.

Burnett, L.S., Wentz, A.C., King, T.M.: Techniques of pregnancy termination. *Obstetrical and Gynecological Survey*, 29:6–42, 1974.

Current Prescribing, p. 13, Jan., 1978.

Grimes, D.A., Cates, W., Jr.: Deaths from paracervical anesthesia used for first-trimester abortion. *The New England Journal of Medicine*, 295:1397–1399, 1976.

Grimes, D.A., Schulz, K.F., Cates, W., et al.: Midtrimester abortion by intraamniotic prostaglandin F$_2$ $\propto$ *Obstetrics and Gynecology*, 49: No. 612–616, 1977.

Hale, R.W., Pion, R.J.: Laminaria: An underutilized clinical adjunct. *Clinical Obstetrics and Gynecology*, 15:829–850, 1972.

Liu, D.T.Y., Black, M.M., Melcher, D.H., et al.: Dilatation of the parous non-pregnant cervix. *British Journal of Obstetrics and Gynaecology*, 82:246, 1975.

Medical World News, pp. 5–6, October 11, 1974.

Moghadam, S.S., Vakizadeh, J., Miller, E.R.: A comparison of metal and plastic cannulae for performing vacuum aspiration during the first trimester of pregnancy. *The Journal of Reproductive Medicine*, 17:181–187, 1976.

Moriyama, Y., Hirokawa, O.: The relationship between artificial termination of pregnancy and abortion of premature birth, in *Harmful Effects of Induced Abortion*, The Family Planning Federation of Japan, 1966.

Nathanson, B.N.: Ambulatory abortion: Experience with 26,000 cases (July 1, 1970, to August 1, 1971). *The New England Journal of Medicine*, 286:403–407, 1972.

Ob. Gyn News, p. 2, May 15, 1974.

Osofsky, H.J., Osofsky, J.D.: *The Abortion Experience: Psychological and Medical Impact*. New York, Harper and Row, 1973.

Roht, L.H., Aoyama, H.: Induced abortion and its sequels: Prematurity and spontaneous abortion. *American Journal of Obstetrics and Gynecology*, 120:868–874, 1974.

Chapter 8—VASECTOMY

Ansbacher, R.: Sperm-agglutinating and sperm immobilizing antibodies in vasectomized men. *Fertility and Sterility*, 22:629, 1971.

Bunge, R.G.: Plasma testosterone levels in man before and after vasectomy. *Investigative Urology*, 10:9, 1972.

Frankel, M.S.: Human-semen banking: Implications for medicine and society. *Connecticut Medicine*, 39:313–317, 1975.

Hackett, R.E., Waterhouse, K.: Vasectomy-reviewed. *American Journal of Obstetrics and Gynecology*, 116:438–455, 1973.

Johnsonbaugh, R.E., O'Connell, K., Engel, S.G., et al.: Plasma testosterone luteinizing hormones and follicle stimulating hormone after vasectomy. *Fertility and Sterility*, 26:329, 1975.

Kohli, K.L., Sobrero, A.J.: *Social Biology*, 20:298–302, 1973.

Leader, A.J., Axelrad, S.D., Frankowski, R., et al.: Complications of 2,711 vasectomies, *Journal of Urology*, 111:365, 1974.

Roberts, H.J.: *Journal of the American Geriatric Society*, 16:267, 1968.

Roberts, H.J.: Voluntary sterilization in the male. *British Medical Journal*, 3:434, 1968.

Rosemberg, E., Marka, S.C., Howard, P.S., et al.: Serum levels of follicle stimulating and luteinizing hormones before and after vasectomy in men. *Journal of Urology*, 111:626, 1974.

Vasectomy reversal that really works. *Medical World News*, pp. 19–21, November 17, 1975.

Vasovasotomy: How effective is it? *Contemporary OB/GYN*, 6:36–42, 1975.

Wieland, R.G., Hallberg, M.C., Zorn, E.M., et al.: Pituitary gonadal function before and after vasectomy. *Fertility and Sterility*, 23:779, 1972.

Chapter 9—TUBAL LIGATION

Berkman, S.: Late complications of tubal sterilization by laparoscopy. *Contemporary OB/GYN*, 9:118–134, 1977.

Brenner, W.E., Edelman, D.A.: Early complications of sterilization in women not recently pregnant. *Surgery Gynecology Obstetrics*, 140:69–74, 1975.

Fishburne, J.I., Edelman, D.A., Hulka, J.F., et al.: Outpatient laparoscopic sterilization with therapeutic abortion versus abortion alone. *Journal of Obstetrics and Gynecology*, 45:665–668, 1975.

Hatcher, R.A., Stewart, G.K., Kline, R.W., et al.: *Contraceptive Technology, 1973–74.* Emory University Family Planning Program, Atlanta, Georgia.

Keith, L., Houser, K., Webster, A., et al.: Puerperal laparoscopy. *The Journal of Reproductive Medicine*, 10:273–275, 1973.

Lecuyer, A.: Reversing sterilization with microsurgery—a report from London. *Contemporary OB/GYN*, 109–114, 1977.

Loffer, F.D., Pent, D.: Indications, contraindications, and complications of laparoscopy.

Obstetrical and Gynecological Survey, 30:407, 1975.

Loffer, F.D., Pent, D.: Laparoscopy in the obese patient. *The American Journal of Obstetrics and Gynecology*, 125:104–107, 1975.

Medical World News, pp. 30–31, May 31, 1976.

OB GYN Observer, Lederle Laboratories, Vol. 15: p. 1, March-April, 1976.

Osathanondh, V.: Suprapubic minilaparotomy, uterine elevation technique: simple, inexpensive, outpatient procedure for interval female sterilization. *Contraception*, 10:251–262, 1974.

Phillips, J., Keith, D., Hulka, J., et al.: Gynecologic laparoscopy in 1975. *The Journal of Reproductive Medicine*, 16:105–117, 1976.

Rioux, J.E., Cloutier, D.: Bipolar cautery for sterilization by laparoscopy. *The Journal of Reproductive Medicine*, 13:6–10, 1974.

Roe, R.E., Laros, R.K., Work, B.A.: Female sterilization. *American Journal of Obstetrics and Gynecology*, 112:1031–1036, 1972.

Wheeless, C.R.: Current contraindications to laparoscopy. *Contemporary OB/GYN*, 3:51–53, 1974.

Wheeless, C.R., Thompson, B.H.: Laparoscopic sterilization: Review of 3600 cases. *Journal of Obstetrics and Gynecology*, 42:751, 1973.

Yoon, I.B., Wheeless, C.R., King, T.M.: A preliminary report on a new laparoscopic sterilization approach: the silicone rubber band technique. *American Journal of Obstetrics and Gynecology*, 120:132–136, 1974.

Yuzpe, A.A., Anderson, R.J., Cohen, N.P., et al.: A review of 1035 tubal sterilizations by posterior colpotomy under local anaesthesia or by laparoscopy. *The Journal of Reproductive Medicine*, 13:106–109, 1974.

Chapter 10—HYSTERECTOMY

Altchek, A.: Guidelines for hysterectomies. *The Female Patient*, pp. 68–73, March, 1976.

Ballard, C.A.: Therapeutic abortion and sterilization by vaginal hysterectomy. *American Journal of Obstetrics and Gynecology*, 118:891–896, 1974.

Barclay, D.L., Hawks, B.L., Frueh, D.M., et al.: Elective cesarean hysterectomy: A 5 year comparison with cesarean section. *American Journal of Obstetrics and*

Gynecology, 124:900–910, 1976.

Bunker, J.P.: Elective hysterectomy: Pro and con. *The New England Journal of Medicine*, 295:264–268, 1976.

Cancer Statistics, 1976. American Cancer Society Professional Education Publications, 1976.

Christ, J.E., Lotze, E.C.: The residual ovary syndrome. *Journal of Obstetrics and Gynecology*, 46:551–556, 1975.

Cohen, M.: Needless hysterectomies. *Ladies Home Journal*, pp. 88–91, March, 1976.

Hysterectomy for sterilization? Symposium, *Contemporary OB/GYN*, 3:141–172, 1974.

Langer, A., Pelosi, M., Hung, C.T., et al.: Comparison of sterilization by tubal ligation and hysterectomy. *Surgery Gynecology and Obstetrics*, 140:235, 1975.

Laros, R.K., Work, B.A.: Female sterilization. *American Journal of Obstetrics and Gynecology*, 122:693–697, 1975.

Ledger, W.J., Peterson, E.P.: Guidelines for antibiotic prophylaxis in gynecology. *Obstetrical and Gynecological Survey*, 30:706, 1975.

O'Leary, J.A., Steer, C.M.: A ten year review of cesarean hysterectomy. *American Journal of Obstetrics and Gynecology*, 90:227–231, 1964.

Rodgers, J.: Rush to surgery. *The New York Times Magazine*, pp. 34–42, September 21, 1975

Schulman, H.: Major surgery for abortion and sterilization. *Journal of Obstetrics and Gynecology*, 40:738–739, 1972.

Chapter 11—THE FUTURE

Another route to contraception. *Medical World News*, 16, p. 58, February 24, 1975.

Antifibrinolytic agent may reduce bleeding after IUD. *Medical Tribune*, p. 6, January 19, 1977.

Azadian-Boulanger, G., Secchi, J., Laraque, F., et al.: Action of a midcycle contraceptive (R 2323) on the human endometrium. *American Journal of Obstetrics and Gynecology*, 125:1049–1056, 1976.

Ben-Aryeh, H., Filmar, S., Gutman, D., et al.: Salivary phosphate as an indicator of ovulation. *American Journal of Obstetrics and Gynecology*, 125:871–874, 1976.

Brody, J.E.: Vaccine to block pregnancy tested. *The New*

York Times, p. 50, March 8, 1976.

Bygdeman, M., Martin, J.N., Eneroth, P., et al.: Outpatient postconceptional fertility control with vaginally administered 15 (S) 15-methyl-PGF$_2\propto$ methyl ester. *American Journal of Obstetrics and Gynecology,* 124:495–497, 1976.

Caldwell, B.V., Auletta, F.J., Speroff, L.: Prostaglandins in the control of ovulation, corpus luteum function, and parturition. *The Journal of Reproductive Medicine,* 10:133–137, 1973.

Cederqvist, L.L., Lauersen, N.H., Donovan, S., et al.: Intrauterine contraception with the Antigon-F device. *Advances in Planned Parenthood,* 10:23–28, 1975.

Chvapil, M., Chvapil, T.A., Owen, J.A., et al.: Reaction of vaginal tissue of rabbit and of cheek pouch of hamster to inserted collagen sponges treated with either zinc or copper. *American Journal of Obstetrics and Gynecology,* 134: 63–70, 1978.

Collagen sponge contraceptive diaphragm. *Modern Medicine,* p. 138, April 1, 1977.

Cooper, D.L., Millen, A.K., Mishell, D.R., Jr.: The Copper T220C: A new long-acting copper intrauterine device. *American Journal of Obstetrics*

and Gynecology, 124:121–124, 1976.

Craft, I.: Induction of midtrimester abortion: intra-amniotic prostaglandins and urea. *Contemporary OB/GYN,* 3:45–50, 1974.

Davis, R.H., Balin, H.: Saliva glucose: A useful criterion for determining the time of fertility in women. *American Journal of Obstetrics and Gynecology,* 115:287–288, 1973.

El-Mahgoub, S.: d-Norgestrel slow-releasing T device as an intrauterine contraceptive. *American Journal of Obstetrics and Gynecology,* 123:133–138, 1975.

The Female Patient, p. 42, April, 1976.

Fiberoptic hysteroscopy for tubal sterilization. *Contemporary OB/GYN,* 2:9–15, 1973.

Fidell, L.S., Keith-Spiegel, P., Hoffman, D.: Complications in selection of sex of children. Letter to the editors, *American Journal of Obstetrics and Gynecology,* 125:280–281, 1976.

Frangenheim, H., Kleindienst, W.: Tubal sterilization under vision with the laparoscope: New techniques and instruments. *The Journal of Reproductive Medicine,* 13:41–43, 1974.

Futoran, J.M.: Experience with a fluid-filled IUD. *Journal of Obstetrics and Gynecology*, 43:82–83, 1974.

Hulka, J.F., Omran, K.F., Phillips, J.M., et al.: Sterilization by spring clip: a report of 1000 cases with a 6-month follow-up. *Fertility and Sterility*, 26:1122-1131, 1975.

The Journal of Reproductive Medicine, Second Trimester Abortion, A symposium by Correspondence. 16:47–64, 1976.

Karim, M., Ammar, R., El-Mahgoub, S., et al.: Injected progestogen and lactation. *British Medical Journal*, 1:200–203, 1971.

Kistner, R.W.: The pill and IUD: not perfect but still the best we have. *Modern Medicine*, pp. 36–44, November 11, 1974.

Lauersen, N.H., Cederqvist, L.L., Donovan, S., et al.: Comparison of three intrauterine contraceptive devices: The Antigon-F, The Ypsilon-Y, and The Copper-T200. *Fertility and Sterility*, 26:638–648, 1975.

Lauersen, N.H., Secher, N.J., Wilson, K.H.: Mid-trimester abortion induced by intravaginal administration of Prostaglandin E₂ suppositories. *American Journal of Obstetrics and Gynecology*, 122:947–954, 1975.

Lauersen, N.H., Wilson, K.H., Birnbaum, S.: Danazol: An antigonadotropic agent in the treatment of pelvic endometriosis. *American Journal of Obstetrics and Gynecology*, 123:742–746, 1975.

Lauersen, N.H., Wilson, K.H.: Termination of midtrimester pregnancy by serial intramuscular injections of 15 (S)-15-methyl-prostaglandin F₂ ∝ *American Journal of Obstetrics and Gynecology*, 124:169–176, 1976.

Leff, D.N.: Boy or girl: now choice, not chance. *Medical World News*, pp. 45–56, December 1, 1975.

Luy, M.L.M.: The male pill—knotty problem or misogynist myth? *Modern Medicine*, pp. 42–46, October 15, 1975.

Maugh, T.H., II.: 5-thio-D-glucose: A unique male contraceptive. *Science*, 186–431, 1974.

Medical News, *Journal of the American Medical Association*, 233:943, 1975.

Medical News, *Journal of the American Medical Association*, 235:2179-2180, 1976.

Medical World News. A contraceptive that's

absorbable. p. 30, May 30, 1977.

Medical Tribune, A long-acting pill implant, bio-erodable for both sexes. p. 8, May 11, 1977.

Medical World News. A machine to predict ovulation time. p. 40, June 13, 1977.

Medical World News. Next, a nonsteroid contraceptive pill? p. 56, Nov. 28, 1977.

Mishell, D.R., Jr.: Intravaginal ring for steroid contraception. *Contemporary OB/GYN*, 2:85–86, 1973.

Mishell, D.R., Moore, D.E., Roy, S., et al.: Clinical performance and endocrine profiles with contraceptive vaginal rings containing a combination of estradiol and d-norgestrel. *American Journal of Obstetrics and Gynecology*, 130: 55–62, 1978.

Moghissi, K.S., Syner, F.N., Borin, B.: Cyclic changes of cervical mucous enzymes related to the time of ovulation. *Journal of Obstetrics and Gynecology*, 48:347/350, 1976.

Neuwirth, R.S.: Hysteroscopy. W.B. Saunders Company, 1975.

Oster, G., Yang, S.: Cyclic variation of sialic acid content in saliva. *American Journal of Obstetrics and Gynecology*, 114:190–193, 1972.

OB/GYN Digest, p. 7, August, 1976.

OB/GYN Digest, p.11, February, 1977.

Rall, H.J.S., Niekerk, W.A., Engelbrecht, B.H., et al.: Comparative contraceptive experience with three-month and six-month medroxyprogesterone acetate regimens. *The Journal of Reproductive Medicine*, 18:55–60, 1977.

Ringrose, C.A.D.: The use of silver nitrate for office tubal sterilization and restoration of menstruation. *OB/GYN Digest*, pp.21–23, February, 1976.

Sakiz, E., Azadian-Boulanger, G., Laraque, F., et al.: A new approach to estrogen-free contraception based on progesterone receptor blockage by mid-cycle administration of ethyl norgestrienone (R2323). *Contraception*, 10:467–474, 1974.

Salhanick, H.A., McIntosh, E.N., Uzgiris, V.I., et al.: Mitochondrial systems of pregnenolone synthesis and its inhibition, *The Regulation of Mammalian Reproduction.* Springfield, Ill., Charles C. Thomas, p. 520, 1973.

Schwallie, P.C.: Experience with Depo-Provera as an injectable contraceptive. *Journal of Reproductive Medicine*, 13:113–117, 1974.

Sciarra, J.J., Osborn, C.K.: Sterilization methods: their potential in population control. *Contemproary OB/GYN*, 8:77–84, 1976.

Segal, S.J.: New approaches to contraception. *Clinical Obstetrics and Gynecology*, 17:157–166, 1974.

Semm, K.: Endocoagulation: A new field of endoscopic surgery. *Journal of Reproductive Medicine*, 16:195–203, 1976.

Soichet, S.: Ypsilon: A new silicone-covered stainless steel intrauterine contraceptive device. *American Journal of Obstetrics and Gynecology*, 114:938–941, 1972.

Soichet, S., Rodrigues, W., Cederqvist, L.: Experience with the modified nulliparous size Ypsilon. *The Journal of Reproductive Medicine*, 13:51–52, 1974.

Stevens,,V.C.: The potential of antifertility vaccines. *Contemporary OB/GYN*, 7:56–60, 1976.

Time of ovulation easily predicted with paper 'testape'. *OB-GYN Observer*, February, 1972.

Ultrasound exposure decreases sperm production in men, animals. Medical News, *Journal of the American Medical Association*, 235:2375–2376, 1976.

Zanartu, J., Aguilera, E., Munoz, G., et al.: Effect of a long-acting contraceptive progestogen on lactation. *Journal of Obstetrics and Gynecology*, 47:174–175, 1976.

The author wishes to express his appreciation to the individuals who gave permission to reproduce the following illustrations:

Figure 1-7 From *Williams Obstetrics*, 15th Edition, Reproduced with permission of Appleton-Century-Crofts.

Figure 3-1 From Hatcher, R.A., Conrad, C.C., Kline, R.W., and Moorhead, F.L.: *Contraceptive Technology*, 1973–1974. Emory University Family Planning Program, Atlanta, Georgia. Reproduced with permission.

Figures 3-2, 3-3, 3-4, and 3-5 Reproduced with permission of Searle Laboratories, Chicago, Illinois.

Figure 3-7 From Tatum, H.J., Schmidt, F.H., Phillips, D., et al.: The Dalkon Shield controversy, *Journal of the American Medical Association*, 231:711–717, 1975. Copyright 1975, American Medical Association. Reproduced with permission of Howard J. Tatum, Rockefeller University, York Ave, New York, N.Y., The Journal of the American Medical Association, 535 North Dearborn Street, Chicago, Ill., and The Population Council, Rockefeller University, New York, N.Y.

Figure 4-5 Copyright 1976, Holland-Rantos Company, Inc., manufacturers of Koromex and Koro-Flex (R) products. Reproduced with permission.

Figure 4-8 Copyright 1976, Holland-Rantos Company, Inc., manufacturers of Trojans. Reproduced by permission.

Figure 5-8 From Zuspan, K.J., and Zuspan, F.P.: Thermogenic alterations in the woman 11. Basal body, afternoon, and bedtime temperatures. *American Journal of Obstetrics and Gynecology*, 120:441–445, 1974. Reproduced with permission of Frederick P. Zuspan, M.D. and The C.V. Mosby Company, St. Louis, Missouri.

Figure 5-10 and Figure 5-11 Reproduced with permission of Maxwell Roland, M.D., Forest Hills, N.Y.

Figure 5-12 From Vorherr, H.: Contraception after abortion and post partum. An evaluation of risks and benefits of oral contraceptives with emphasis on the relation of female sex hormones to thromboembolism and genital and breast cancer. *American Journal of Obstetrics and Gynecology*, 117:1002–1025, 1973. Reproduced with permission of Helmuth Vorherr, M.D. and C.V. Mosby Company, St. Louis, Missouri.

Figures 7-1, 7-2, 7-3 Reproduced with permission of Berkely Bio-Engineering, Inc., 600 McCormick Street, San Leandro, California, 94577.

Figure 7-5 Reproduced with permission of C.J. Eaton, M.D.

Figure 8-1 From *AVS News*, Association for Voluntary Sterilization, March, 1975. Reproduced with permission of Association for Voluntary Sterilization, Inc., New York, N.Y.

Figure 9-8 Reproduced with permission of Clifford Wheeless, M.D.

Figure 9-9 From Wheeless, C.R., Thompson, B.H.: Laparoscopic sterilization: Review of 3600 cases. *Journal of Obstetrics and Gynecology*, 42:751–758, 1973. Reproduced with permission of Clifford R. Wheeless, M.D., and Harper and Row, Publishers, Inc.

Figures 9-10 and 9-12 Reproduced with permission of Sostheme Casthely, M.D.

Figure 9-14 and Figure 9-15 Reproduced with permission of KLI, Inc., Ivyland, Pa.

Figure 11-1 Reproduced with permission of Dr. Daniel Mishell, Jr.

Figure 11-3 Reproduced with permission of Jack Futoran, M.D.

Figure 11-4 and Figure 11-5 Reproduced with permission of Lars L. Cederqvist, M.D.

Figure 11-6 Reproduced with permission of Professor E. Sadovsky.

Figure 11-7 and Figure 11-8 Reproduced with permission of Harold J. Kosasky, M.D., Boston, Mass.

Figure 11-9 Reproduced with permission of Department of Obstetrics & Gynecology, School of Medicine, University of North Carolina, Chapel Hill, N.C.

Figure 11-13 Reproduced with permission of Mostafa S. Fahim, Ph.D., University of Missouri-Columbia patent disclosure #674,110

Table 2-4 and Table 2-6 Reproduced with permission of Executive Editor of "Dialogues in Oral Contraception," Health Learning Systems Inc., Bloomfield, New Jersey.

Table 2-5 From Nelson, J.H.: Selecting the optimum oral contraceptive. *The Journal of Reproductive Medicine*, Volume 11,

Number 4, October, 1973. Reproduced with permission of James H. Nelson, M.D. and The Journal of Reproductive Medicine.

Table 2-8 From Tietze, C., Bongarts, J., and Schearer, B.: Mortality associated with the control of fertility. *Family Planning Perspectives*, 8:6–14, 1976. Reproduced with permission of Dr. S. Bruce Schearer and Family Planning Perspectives.

Tables 3-1, 3-2 and 3-3 From *Contraceptive Technology 1974–1975*, Hatcher, R.A., Stewart, G.K., Kline, R.W., and Moorhead, F.L., The Emory University Family Planning Program, Emory University School of Medicine, Atlanta, Georgia. Reproduced with permission.

Table 3-4 Reproduced with permission of Alza Pharmaceuticals, Palo Alto, California.

Table 3-5 From Kahn, H.S., Tyler, C.W.: IUD-related hospitalizations. *Journal of the American Medical Association*, 234:57–59, 1975. Reproduced with permission.

Table 5-3 From Vorherr, H.: Contraction after abortion and post partum. *American Journal of Obstetrics and Gynecology*, 117:1002–1025, 1973. Reproduced with permission of Helmuth Vorherr, M.D.

Table 6-1 From Kuchera, L.K.: Postcoital contraception with diethylstilbesterol—updated. *Contraception*, 10:47, 1974. Table 3 reproduced with permission of Lucile K. Kuchera, M.D., M.P.H and Geron-X Publishers, Los Altos, California.

Table 6-3 From Sonek, M., Bibbo, M., Wied, G.L.: Colposcopic findings in offspring of DES-treated mothers as related to onset of therapy. *The Journal of Reproductive Medicine*, 16:65–70, 1976. Reproduced with permission of Mojmir G. Sonek, M.D. and *The Journal of Reproductive Medicine*.

Table 7-1 From *Abortion Surveillance 1974*, U.S. Department of Health, Education, and Welfare, Public Health Service, Center for Disease Control, Bureau of Epidemiology, Family Planning Evaluation Division, Atlanta, Georgia. Reproduced with permission.

Table 9-1 From Phillips, J., Keith, D., Hulka, J. et al.: Gynecologic laparoscopy in 1975. *The Journal of Reproductive Medicine*, 16:105–117, 1976. Reproduced with permission of Jordan Phillips, M.D., and *The Journal of Reproductive Medicine*.

Table 9-2 From Brenner, W.E., and Edelman, D.A.: Early complications of sterilization in women not recently pregnant. *Surgery*,

INDEX